NEVER LOOK A
POLAR BEAR
IN THE EYE

NEVER LOOK A
POLAR BEAR
IN THE EYE

*A Family Field Trip to the
Arctic's Edge in Search of Adventure,
Truth, and Mini-Marshmallows*

Zac Unger

DA CAPO PRESS
A Member of the Perseus Books Group

Some names have been changed and dialogue is to the best of the author's recollection.

Designed by Pauline Brown
Set in 11.5 point Minion Pro by the Perseus Books Group

Library of Congress Cataloging-in-Publication Data

Unger, Zac.
    Never look a polar bear in the eye : a family field trip to the Arctic's edge in search of adventure, truth, and mini-marshmallows / Zac Unger.—First Da Capo Press edition.
        p.   cm
    ISBN 978-0-306-82116-5 (hardcover : alkaline paper)—ISBN 978-0-306-82163-9 (e-book) 1. Polar bear—Manitoba—Churchill. 2. Polar bear—Conservation—Manitoba—Churchill. 3. Human-animal relationships—Manitoba—Churchill. 4. Unger, Zac—Travel—Manitoba—Churchill. 5. Churchill (Man.)—Description and travel. 6. Churchill (Man.)—Environmental conditions. I. Title.
    QL737.C27U58 2013
    599.7862097127—dc23

                                                                                          2012033743

First Da Capo Press edition 2013

Published by Da Capo Press
A Member of the Perseus Books Group
www.dacapopress.com

Da Capo Press books are available at special discounts for bulk purchases in the U.S. by corporations, institutions, and other organizations. For more information, please contact the Special Markets Department at the Perseus Books Group, 2300 Chestnut Street, Suite 200, Philadelphia, PA 19103, or call (800) 810-4145, ext. 5000, or e-mail special.markets@perseusbooks.com.

10 9 8 7 6 5 4 3 2 1

For Shona

Such is the economy of nature, that no instance can be produced of her having permitted any one race of her animals to become extinct; of her having formed any link in her great work so weak as to be broken.

—THOMAS JEFFERSON, 1781

The complete extinction of the species of a group is generally a slower process than their production. . . . So profound is our ignorance, and so high our presumption, that we marvel when we hear of the extinction of an organic being; and as we do not see the cause, we invoke cataclysms to desolate the world.

—CHARLES DARWIN, 1859

More than 99 percent of all species that ever lived are extinct—and disappearance cannot be the biological equivalent of a scarlet letter.

—STEPHEN JAY GOULD, 1992

CONTENTS

CHAPTER 23   The Bear Whisperer   227

CHAPTER 24   Bunny Huggers   237

CHAPTER 25   They Know They Are Safe Here   245

CHAPTER 26   Circus Bears   253

CHAPTER 27   Bear in the Air   261

CHAPTER 28   All Creatures Great and Small   267

CHAPTER 29   The Heavy Hitters Speak   273

CHAPTER 30   Apocalypse Now. Or Maybe Later.   283

                Epilogue   291

                Acknowledgments   295

                Illustrations follow page 138

O N JANUARY 24, 2004, in the frigid moonscape of an Arctic winter, wildlife biologist Steven Amstrup rode shotgun in a helicopter flying low over the ice. He aimed an infrared heat detector at the ground, hoping to find polar bears in their dens. He'd been tracking bears for years, and the chopper-mounted heat gun was a great modern tool, one that would reduce the amount of time he would have to spend slogging through the tundra on foot and by snowmobile.

When the gun recorded a hit, Amstrup circled around for a closer look. What confronted him was something he had never seen or heard of in thirty-four years of polar research. The mouth of the den was open, and a smear of bright red blood stretched away for two hundred feet. There, at the end of a long drag trail in the ice, lay the still-warm body of a mature female polar bear. Given that the air temperature was 20°F below zero, this bear could not have been dead for more than twelve hours. But the helicopter was running short on time, and Amstrup reluctantly left the scene of the carnage before he was able to figure out what had happened.

POLAR BEARS DO NOT HAVE ENEMIES. A male can weigh up to 1,500 pounds, with paws a foot wide and rows of savage teeth that are deadlier than a grizzly's. They are the unchallenged master predators in one of the harshest environments on earth. A full-grown bear slaughtered in her den is far outside the ordinary.

Amstrup and his team returned by snowmobile. Only a little additional snow had fallen, and the subzero temperatures were a crime scene analyst's dream. The dead female had multiple wounds to her neck and head, and the snow was stained by heavy arterial bleeding. She had multiple bite wounds to her head, and her skull had been pierced by a long tooth that had slammed into her brain. Her hindquarter, belly, and mammaries had been partially eaten. Although they don't hibernate, pregnant mothers do build snow caves in which to deliver their fragile cubs. When Amstrup walked to the den, he peered beneath the collapsed roof. Inside he found two tiny cubs, each weighing less than five pounds. And both of them were dead, suffocated by the thick snow of the ruined cave.

There was only one explanation for this carnage. A single set of massive footprints led directly to the den. This bear and her cubs had been killed by another polar bear.

Cannibalism is not normal polar bear behavior. Ringed seals are easier to catch and have more calories per pound than bear meat. But over the course of that single field season, Amstrup witnessed two additional instances of polar bear cannibalism. On Herschel Island in the Yukon Territory, a fifteen-year-old female was found frozen and dead, her subcutaneous fat and most of her muscle eaten away. Her dependent yearling cub had escaped; a set of tracks led away to the northwest and then disappeared. The cub's chances of survival on its own were zero. A few days later and around sixty miles away, researchers witnessed an adult male bear feeding on a dead yearling. The younger bear's skull had been savagely crushed; footprints revealed that the larger male had stalked this young bear, then set upon him as he lay sleeping.

Having never seen anything like this, Amstrup was shocked to stumble across three separate incidents of polar bear cannibalism in one season. But as he spoke to colleagues, he found that what he was seeing was becoming more common. Several thousand miles away, on the eastern edge of the Canadian Arctic, an adult male was reported to have consumed most of the carcass of a yearling male he had killed. The dead bear's mother hovered around for two days, watching as her cub was picked apart. And a few years earlier in the Svalbard Archipelago, four hundred miles north of Norway, three small cubs were found dead inside their den. Autopsies revealed the presence of fresh milk in their stomachs; their mother had not abandoned them, yet she did not attempt to intervene as a powerful male bear killed them one by one. Elsewhere in Svalbard, researchers observed a male pursuing a mother bear and her yearling, doggedly chasing them over broken spits of ice, in and out of the frigid waters. Finally, cornered at the base of a sheer cliff, the yearling was killed by a blow to the skull. The mother fled along the coast, and the aggressive male dragged the yearling carcass to an ice floe six hundred feet offshore, where he feasted on it for days.

Back at the ravaged den he had discovered, Amstrup followed the paw prints and analyzed the blood spatters. The offending male bear hadn't just chanced upon this site. He had actively stalked it, much the way bears sneak up on the lairs of ringed seals. The footprints followed the typical hunting pattern—the bear meandered around in a wide arc, then made a beeline for the spot where mother and cubs were resting. He had crashed through the roof, collapsing the snow cave and suffocating the cubs. Once inside, he held the female in place with his paws and crushed her skull with his teeth. After the struggle, the male dragged his feast to a patch of clean snow. Although polar bears have killed other polar bears in the past, this was the first recorded instance in which the killing took place at the supposedly safe haven of a denning site.

Even before the killings began, the year 2004 had been particularly difficult for polar bears. Warm temperatures had been shrinking the pack ice for a decade, but the summers of 2002, 2003, and 2004 had seen a rapid melt and a resultant sharp increase in the amount of area covered by open water. Between 1987 and 2003, scientists conducting aerial surveys observed a total of twelve polar bears swimming in open water, miles out from the edge of the pack ice. But in 2004 alone, an aerial survey showed ten bears swimming in open water, several of them as far as sixty miles offshore. Even more alarming, scientists observed four polar bear carcasses floating in the sea; the bears had apparently drowned while attempting to make it from one chunk of ice to the next. Never before had scientists seen even a single drowned bear. On land, as they trapped bears in the course of their normal research, the scientists found that fully half of the bears they were seeing were in a lean or emaciated condition.

In western Hudson Bay, near the town of Churchill, Manitoba, a 2006 study told a grim tale. In twenty years, the local bear population had plummeted from 1,194 bears to 935, a decline of over 20 percent. Similar numbers were coming in from all across the Arctic. In Baffin Bay, just off the coast of Greenland, the bear population was down by one-third from its high point. And on the ice shelf off Alaska's northern coast, bears were becoming smaller and cubs were less and less likely to survive into adulthood. All around the Arctic Circle, from Canada to Russia to Norway, the pattern was consistent, and scientists were building the case that polar bears were the first in a long series of future calamities attributable to global warming.

Steven Amstrup, who had written many of the papers detailing the bears' precipitous decline, was beginning to understand the carnage. As global warming shrank their hunting grounds, the polar bears were becoming more and more desperate. The sea ice was in full retreat. The seals were nowhere to be found. Polar bears were turning to cannibalism because they were starving to death.

Or, at least that's how it got reported . . .

CHAPTER 1

Let's See
What We've Got
Bear-Wise

The more I study these animals the less I know.
—MALCOLM RAMSAY, POLAR BEAR SCIENTIST,
UNIVERSITY OF SASKATCHEWAN

NESTOR TWO ... *scratch* ... Rocky ... *scratch* ... bear ... Nestor ... be careful ... *scraaaaaatch* ... bear." The radio on my hip crackled, but the static made it impossible to pick out anything specific. The bugs in my ear didn't help, either, as they launched kamikaze missions toward my face, gorging themselves on the sweet juices running from the corners of my eyes. A minute ago I'd splashed my face and hair with pure Deet bug repellent, but it had had no effect other than to give the blackflies a caustic aftertaste as they committed suicide against the back of my throat.

In the distance, a man stood on the roof of a building that looked as though it had fallen from the sky into the middle of a river. This wasn't like any river I'd seen before—no babbling waters, no cool shade trees. Instead, it was impossible to tell where the water ended and the land began. Clumps of ragged grass sprouted from the muck, cutting the waterway into a thousand braided channels; in most places the water was less than a foot deep and flowed so slowly that when the wind picked up, the current seemed to change direction. The highest natural feature in miles was the top of my head. The man on the rooftop waved his arm as he called on the radio, repeating his garbled message about a bear and the need to be careful.

It was 2008, and I was standing in the river itself, in water that was ice cold despite this being the middle of July. I had bought a mesh bug mask in preparation for the trip, but the packaging didn't mention how unpleasant it is to wrap your head in a poison-impregnated swath of green gauze. Suffocating inside the torture hood was marginally better than being enveloped by the waiting clouds of gnats. Someone had loaned me a pair of hip waders with a leak in the left toe, and now I staggered through the shallows with a dead-frozen foot, bug repellent running into my eyes and accumulating in my liver, and a hungry polar bear somewhere behind me, watching the whole mess and licking his lips. Ah, the sweet serenity of nature.

The river was called the Mast, and it flowed through Wapusk National Park and into Hudson Bay, thirty miles east of Churchill, Manitoba. In the fall, the town is literally overrun with polar bears waiting for the sea ice to form; come the November freeze-up, the bears head out and disappear from view. The bears attract tourists, and for six weeks in October and November, this little town of nine hundred people becomes a world-class ecotourism destination as 10,000 visitors descend on a slightly shell-shocked local populace.

But in the summer, with the bears not yet in residence within city limits, there's little reason to visit. In the hot months, the bears bed down, wallowing in the shallows of Hudson Bay and the cool bogs of Wapusk National Park. Wapusk, which means "white bear" in Cree, is one of Canada's most rugged and least accessible parks, an inhospitable jumble of tundra and willow bogs. (One park ranger remarked that he'd put up a signpost a few years earlier and "can you believe that it doesn't even have a single bullet hole in it yet? There really must be nobody coming here.")

There are differences in behavior among bear species. Black bears and grizzlies hibernate, but polar bears just starve. Whereas other bears are omnivorous, polar bears are said to feed almost exclusively on meat, on seal blubber in particular. In Hudson Bay, the seals don't come ashore, so the bears go onto the ice to find them. The seals scratch air holes in the ice, and the bears wait to pounce, motionless—sometimes for days—until the seals surface. Sometimes a bear will slip into the water and blast up underneath a seal, forcing the terrified animal up through the air hole and to its death. When they hunt, bears are both cunning and infinitely patient. They'll build walls of snow for camouflage, or even hide behind blocks of ice that they push along the surface of the frozen sea.

But sea ice is a winter thing. After gorging all winter, the summer and fall is a time of steady weight loss. During the late stages of the fast, which lasts for up to five months, bears drop two pounds a day. For pregnant females, the lean season is even worse. Typically, they'll go inland and dig a lair in September, emerging eight months later without having eaten a bite. They can gestate, deliver their babies, and nurse them into solid cubs, all without taking a single meal.

And that is why a loss of ice is such a problem. Each degree of temperature rise means one more ice-free week per summer. In one week of hunting, a female polar bear catches an average of one and a half seals. This translates into twenty-two pounds of blubber that the bear can store for the lean months. Add the opportunity cost of lost hunting to the actual cost of more fasting, and some bears drop thirty-five pounds in a week, nearly one-tenth of the body weight for a younger bear. As the falls get warmer and longer, what should be a time of getting bigger has turned into a time of increasing desperation. Female bears are now less likely to have triplets; the energy demands of raising so many cubs are simply too great. Even with litters of one or two, fewer youngsters are surviving to adulthood. There's no better way to destroy a population than to decimate its youth.

Polar bears don't love hot weather, but they can suffer through it. The problem with global warming is that without ice to stand on, it's very difficult for bears to hunt. Nobody knows exactly what will happen with sea ice in the future, but recent years have seen dramatic shrinkage. In the last two decades of the twentieth century, Arctic sea ice disappeared at a rate of about 3 percent annually. In the summer of 2007 alone, over 1 million square kilometers of ice were lost, an area equivalent to Texas and California combined. Some scientists predict that the Arctic will be ice-free in summer by the middle of this century.

Of course, not everyone is willing to believe the dire predictions. The summer of 2008 was significantly colder than previous years, causing climate change skeptics to crow that warming was a myth. Climate scientists countered that the summer of 2008 still had significantly less ice than was average thirty years prior. One thing everyone agreed on was that whenever you talked about sea ice, you had to show a picture of a polar bear. It only made sense; it's hard to get people excited about ice without crushing it in a blender and adding tequila. Environmental groups warned that if trends continued, the polar bears would all die. Global warming deniers said that fluctuations in sea ice were normal and unconnected to human activities. Besides, they said, doing anything about it would bankrupt every nation on earth. Neither side of the screaming match really mentioned that it was *summer* sea ice that was shrinking; nobody was going so far as to predict ice-free winters anytime soon. And, at least in Churchill, polar bears had been living through ice-free summers for as long as anybody could remember.

MY COMPANION IN THE MAST RIVER, Dr. Robert Rockwell, held his radio high in the air and spun around like a homing beacon, bending one way and another until the signal became clear. This operation was made more difficult by his MacGyver-style vest brimming with gadgetry, and the short-barreled shotgun slung over his shoulder. Face and hands uncovered, Rockwell had no patience for bug jackets or other such sissy accoutrements.

"You've got a bear to the south of camp a bit," the radio announced, the static breaking momentarily. "He's sniffing around. Looks like maybe a subadult."

"Cool!" Rockwell responded, with the enthusiasm of a teenager, and then signed off. He holstered his radio and untangled the strap of his shotgun, a Remington 870 pump action with the words "FOR LAW ENFORCEMENT ONLY" etched onto the side. Rockwell wasn't exactly a cop, but out here in the land of nobody and nothing, he was as close as it got. He explained to me that he liked a short gun because it didn't stick up too far over his shoulder, a handy feature when your commute vehicle is a helicopter. Also, when he was walking through waist-high willows, it rested easy in his hands, Rambo style, so he could wheel quickly and shoot from the hip if a bear came crashing on him from close range. Mostly though, it was just damned cool. And Rockwell liked being cool.

Showing no obvious signs of worry about the fact that there was a polar bear in our general neighborhood, Rockwell picked up where he had left off a minute ago, in the middle of an enthusiastic description of the migratory habits of the lesser snow goose. To my untrained (and decidedly bear-phobic) eye, he seemed completely unconcerned about being on the ground with one bear—and possibly many more—lurking in the shallows nearby. But this was—I hoped—probably just the result of confidence and caution rather than the opposite. He'd spent forty summers in polar bear country, studying their behavior and getting comfortable with the feeling of being within sniffing distance of a thousand-pound carnivore. Birds, bears, blades of grass—to Rockwell they were all just happy little links in the circle of life.

I, on the other hand, was feeling a bit like bait.

"Should we maybe head back in?" I asked.

"A million and a half geese coming up the Mississippi and Central flyways," he said, ignoring me. He pulled a bottle of Deet from one of his pockets and dabbed it on himself like a socialite applying Chanel. "Just imagine that . . . a million and a half!"

"Yeah, I'm pretty sure I read that in one of your papers," I said. "I wonder if that bear's still where he was a minute ago?" If this particular bear wanted to get to the bay from his current inland position, he'd have to come right through us. As the wind shifted, beginning now to blow from our back and toward the bear's nose, my mind turned to the

pork-chop sandwich and granola bar in my backpack. "He must be getting a pretty good whiff of us right now," I said.

"But even if you get your *lambda* value down to one," Rockwell continued, "it's going to take years or even decades before you see any significant changes in a goose population like that. A population that big
is like a battleship—you can't just turn it around on a dime!" I couldn't
tell if Rockwell was really this comfortable with what I assumed was our
impending mauling, or whether I was overreacting. I felt like the dumb
new kid on a military patrol, hunkered down in the river and jumping
at every rustle in the bush. I edged away from Rockwell in the direction
of camp, hoping that maybe I could get him moving.

"Oh, by the way," Rockwell said, looking down at a bird skeleton
he'd found in the water. "Don't get too far ahead of me, because the bears
just love to hide out on these little islands." I stepped back, climbing out
of the water onto a tuft of grass the size of a VW Bug. All of a sudden,
an eider flopped out of the bushes in a tumble of flailing wings and aggrieved squawks. I jumped ten feet in the air while Rockwell chortled
happily alongside me. The bird darted around my feet, making furious
noises and hazing me away from a nest hidden in the grass. As I moved
past, she waddled onto the dirt and shot me a menacing glare before set-
tling back down with her eggs.

"This is a *coooooool* feather," Rocky said, handing me something
gray and matted, which looked a lot like a wet version of every other
feather I'd ever seen.

"Very cool," I said.

"It's incredible what you can find out here," Rocky said, rattling off
a list of birds and grasses that I forgot as quickly as he could say them.
I'd come out to this desolate spot because I wanted to see polar bears,
but it was starting to dawn on me that Rockwell was the kind of naturalist
that has always filled me with dread: strip away all of his illustrious degrees and well-reviewed publications, and Rockwell was, deep down inside, a birdwatcher.

And Rockwell wasn't playing around. The personal and the professional were in perfect harmony; he had binoculars that were probably

worth more than my car, had seen more animal species than Noah, and was cheerily willing to talk about them, one critter at a time, until everyone within earshot had died. I'd met his type before, but I was only just realizing that the only thing worse than spending time with a birder is spending time with a birder while you're worried about being stalked by a polar bear.

After quite a bit more detail than I cared to hear about snow goose mating, Rockwell finally started to amble back toward safety, with frequent stops to inspect bits of moss or feathers that he found hidden among the river rocks. Half an hour later we reached the camp, known for some reason as Nestor Two, which was ringed by an electric fence sunk into the riverbed. I grasped the plastic handle of the gate and stepped over the bottom wire, dripping water onto the electrified coils. When you come back from a walk in Manitoba you don't brush off the dust; instead, you clean Manitoba out from between your toes.

"Here we are," Rockwell said. "Now let's see what we've got bearwise."

To say that Nestor Two was on an "island" would be too generous. Really it was more like a dirty lump the size of a football field. Half a dozen buildings were scattered about at haphazard angles and a low haze hung in the air, along with a cloud of toxins emanating from a decrepit steel drum that glowed red with fire.

"That's the best spot on the island," Rockwell chirped, pointing to some broken lawn chairs next to the flaming barrel. "The bugs won't come near you there!" The entire place had a post-apocalyptic feeling of isolation and despair. The hot fence completed the prison camp ambiance.

I followed Rockwell along a series of wooden pallets and broken stretches of boardwalk that were sunk into the pernicious mud. He moved lightly over the uneven pathway, and when we reached the far end of the camp, he scampered up a ladder that was nailed to the side of a building. As I scrambled to secure my footing, Rockwell straddled the peak of the roof and raised a pair of binoculars. "Yup, there he is," he said, and handed me the field glasses.

A few hundred yards away, a polar bear moved from left to right over broken ground. His white fur stood out against the green islands, but when he slipped into the water, he disappeared. I was amazed by how well this giant animal could camouflage himself. It was the height of summer, not a patch of snow in sight, and still this immense white beast was impossible to get a bead on. One moment I'd be looking right at him, watching him move smoothly over an island or through a pool, and a second later he'd vanish. The terrain seemed incidental to him; in the water he didn't splash, and on land he didn't disturb a leaf. I've always imagined bears as crashing through the underbrush, substituting speed and brute force for their lack of stealth. But this guy was pure poise, utterly in control of every inch of his frame. His silence was more unsettling than his strength could ever be. Soon, as I spun around on the roof to take in the vast emptiness surrounding me, every distant rock and unidentifiable lump became suspect. We could be under wholesale bear attack for all I knew, and have absolutely no idea until the moment they hit the fence.

The bear appeared to be looking for something. He lingered on each island, head down, pawing in the dirt. I watched as he ripped up a large bush as if it were a tiny weed. Occasionally he lifted his snout and stood frozen, smelling the mixed odor of food waste, plastic, and general humanity wafting out of the burn barrel.

"Definitely a subadult," Rockwell said. "He looks good, too. Here fatty fatty, heeeere fatty," he cooed, as though calling a puppy. "I guess he didn't get the memo."

"Which memo is that?" I asked.

"The one that says he's supposed to be starving to death." Rockwell lowered his binoculars and laughed out loud.

CHAPTER 2

The James Bond of
Vertebrate Zoology

I DIDN'T END UP IN polar bear country by accident. I went there because I wanted to be a hero of the environmental movement. What spotted owls and baby harp seals were to previous decades, polar bears were to the 2000s. Their coming annihilation at the hands of callous consumerism was Love Canal, Three Mile Island, and the *Exxon Valdez* all rolled into one sad, furry face. Everything that was bad about the world could be easily expressed by the image of a lone bear on a melting piece of ice. And I was going to be the one to write the book that brought it all together in one tidy package. I'd be as sensitive as Aldo Leopold, as persuasive as Rachel Carson, and as angry as Ed Abbey. Hell, I'd be Henry David Thoreau, and Hudson Bay would be my Walden.

This wasn't a passing fancy or some half-baked lunge at eco-stardom. I'm not a nutcase with a bear fetish or a shrill environmental warrior who wants to smash the technological paradigm while also seeing his face on television as much as possible. Instead, I am that other species of treehugger, the kind who drives a minivan that gets only seventeen miles to the gallon but who at least has the good sense to feel really, really guilty about it. I go to websites that help me analyze my global warming footprint and (sometimes) I even (occasionally) buy carbon offsets when I book an airplane flight. I've replaced the light bulbs in my house with compact fluorescents, bought energy-efficient windows, and planted a little victory garden in my backyard. I eat organic, bicycle to work, and do a totally kickass job of remembering to turn off the computer before I go to sleep. By the standards of the Supersize Society, I'm practically a monk.

I CAME BY MY ENVIRONMENTALISM HONESTLY, with a childhood that included a lot of sleeping in the dirt. I was a Junior Ranger without peer, the kind of kid who can't really catch a baseball but can tell you the difference between igneous and metamorphic rock. When it came time for college I chose Brown University, in part because of its reputation for aggressively left-leaning crunchiness. I convinced myself that Brown alums all shunned the stuffy investment banker/corporate lawyer route that was the stuff of dreams for Harvard and Yale men, those scholastic automatons whose only ambition was to crush the little guy like their daddies did.

In the end, the only difference between Brown and the rest of the colleges on the East Coast was that we did our laundry less frequently. We were also more prone to shoulder injuries as a result of so vigorously patting ourselves on the backs for our moral rectitude. As it turns out, getting a bunch of well-off eighteen-year-olds to convince themselves that they're going to save the universe doesn't exactly require sorcery.

I gravitated to that temple within a temple, the Environmental Studies Department, where I imagined I would find like-minded students with whom I would spend the following years on an extended backpacking trip with occasional breaks for class work. The department was located in a funky old carriage house, grandly renamed the Urban Environmental Laboratory. There were solar panels on the roof, alfalfa sprouts grew in a jar on the windowsill, and everybody toted Nalgene water bottles from which they hydrated themselves madly without succumbing to the evils of disposable cups. Some students even slept on an upstairs deck, talking late into the night about how they were going to make a difference in the world.

THE JAMES BOND OF VERTEBRATE ZOOLOGY 15

Unfortunately, environmental science was not what I had imagined it would be. Having been raised in the West, my conception of environmentalism was decidedly wilderness-based. I thought environmental science meant wild beasts and mountains and rivers; I thought I might get the chance to see a tree or two during the course of my studies.

But the East Coast race of my species, *Homo environmentalis,* was a foreign animal. These greens eschewed extended romps in the dirt; instead they migrated in herds along the I-95 corridor, making themselves at home in Regional Sustainability Planning Commission meetings and public hearings about the use of pesticides on golf courses. This was important stuff, to be sure, but I couldn't get excited about leaking underground storage tanks or subsidies for mass transit. What sort of people become environmentalists because they dream of attending meetings where the topic of discussion is literally about the way paint dries?

I couldn't quite put it into words, but what I really wanted to be when I grew up was Steven Amstrup, the polar-bear-tranquilizing, helicopter-flying, cannibalism-witnessing, tough-as-nails, intellectual adventure junkie whom I wouldn't meet until almost two decades later. No committee meetings or long nights stuck inside a sterile laboratory testing soil samples for trace pollutants for me! I'd be one part mountaineer, one part scientist, and 100 percent badass. (All right, so maybe being the James Bond of vertebrate zoology doesn't have exactly the same cachet as being plain old James Bond, but for a nerdy kid who likes to walk in the woods, it's the next best thing.) I didn't want to *think* about things, I wanted to *do* them; I wanted to build trails, not make policy.

Hoping things would get better, I upped the ante on environmental science and enrolled in graduate school at Berkeley. When classes started, it didn't take me long to appreciate the fact that when you studied ecology in California, you occasionally got to go outside. San Francisco Bay sparkled in the sunlight, and the California hills were green with life, a refreshing corrective to the brown slush and exhausted postindustrial landscapes of the urban East. That first semester I even met my future wife, Shona, an environmental lawyer who was not only smart and funny and cute, but who also came complete with her own mountaineering gear and an extended family in the Yukon, both of which were major pluses.

But Berkeley wasn't a perfect fit, either, at least not for the kind of principled, rugged eco-warrior I hoped to become. There was a bit of cowboying, sure, but there was also a hell of a lot of minutiae. I was expected to master the life cycle of soil microbes and deeply understand the "woody debris" problem as it related to dynamic riparian ecosystems. There was calculus galore, and actual experiments with lab coats and beakers. Apparently, the Steven Amstrups of the world weren't just darting bears in the ass and then retiring to their igloos for a beer. Instead, they actually had to collect data and then do actual math. Why was it so hard for a guy to make a living doing macho, fun stuff in the woods? If the Navy SEALS had a small division for peacenik forest rangers, that would have been ideal.

I survived at Berkeley long enough to get my master's, though I'm convinced I only graduated because the professors didn't want me hanging around any longer. But before the ink on my diploma was dry, I cast environmental science aside and joined the Oakland Fire Department. If I wasn't smart or patient enough to save the earth, I was at least strong and reckless enough to save some of the people on it.

Becoming a fireman was an unassailable choice, but I still felt as though I had betrayed some essential part of myself by officially admitting that I was no better than the next guy when it came to saving the planet. Sometimes I would run into my professor on the street, and I always felt like apologizing for having tied up a spot in his graduate program. Eventually, the professor's wife even hooked me up with a freelance job writing florid ad copy for an adventure travel company. "Come gaze at the last remnants of the once mighty elephant herds," I'd write. "Test your mettle in the alligator-filled rapids before a proposed dam floods the canyon forever!" The pay was decent, but the feeling was all wrong. Cajoling people into going on luxury safari trips to gawk at darling native children is pretty much the opposite of what an environmental studies education is supposed to prepare you for.

And though I may have left academia behind, I did my best to keep environmentalism alive. At home I taught my three kids that the little things they did could make a difference. My five-year-old daughter, Percy, a congenital worrier like me, grew concerned about her carbon footprint whenever we flew to Canada to see her grandparents. My four-year-old son, Mac, helped install a drip-irrigation system in our drought-tolerant yard; he even cited environmental concerns as the reason he refused to bathe. And Zeke, the two-year-old, would yell, "No driving! Wanna walk!" no matter how long a trip we were planning to take. And usually we obliged him. I tried not to worry that my decision to have three kids negated any possible conservation efforts we could ever make.

Around the firehouse I was known as the guy who rode his bike everywhere, the guy who pestered people about recycling. The worst fight I ever got into was when another fireman exploded after I'd hassled him one too many times for running a half-empty dishwasher. I wasn't saving the world the way I once thought I might, and I wasn't out on the front lines, but it was the best I could do, and I did it with fervor. When you've got a green tinge to your soul, you're always going to be a little bit insufferable.

And yet, for all of my conservation cheerleading, I was starting to have a hard time believing in my own sales pitch. I'd performed the requisite viewings of *An Inconvenient Truth*, and when I got together with friends, we had dorky arguments about whether fuel efficiency standards or increased gas taxes were the best way to reduce greenhouse gases. But to be honest, I really wasn't seeing it. Global warming was so damned theoretical. The summers, like the winters, were either a little hotter or a little colder from one year to the next, just like they'd always been. I looked out at San Francisco Bay almost every day, and even when I went right up to the water's edge, it didn't look to be any higher than it had been when I was a kid. The Berkeley hills were green in winter and brown in summer; nothing new there. Where were the Africanized killer bees and poisonous snakes that were supposed to be marching relentlessly northward? Where were the malarial mosquitoes and the senior citizens dropping dead of heat stroke? I wasn't looking forward to that stuff, but I'd been trumpeting its arrival for so long that I felt almost cheated by the general harmony of things.

I wasn't so naïve as to think that global warming would revolve around me. And I wasn't so weak a scientist that I couldn't understand the principles of incremental change and large-scale trends. Just because I couldn't see climate change with my own eyes didn't mean it wasn't happening. Nonetheless, at some point you want to see a little return on investment, even when the currency is worry and the payoff is total global apocalypse. Maybe if I could see glaciers calving from my kitchen window every morning I would have felt differently, but honestly, it was hard to get excited about graphs detailing the potential changes in spatial distribution of conifer woodland.

The simple presence of doubt in my mind began to make me uneasy. Everybody I knew believed in global warming. Well, not everyone; the fireman who blew his stack at me over the dishwasher thought that climate change was a vast left-wing conspiracy, and he never failed to bring my attention to weather reports calling for snow. Then again, he probably also thought that Democrats wanted to euthanize old people and that Barack Obama was a Kenyan terrorist who rigged the 2008 election. Still, the thought that my opinions could ever occupy the same airspace as his was a little upsetting.

Meanwhile, bears had become as much of a rallying point for the right as they were for the left. Environmentalists used polar bears to symbolize the excesses of civilization, and conservatives used polar bears to symbolize the excesses of the left. Websites hawked T-shirts that proclaimed, "I DIDN'T FALL FOR THE POLAR BEAR EXTINCTION HOAX," and climate change skeptics bent over backward to prove that bears were healthier than they had ever been. Oklahoma Senator James Inhofe released a paper entitled, "U.S. Senate Report Debunks Polar Bear Extinction Fears." He even went so far as to compare global warming activists to "the Third Reich, the big lie." What you thought about polar bears revealed less about your understanding of science than about where you positioned yourself in the culture wars. I didn't want my nagging doubts to imperil my lifelong membership in the crunchy granola club. The certainty of the polar bear's extinction was one of those things that didn't need any more analysis, like the fact that cigarette smoking gives you cancer or that clubbing baby seals to death is in bad taste.

Watching a polar bear starve to death in front of me was, I became convinced, a surefire way to reconvince myself of the truth of global warming. My home environment was too temperate and adaptable to see any real change, and besides, I was too close to it to notice, the way you can't tell that your kids are growing until the day they grab something off the top of the refrigerator. Going to an extreme place would show me the truth; it would allow me to be a believer again. And I was sorely in need of some reassurance that the entire planet was doomed.

Moreover, my comfortable yuppie lifestyle had begun to feel a little mundane. I made Rice Krispies squares for Mac's preschool fund-raisers, I obsessed over my 401(k), and I changed the oil religiously on our new minivan. We'd moved into a house on the same street where I grew up, meaning that after thirty-five years, my life had gone precisely nowhere. On Tuesdays the kids had piano, on Thursdays they had ice skating, and on Sundays we went to the farmers' market, where we saw the same people buying the same whole-wheat scones and drinking the same fair-trade coffee that had been shade-grown by an enlightened cooperative of proto-Marxist peasants in the high Andes.

Every man's midlife crisis is different, of course, but it was becoming clear that mine was going to involve some serious face time with a really big carnivore. When I try to explain it, it doesn't make a whole lot of sense. But I needed some adventure, some discomfort, some way to reconnect with that idealistic kid who used to think he could save the world. I needed to see the great bears before they died, to witness man's destruction of one of the last great things on earth, to do my small, smug part to educate the folks down south about the heavy consequences of our actions.

"Would you like to go see a polar bear?" I asked Mac one day, as he whacked a hatchet against our back fence for no apparent reason. He lowered the weapon tentatively, looking out at me from beneath matted blond hair. I was struck by how much my reckless son looked like a poster kid for an anti-child-abuse public service announcement. His left eye was black, half a dozen bruises ranging from deep purple to light yellow dotted his bare legs, and a trail of dried blood flaked off his shoulder. Given the choice, he would almost certainly prefer to be raised by wolves than by my wife and me.

"A real polar, Daddy?" he asked.

"Yes."

"No, no . . . I mean a real polar bear. Not the kind that lives in a zoo and eats dog food."

"Those are real," I said.

"They're real but they're not *real*," he said. "I only want to see the kind that live on the ice and still kill people. Can you take me to see that kind?"

"No promises," I said, beginning to hatch a plan. "But I'll see what I can do."

CHAPTER 3

The Polar Bear
Capital of the World

The polar bear is an intelligent and crafty animal,
but it is cursed with intense curiosity.

—FRIDTJOF NANSEN, LEGENDARY
NINETEENTH-CENTURY POLAR EXPLORER

I F YOU'VE EVER SEEN a picture of a polar bear, chances are that it was taken in Churchill. And if you've ever seen a picture of a polar bear that was taken by someone you know, then the odds of it being from Churchill rise to nearly 100 percent. Churchill isn't just the Polar Bear Capital of the World; perhaps more important, it's the Polar Bear *Tourist* Capital of the World. After a few long nights of Googling, it became abundantly clear to me that the route to saving the world led right through the heart of Churchill.

During the winter, the town has a population of under 1,000. By January, the Arctic night is endless and the temperatures are so low that just walking around outside is dangerous. In Berkeley, if you get drunk and fall asleep underneath a lamppost, the worst that happens is you'll wake up with a mouthful of gutter water. But in Churchill, such things can be fatal. Churchill isn't a bad place, but it is unremittingly harsh. Whether it's the summer bugs, the pitch-dark winter, or the epic bouts

21

of unemployment, only a very special kind of person chooses to make this place home. Even the mayor doesn't live in town full-time; his family all moved to Winnipeg years ago.

If Churchill had a flag it would be gray on a gray background, with gray trim. Just as Ireland is associated with green and Arizona with rusty red, things in Churchill are notable mostly for their lack of any color whatsoever. Even polar bears, as it turns out, look as though they've been smudged nose to tail by a dedicated charcoal artist. And in the fall, when the sun dips permanently below the horizon, the people themselves take on a sickly hue, except for when they're florid red, testament to the rigorous drinking required to banish the grayness from their lives.

Churchill's main street does not scream "vacation destination." There are no decorative streetlamps, no sidewalk cafés. In fact, on one side of the street there's no sidewalk at all, just a sign telling snowmobilers to take it easy. Churchill's main street isn't even named Main Street; instead, it honors Henry Kelsey, a lifelong employee of the Hudson's Bay Company whose main claims to fame are that he had an excellent ear for Native dialects, that he was twice captured and imprisoned by the French, and that he *may have been* the first white man to see a buffalo. A modest hero for a modest town.

At one point, though, the town was full of heroes. In the early 1940s, World War II was in full swing, and there were reports of German subs in Hudson Strait. Any military strategist with a globe on his desk couldn't help but notice the potential geopolitical significance of the Far North. If you started out in Churchill, it was a straight shot over the top of the world to the Soviet Union, and the Allies were not about to leave their northern flank unguarded.

By 1942, there were 2,200 American soldiers living in Churchill. The plan was for wounded servicemen from Europe to be evacuated to Churchill, where they could recuperate before being sent back to the front. The town's position on Hudson Bay was also mentioned as a potential key link in the supply chain of food and materiel between North America and Europe.

But the bad guys never snuck over the top of the world, and the base was eventually converted to a scientific rocket range. Churchill is famous for the frequency of its northern lights, and the military wanted to know more about them. Specifically, military scientists wanted to know how to turn them off, because the aurora interfered with communications equipment. Today, the ground around Churchill is littered with bits of abandoned rocketry, from unidentifiably twisted metal to fully intact nose cones. Before long, the rocket range was abandoned as well, and the entire military infrastructure crumpled into the snow, a monument to the coldest front of the cold war.

The town of Churchill is like an archaeological dig with no archaeologists. Layers of history, the very ancient to the merely old, sit atop each other in various states of ruin or simple neglect. Nothing ever disappears here: structures are built, abandoned, reclaimed, repurposed, and abandoned again. There's so much land, and demolition takes so much effort, that the easiest thing to do is build anew in the shadow of the old, maybe stealing a few boards as necessary but leaving the skeleton to stand as a neighbor.

For the parts of town that are at least nominally in use, the general aesthetic is that of a plucky trailer park. Because there is no road connecting Churchill to the rest of the world, and the nearest spindly timber is many miles away, everything in town has been shipped by rail at great expense. You might enjoy some decorative trim around your windows, but do you really want to fly to Winnipeg, rent a car, pick out your samples, box them for shipping, fly home, meet the train at midnight three weeks later, and keep your fingers crossed that your prized molding wasn't crushed en route by a box of canned pears in heavy syrup? Better just to stick with simple two-by-fours and tack a pair of antlers over the front door.

Kelsey Boulevard boasts one grocery store, five restaurants, a hardware store, and sixty-three fake polar bears. I know because I counted; there's not a lot to do in Churchill. Nearly every building—businesses, private residences, and government offices—has its own polar bear of one kind or another. The polar bears come in all shapes and sizes, both realistic and abstract. They exist as paintings, statues, etchings; every form of art known to man has been pressed into service in order to render the polar bear. To say that Churchill is bear crazy is an understatement; if you were to remove everything with either a picture of a bear or the word "bear," the town would probably fall to pieces.

THE AUTUMN MONTHS are the sweet spot in Churchill. In the fall, the temperatures are mild (by Arctic standards), there's a solid block of daylight every twenty-four hours, and the bugs have taken a breather, doing whatever it is mosquitoes do when they're not sucking human blood. And, at the same time, a thousand bears arrive on the outskirts of town, lean and hungry and impatient. Because of a few geographical oddities, the coastline off Churchill is the first spot in Hudson Bay to freeze solid. The bears know this, so with the first chill of fall, they mass on the tidal lowlands, waiting for the slush to turn solid so they can head out and hunt.

Over the years, the ecotourists of the world have acquired the same seasonal knowledge. Come mid-October, Churchill transforms from a sleepy nowheresville to a galloping boomtown. The six-week bear-watching season is a brief window that brings in 10,000 tourists, not to mention most of the money that sustains the townsfolk for the remaining forty-six.

As long as the bears keep coming, so will the tourists. Thousands of tourists from every corner of the earth: German nature lovers and Japanese photo-safarians, and slightly unhinged American I-came-so-close-I-almost-got-my-hand-bitten-off adventure-travel yahoos. As the temperatures plunge and the kitsch salesmen feverishly rake in foreign currency, the gawkers compete for space with the scientists, the wildlife management officers, the conservationists, and the regular people of Churchill, who just want to get their kids to school without having them eaten by a bear or run over by a herd of senior citizens in matching parkas midway through their "Elder Hostel Trip of a Lifetime."

The crush of wannabe Bear Whisperers is so strong that the locals have even created an entirely new mode of transportation. Known as Tundra Buggies, these glorified RVs have wheels as high as a man's head, reinforced walls, and windows just out of reach of prying snouts or paws. From the outside, a Tundra Buggy looks like an unholy union between an RV and a FEMA trailer. It is boxy and rectangular, wider than a school bus, and it floats high off the ground on tires that are five feet across. Inside there is a tiny bathroom, as on a Greyhound bus, and a heater powerful enough for on-the-spot cremations, should the need arise. On the back of the buggy, there is an "observation deck" that protrudes out over the rear wheels, its floor made of see-through metal mesh to allow riders to watch as bears pass underneath. The deck is surrounded by chest-high wooden walls to keep the people in and the bears out; the aggregate effect feels something like a penalty box or an Arctic chicken coop. People pay thousands of dollars for the privilege of being packed inside like schoolchildren and driven along the coast in circles, eyes peeled for bears.

A Churchill vacation isn't a study in luxury. But for the hardcore animal lover who needs to tick the polar bear box on his list, there's no spot on earth better suited for the task. For a northerly place, Churchill is fairly far south, and as easily accessible as a place with no road access can be. There are motels and gift shops, Internet access, and even a small movie theater (because you can't talk about bears *all* the time). Scientists flock to this spot, too, as do photographers, movie stars, politicians, and the occasional member of one royal family or another.

The travelers who show up belong, almost exclusively, to the camp for whom global warming is both real and immediate. A climate change skeptic wouldn't waste the time on a trip to see what are essentially overgrown dogs rolling around in the dirt. But for the true believers, a trip to Churchill is a chance to decry the ills of modern society and congratulate themselves for being aware enough to head off the beaten path in search of Truth—never mind the carbon footprint of the trek. These are the select few with the desire and the money to go beyond the *National Geographic* article and experience climate change firsthand. But even more than that, there's no price too large for the *Holy Shit!* that comes from seeing those powerful jaws just a few feet from your throat.

I figured that the best way to get beneath the surface of the tourist circus was to offer myself as a volunteer with one of the big-name researchers. Every fall, these scientists did population surveys by shooting tranquilizer darts out of helicopters, weighing and measuring the drugged bears, then radio-collaring them or tattooing their gums with a unique identification number. I figured I'd ride shotgun in the helicopter, kneel in the snow next to a groggy bear, entertain the tiny cubs until mom woke up. When I'd earned the scientists' trust, maybe they'd even let me shoot the tranquilizer dart myself. This was going to be awesome.

"You can't come with me."

"I won't be any trouble, I promise," I said.

"You can't come with me." At long last I was talking to Steven Amstrup, and it was not going well. I'd left him multiple voice mails, tried to get at him through the most tenuous strings of personal connections. I'd finally caught him in person and he sounded deeply annoyed, as though he'd picked up the phone expecting someone else and instead gotten me, yet another in a long string of people who wanted something.

"I'll pay my own way. I'll charter a helicopter, I'll work for you for free, just please let me come along next time you do a bear survey."

"It's simply not possible," he said. I'm not averse to groveling, but this was low even for me. I felt like I was begging an old girlfriend to take me back after she'd already gotten married and had twins with the new guy.

"Well, if there's ever any way . . ."

"There won't be," he cut me off. "Good luck."

I wanted Steven Amstrup badly. He wasn't a musty academic, but a researcher for the United States Geological Survey. I hadn't known that the USGS cared about anything that was actually alive, but Amstrup was a dynamo when it came to wildlife management. In his résumé he stated flatly that "I am the senior polar bear specialist in the US Federal Government." He was based in Anchorage, Alaska, but traveled all over the world, penning countless papers with titles like "Forecasting the Range-wide Status of Polar Bears at Selected Times in the 21st Century."

Whenever anybody needed a prediction about the future of polar bears, Amstrup was the crystal ball into which they gazed. He was the go-to guy, the public face of the polar bear. One minute he'd be testifying before Congress, and the next he'd be chatting with a television host, detailing the crisis in calm, measured tones. He was never hysterical and he always struck the right balance between scientific jargon and a heartfelt appeal to humanity's better impulses. It didn't hurt that he was tall and better looking than anybody with a PhD has a right to be. With sandy blond hair, a square jaw, and broad shoulders, it was no wonder the cameras loved him. He wore flannel shirts and blue jeans and looked as if he'd climbed down from a Marlboro billboard. To this day, he remains the only person I've ever met who can look cool when wearing three layers of thermal underwear and a hat with chinstraps. Not only was he living my adrenaline-junkie's dream, but he was saving the world in the process. At least when we'd talked on the phone I'd preserved enough dignity to avoid mentioning that he was what I wanted to be when I grew up.

Amstrup wasn't the only polar bear scientist in the world, but I quickly learned that he was not alone in his desire to completely blow me off. Getting a polar bear scientist to return your calls is as easy as convincing Mick Jagger to sing at your Labor Day picnic. I pursued the top guys with a vengeance, firing off emails and cyber-stalking their graduate students. Part of the problem was that there just weren't many of these guys to choose from. Unlike the group of academics who work with, say, white mice, the North American cohort of polar bear scientists is small enough that they can share a hotel suite when they go to a conference. They were deluged by media requests, savaged by skeptics, and put under the sort of public scrutiny that most ecologists never face. It wasn't their fault; when most of them got into the field decades ago, they weren't signing up for what most scientists would consider to be a plum assignment. The fact that it had become sexy over the years was one of those unforeseeable blips in the public's interest. Now they had become the kings of the realm. One biologist friend of mine lamented that the big mammal guys like Amstrup rake in grant money by the barrelful, while she has to struggle for every dollar for her research on salamanders. Well, *duh*.

The newfound stardom being enjoyed by Amstrup and his colleagues was putting a serious crimp in my plans. I started to refer to the group as the Heavy Hitters, a secretive cabal of ecological geniuses who rarely deigned to speak with commoners. One scientist pleaded overload, saying that he'd had his fill of media and couldn't do any more. Then he piled on: "I cannot accommodate everyone and . . . the end product of that collaboration has to be 'scientific,' focus on the polar bears, and have a strong conservation message." Did he think I didn't have a conservation message? Wasn't I making myself clear? I needed to feel fur between my fingers, to look into those big, watery bear eyes and say, "I'm here for you guys. Just let me tell your story." All I wanted from the scientists was for them to let me join their cause, so why wouldn't they hurry up and love me?

Finally, somebody asked me if I'd talked to Dr. Robert Rockwell and his grad student Linda Gormezano. Not only had I not talked to Rockwell, I'd never even heard of him. My initial search was unpromising; Rockwell's website had a tribute to the heroes of 9/11 and an enormous list of publications with such titles as "Effects of Declining Body Condition on Gosling Survival in Mass-Banded Lesser Snow Geese." But according to my source, Rockwell had spent forty summers in the bear-heavy tidal marshes to the west of Churchill. Reportedly, he'd had more polar bear encounters than all of the other researchers put together. It was worth a try; the Heavy Hitters had already rejected me, so how much worse could it be to get stiffed by an expert on the sexual habits of geese?

CHAPTER 4

Vacation in Bogland

A monstrous blot on a swampy spot,
with a partial view of the frozen sea.

—ROBERT BALLANTYNE,
HUDSON BAY COMPANY CLERK, 1846

MUCH TO MY SURPRISE, Dr. Rockwell was every bit as accessible as the Heavy Hitters were reclusive. He even picked up his own phone on the first ring. I stammered out my usual introduction about how I was conservation minded, scientifically oriented, totally not an asshole, and really good at buying beer for people who helped me. "Sure!" Rockwell hollered into the phone. His manner edged into the upper reaches of appropriate friendliness. "Do you want to come for one week or two?" he asked, inviting me to join him at his research camp. "You can bunk here for free and I'll pay for all the food, unless you like to cook, in which case you should bring up any special ingredients you need, but otherwise I do most of the cooking and we usually eat pretty well up here."

"I can't tell you how much I appreciate this," I said. "I've been trying and trying to get on with Amstrup and those other guys, but I haven't had any luck."

"Of course you haven't," Rockwell snorted. "Believe me—you're not alone." My failure to score an interview with the Heavy Hitters only seemed to make Rockwell like me more. And just like that, I was set: ten days in polar bear country coming right up. It seemed almost too easy, but I was hardly in a position to be picky. Given the generally annoying nature of reporters—not to mention reporters in bear country—Rocky probably had some misgivings about me. But if he did, he kept them to himself.

"If you mean what you say about wanting to get the science right, then coming up here will really open your eyes," he said. "You can't believe everything you're reading about polar bears in the papers." It was just cryptic enough to be absolutely intriguing.

THERE'S NO EASY WAY to get to Churchill, Manitoba. The town sits on the edge of Hudson Bay, six hundred miles north of Winnipeg. The next-closest town is Arviat, a predominantly Inuit community in the Canadian territory of Nunavut. There's no road to Arviat, either. Most people arrive in Churchill by way of a painful rail odyssey, several days of bone-rattling tedium through midcontinent nothingness. The sleeper cars book up quickly, consigning many travelers to two nights in their seats, shoulder to shoulder with trappers and semi-feral homesteaders who disembark along the route and disappear into the bush. In summertime, the sun hardly sets, and the view from the coach cars is fantastic, provided that you're a fan of bogland.

If you think of Canada as nothing but frozen tundra and windswept grasslands, then you obviously haven't experienced Manitoba. Manitoba is the ooziest place I have ever been. Manitobans boast that their province is home to 100,000 lakes, but that understates how watery everything is. Depending on your criteria for use of the word "lake," Manitoba could easily have a million of them. Spidery networks of creeks and rivers stretch out in every direction, linking pond to rivulet to brook to any other word ever invented to describe a body of water. Even solid ground looks unstable; I suspect that anything in Manitoba that isn't paved over could be drunk through a straw.

Manitoba's most prominent natural feature is Lake Winnipeg, a long, ragged fissure in the earth just north of the city of Winnipeg. It has a shallow bottom, an irregular coastline, and dozens of tiny islands. The lake is 258 miles from north to south, and covers about 10,000 square miles; nearby, Cedar Lake, Lake Manitoba, and Lake Winnipegosis cover another 5,000. The word "Winnipeg" is Cree for "muddy waters," an accurate if somewhat uncharming description if that's your home region's capital city and main geographical feature. Although Lake Winnipeg is not large enough to be affected by lunar tides, the wind whips up waves as high as four feet, and the water levels are so variable that you can bring a towel and a picnic to your favorite beach spot only to find a long pier leading out to a mile of pure mud. Which may be for the best, because Lake Winnipeg is subject to regular explosions of blue-green algae called neurotoxic cyanophyte, which, if inhaled, can cause vomiting, diarrhea, liver and brain damage, and sometimes death. Nothing puts a damper on summer vacation quite like liver failure.

A CANADIAN FRIEND OF MINE once told me that Manitoba is "easily the worst place in the country." When I asked why, she said that "it's got the coldest winters, the hottest summers, and the most mosquitoes." In a country that's world famous for its cold and its bugs, this is a pretty serious charge. (The oppressive summertime heat is just an added bonus.)

Because trains to Churchill are often hours late—and have been plagued by a series of derailments in recent years—air travel is a better bet. Churchill is a gateway to the remote Canadian territories of Nunavut and the Northwest Territories; Calm Air—sometimes referred to as Calamity Air—shuttles to half a dozen remote communities. A round-trip from Winnipeg to Churchill costs $1,100, and that's only if you can get a seat, which is next to impossible during the tourist season. Because of the harsh northern weather, flights are often turned back midway, and seatmates swap stories of the days they've spent bouncing back and forth between Rankin Inlet and Repulse Bay before finally arriving at their destination. Still, the airline gives out free coffee in the boarding area and giant chocolate chip cookies on board, extra touches that go a surprisingly long way toward making up for the other indignities.

As I settled into my seat for the long flight northward, I noticed that many of the people on the plane had requested seatbelt extenders, an obesity accessory that I had never known existed. In the airport, the gate attendant had weighed my carry-on bag and entered the result into a complex seating chart formula. My decision to bring a few extra books apparently mattered more than the fact that my seatmate was the functional equivalent of two seatmates.

Sitting across from me were two Native men in dirty jeans and tattered ball caps. I'm never sure what to call people like that when I'm in Canada. "Native American" is surely wrong, and "Native Canadian" sounds forced and derivative. "Indian" is just as loaded in Canada as it is in the States and misses the fact that there are actually six hundred–plus different kinds of indigenous people in Canada. "Indigenous" makes them sound like plants, and "aboriginal" is too Australian. The preferred term these days is "First Nations," an appellation clearly designed by committee, with the added disadvantage of being grammatically maddening. What would you say: I am a First Nations? A First National? I hail from the First Nations . . . and also from a suburb near Toronto?

"Are you guys from Churchill?" I asked, hoping for a little of that small-town friendliness that rural people are always congratulating themselves for.

"Yup," said the guy on the aisle.

"Have you lived there your whole lives?"

"Yup."

"So what were you doing down in Winnipeg? Did you have a good time?"

"Nope."

I'd been warned that First Nations people were a reticent bunch, but this was an even more difficult conversation than I could have imagined. Maybe their silence was a generations-old adaptation designed to avoid losing body heat through an open mouth. Then again, I probably wasn't helping myself with the scientific article I had splayed across my lap, recommended reading from Dr. Rockwell and his colleagues entitled, "Facts from Feces Revisited."

"Seen any polar bears recently?" I asked.

"Yup."

"Where were they? Can you tell me anything about them?"

"Nope," the guy said, at which point I gave up.

Outside the window, the Nelson River came into view, and then the Churchill River after it, two broad currents running hard to the northeast, relentless sluiceways of frigid water. And finally Hudson Bay itself appeared, the great thirsty basin that all of Manitoba's waters labor so hard to reach. Hudson Bay is an immense, kidney-shaped body of water with a suggestively shaped protruding appendage called James Bay. For teenage Canadian boys, the lower reaches of Hudson Bay must serve the same snicker-inducing function as Florida does for adolescent American geographers. Hudson Bay is technically a part of the Arctic Ocean, though the only passage out of it is a jumble of islands, backwaters, and randomly placed ice shelves. This area, known as Hudson Strait, was a deathtrap for early explorers who got frozen in place when winter suddenly arrived. Today, with GPS equipment, ice-breaking ships, and satellite weather-prediction capabilities, Hudson Strait is merely a monumental headache and perennial financial sinkhole. Winter still sneaks up on sailors, although scurvy and dysentery are no longer in vogue.

DR. ROCKWELL'S CAMP is not located in Churchill proper. Instead, it is at La Perouse Bay, a V-shaped notch in the coastline thirty miles away. Unless you want to hoof it overland through a long expanse of marshland, your only option is a helicopter journey, which costs $1,500 an hour. Plus fuel. Unfortunately, Rockwell's hospitality did not extend quite that far. I tried not to think about how I should be saving for my kids' college education rather than chasing bears around northern Manitoba. But if you want to fight global warming and save the polar bears, you've got to spend big money and burn lots and lots of aviation fuel. Everybody knows that.

I hitched a ride from the Churchill airport to Hudson Bay Helicopters, a small trailer among many others on the town's main drag. There were four helipads out back, though I could see only one helicopter, and its blades were tied down tightly, lest they start spinning uncontrollably in the heavy winds. There was a tall fence, but if you wanted to get to the aircraft, all you would have to do is walk a hundred feet to the end of the fence line and turn the corner. No Department of Homeland Security here, apparently. At the Churchill airport, I later noticed, nobody bothers to check your identification, and they don't even have a metal detector. I once saw a man with a chainsaw as his carry-on luggage. It was in a plastic case, but still. A chainsaw.

I opened the door to the office and stepped inside to find Joan, the company's manager, admiring a small watermelon.

"It's a beauty, eh?" she said, with a broad smile and a Canadian accent as thick as whale blubber.

"Best I've ever seen," I replied, as I handed her three bars of dark chocolate. Never underestimate the power of minor bribery in a town with no road access. She thanked me profusely, but the candy was a minor prize compared to the watermelon.

"It just came in today," she said, resting her hand on the fruit as if it were a newborn. Thinking about the journey that melon must have made—not to mention the cost—I could understand her excitement.

During the fall tourist crush, she would have half a dozen helicopters at the ready, but because it was only July, the fleet was smaller, and she wasn't quite sure where one of the helicopters was at the moment. She hailed the pilot on the radio a few times, but nobody answered. "He's gotta be out there somewhere," she shrugged, seeming unconcerned about being unable to get a solid bead on a helicopter and pilot somewhere in the tundra. "I'm going to go pull my nets out of the river."

"Your nets?" I asked.

"Yeah. Fishing. This helicopter stuff is just part of it. I work four jobs to cover for all the other people in town who can't be bothered to even work one." And with that she scooped the melon off the table, eyeing me with mistrust, and squirreled the fruit away in a back room. "You can wander around town if you like," she told me. "Just come back when you hear the machine coming in."

CHAPTER 5

Pretty Dumb
for
Being So Smart

A S WE CHOPPERED OUT OF TOWN, the pilot, who seemed about twelve years old, pointed out the notable features of the landscape. "There's the ruins of the army base," he said, indicating a series of collapsing gunmetal gray buildings. "That's the wreck of the *Ithaka*." He jutted his chin toward an enormous abandoned cargo ship marooned in the shallows just offshore. Its ancient hull was rusted clear through, and gentle waves surged through the midships. "And that," he said, banking harder than seemed strictly necessary, "is *Miss Piggy*." He grinned beneath his flight helmet; evidently this was his favorite bit of annihilation, an immense freight plane nestled into a rocky hillside, a hundred yards above the high-tide mark and shy of the airport by a good two miles.

Miss Piggy fell out of the sky in 1979, when the pilot experienced mechanical trouble. He lived. The sinking of the *Ithaka* in 1959 (or 1960, or 1961, depending on whom you believe) is a little less straightforward. The ship, which may or may not have once been part of Mussolini's navy, either ran aground in a gale or was purposefully scuttled for insurance money. The cargo was either carefully removed by investors or pillaged by locals. One of the wonderful things about a town this remote is that actual events become myths in no time flat. Although there are probably several dozen people who saw the *Ithaka* go down, getting an accurate account is about as easy as getting a description of the sinking of Atlantis.

I'd noticed that similar exactitude applied to the received wisdom regarding polar bear populations. One old-timer would say that before World War II, there used to be bears everywhere; another would proclaim that now is the heyday, and the population has never been healthier. And really, who's to say which craggy old drunkard is right? Until American popular interest shifted north, polar bears were the proverbial tree falling in a forest. If a bear dies on an ice floe and nobody gives a shit, was he ever really there to begin with?

Even beyond the glaring mechanical failures of the *Ithaka* and *Miss Piggy*, the entire countryside was a palimpsest of ruin and neglect. Empty fuel barrels were as common as boulders, red with rust and leaking mystery toxins into Hudson Bay. Dirt roads and four-by-four tracks wove circles into the ground, each beginning in some vaguely defined nowhere and ending someplace else, far away, in a spot that looked exactly the same as the starting point. The earth was cratered with sunken pits and the piles of dirt that had once filled them. Twisted metal, burned cars, barely concealed garbage dumps . . . the outskirts of Churchill looked as if my son had been set loose with backhoes, dump trucks, and a few sticks of dynamite. Muscle and energy and intent abounded, but finished projects were hard to come by.

As the battered outskirts of town fell behind us, the view yielded to unvarying emptiness. A topographical map wouldn't require even a single contour line. Odd-shaped ponds were dolloped across the ground like splotches from an abstract artist shaking out brushes. The vegetation was low and stunted, a uniform gray-green where endless wind and incessant mud had conspired to dirty every leaf. Long swaths of rock erupted from the ground like the backs of breaching whales. The only thing that looked truly animated was the shadow of our helicopter, tracing a path across the endlessly replicating bands of earth. It was impossible to tell where the water ended and the mudflats began.

After twenty minutes, the camp came into view. It was built roughly in the style of the Churchill "suburbs," call it Modern Bomb-Blast, or Shantytown Revival. The pilot went into a tortuously slow, circling approach.

"What are you doing?" I asked, keenly aware of the effect that this circuitous path was having on my $30-per-minute bill. Helicopter rides are fun, but only if somebody else pays. If you're footing the bill, then it's like the worst taxi ride ever, the kind that requires a home equity loan if you get stuck in traffic.

"We always do this on approach," he said. "To look for bears." I scanned the ground like an airborne sniper, and sure enough, I saw two bears, one on either side of camp. The bear on the bay side of camp walked slowly, head down and shoulders hunched as if in the final stages of an exhausting hike. On the inland side of camp, another bear slept in a shallow puddle, its head resting on its forearm. Neither of them paid us the least bit of attention; either they were accustomed to constant overflights or they were both stone deaf. They didn't look particularly big, but then again, I had nothing to compare them to.

The helicopter maneuvered downward, though I wondered whether the murky island would support our weight. When quicksand failed to devour the skids, I hopped out, falling headfirst into a bush in my exaggerated attempts to avoid being decapitated by the rotors. Dr. Robert Rockwell stood off to the side to greet me. The helicopter blades slowed, but never stopped, which was fine by me, as I was paying for the pilot's empty return flight as well and I wanted him to get on with it.

Rockwell grinned as he pumped my hand. Compared to Amstrup and the other Heavy Hitters who acted as though they barely wanted to let me read their journal articles, this was practically a hero's welcome. Rockwell wore knee-high rubber boots, a radio on his hip, and a shotgun over his shoulder. His graying hair stood upright and his shirt was untucked, as if he'd just been unexpectedly called away from the bathroom. He looked less like a tenured professor from New York City and more like a friendly guy who might sell you some nightcrawlers and help you find a place to launch your houseboat into the reservoir.

"Lemme give you the nickel tour," Rockwell said, as soon as the thwup-thwup of the helicopter died down. "That's where we eat, that's where we sleep, and that's where we shit." He pointed out one building after another without moving from the helicopter pad. I was also introduced to three or four other members of the camp, none of whom appeared to have changed clothes in quite some time. It was hard to imagine spending an entire summer here, much less forty consecutive summers, as Rockwell had done. You'd need to have a real love of swamp grass or a terminal allergy to shade. I guessed that the temperature on the island was close to 90°F.

Although every building was different, one consistent element was the electric fence ringing the camp. It consisted of a few thin strands of wire. "Is this thing really strong enough to keep the bears out?" I asked, thinking of the two that I'd seen on approach. It seemed as though any self-respecting bear could barrel through the fence and be inside with us before even feeling the shock.

I followed Rockwell as he walked the perimeter of the camp, checking for fraying wires and bits of overgrown brush that might impede the electrical current. As it turned out, the fence was just one part of the defense system. The other part involved all hands on deck and a whole lot of guns.

When a bear comes near camp, Rockwell said, everybody gets on the roof of the kitchen building, sometimes staying for hours, waiting for the animal to touch the fence. When it does, the researchers unleash a volley of nonlethal firecracker shells, scaring holy hell out of the largest terrestrial man-eater on earth at the same time the beast is being soundly electrocuted on the tip of its wet nose. If the idea were to infuriate the animal so that it redoubled the effort to get at you, then I could hardly imagine a better plan. But Rockwell assured me that a bear so assaulted would take off running in the opposite direction. "They learn that the sound of the shells and the pain of the fence go together," he said. "But they're not necessarily good at remembering the order."

Some bears have learned to run as soon as they hear the sound of a shell being racked into the chamber. Others are not so smart—or so timid. "There was this one big old male who came back year after year. We knew it was him because he had this giant scar on his face," Rockwell said. "And he'd stand there for hours. You could almost see him thinking to himself, 'I wonder if they have that fucking fence turned on or not.'" Eventually, a zap from the fence or a volley of cracker shells would drive him away, just the same as the last time, and the time before that. "They can be pretty dumb for being so smart sometimes," Rockwell said, laughing.

The fence went up in 1984, sixteen years after Rocky first started working here. I asked him what life was like before that. "Tense," he said. In the twenty-five years since, the perimeter defenses have been breached only twice, which seems like a pretty good ratio until you remember what a determined half-ton animal with lethal claws can do. Even a single polar bear attack is enough to make you wish you'd majored in art history rather than doing bear patrol 1,000 miles from the closest competent trauma center.

Once, the wire was accidentally lowered and a curious bear simply stepped over it and into the camp. Of course, the odds of him finding the same way out were virtually zero, leaving him trapped inside the same hot fence that was supposed to repel him. Finally, one intrepid team member snuck down from the roof and turned off the power, which is the kind of thing that really ought to earn you tenure if the world were fair. In the second instance, a cub squirted under the fence, while mama, enraged and confused, was stuck outside. When the little guy hit the fence and let out a yelp, mama came crashing through the wires, oblivious to the shocks. Eventually, the pair made its way back outside the wire, and nobody had to die.

"The whole idea," Rockwell said, "is to make coming close to camp as noisy and uncomfortable for the bears as possible. You don't want them getting habituated to people, because, you know, they *are* pretty large carnivores." Which sounded like the understatement of the year to me.

CHAPTER 6

The Truth Is That
We Just Don't Know

*Science is organized common sense where many
a beautiful theory was killed by an ugly fact.*

—THOMAS HENRY HUXLEY,
NINETEENTH-CENTURY BIOLOGIST

ONE MAJOR DIFFERENCE between Rockwell and the Heavy Hitters was that Rocky didn't just work with polar bears themselves. He also worked with their shit.

"This polar bear stuff isn't all about helicopters and guns," he said. "Although I do like both of those things quite a bit." We were standing on the roof of the kitchen building, watching a bear rooting around on a nearby island. "You can learn a lot from looking at their feces, a lot that you can't get just by darting them and measuring them." Rockwell shifted his weight to adjust his shotgun, and the roof trembled a little. He seemed totally at ease standing on the pitched slope, but I was kneeling. Things felt a lot less dangerous once I was on all fours.

I took the binoculars and stared hard at the bear, who was splashing around in the water and digging in the mud like a kid at the beach. He was a fairly small bear, Rockwell told me, but from this distance it was impossible to determine the gender. Even up close it's difficult to "sex" a bear; one of the best ways is to look at the pattern of urine stains on the fur, which are in different places for males and females. Presumably the bears themselves have a more elegant way of determining who's who.

Even though there were a few hundred yards, an electric fence, and an accomplished gunman between me and the bear, I couldn't help but feel a jolt of excitement. It's rare to be in the presence of a true carnivore, and there's something about knowing that an animal wants to eat you that makes a man feel alive. You don't even have to see the teeth to get the full effect, although it certainly helps.

One thing that happens when you first see a polar bear is that, in that instant, you become suddenly cooler and more interesting than almost anyone you know.

You may be less attractive than your friends, or have less money than your enemies, but as soon as you see those giant paws with your own eyes, you've done something they haven't and probably never will. It means that you've gone to extremes, that you have the courage of conviction to spend a lot of money to go someplace that seems really important.

I felt like I could watch that polar bear forever. I also felt like I might like to climb off the roof and make a sandwich. I tried to ignore that second thought, because it's important to be able to kind of mean it when you tell your friends that you felt like you could have watched that bear forever. Rockwell stared at the bear.

"So what exactly can you learn from looking at their shit?" I asked.

"All kinds of stuff. Mostly you can tell what they've been eating."

"Seals, right?"

"That's what *they* want you to believe," Rockwell said, referring to the Heavy Hitters. The whole story about bears and starvation and global warming relies on the assumption that polar bears subsist on seal meat and nothing else. If they had variety in their diet then the loss of the sea-ice hunting grounds wouldn't be such a big deal. "We're finding that they aren't really the 'true carnivores' they're always made out to be," Rockwell continued. "They're eating geese and caribou and vegetation and all sorts of things."

Sure enough, the bear appeared to be eating something. He wriggled his head around like a dog, snapping his jaws and extending his neck for a good swallow.

This was tricky to wrap my head around. I'd read just about every scientific journal article on polar bears that had been published in the past ten years, and if there was one thing that the scientists generally agreed on, it was that polar bears were seal eaters. Sure, you might catch a bear eating the odd goose or nibbling on a caribou carcass it came across, but the suggestion that polar bears could be as omnivorous as grizzlies sounded like fiction.

"I haven't really read too much about that from Amstrup and the other guys," I said.

"And you won't," he countered. "Because it challenges their thesis that everything is hopeless." Rockwell stood astride the peak of the roof, with one foot firmly planted on either side, binoculars in hand. Ten miles to the east was the leading edge of the boreal forest with its shimmering promise of shade and living trees. Knight's Hill rose in the northwest, a low, wedge-shaped mountain of rock that had been deposited by some ancient glacier and was now the only vertical topography for hundreds of miles. To the north were the mudflats, picked down to bare dirt by the geese. And of course, directly in front of us was a polar bear, one of the most ferocious creatures known to man. When Rockwell raised his binoculars, I felt as though we were manning the last civilized outpost in some dystopian future world. The pod people should be emerging from the marsh any minute.

Rockwell made a mental note of the bear's location. "God, I'd sure love to go over there and see if he left a big steaming pile full of goose feathers," he said. "That would be awesome, wouldn't it?"

"It would be OK," I said.

"Tomorrow, after he's gone, let's go and see what treats he's left for us." Rocky was giddy, more so than I'd expect for a man in his sixties, especially given the subject matter. A bird skeleton—and a fresh poop proving it—would show that bears were not as strictly seal-centric as

Amstrup always asserted. Rockwell climbed down and left me alone on the roof with the bugs, the heat, and the increasingly lethargic bear, who was now wallowing in the river to stay cool. *My god*, I said to myself. *I'm marooned on an island with the only scientist on earth who doesn't believe that polar bears are starving to death.* No wonder this guy seemed so eager to have me join him. Here I'd been assuming that one polar bear scientist was as good as the next. But instead I'd pinned my star to a happy renegade. And I'd just emptied my bank account to listen to what seemed to me like a whole bunch of fringe theories.

Robert Rockwell looks almost cherubic, if you can imagine a cherub with a sunburn, a goatee, and incipient jowls. He is surrounded by a bubble of gusto and good humor that can't be dissipated, despite bad weather, long hours, and cramped living conditions. I always suspected he was remembering a private joke, or maybe having some silent fun at my expense. If you spend enough hours in his company, you're assured of hearing the same stories many times over, yet his rollicking delivery ensures that they don't get stale, at least through the first three or four iterations. One thing he never forgets is his life's work: he can tell you which professor published in which journal in 1973, who peer-reviewed the article, and what the limitations of their statistical methods were. The downside of this is that he also has perfect recall of every academic slight, real and imaginary, that has accumulated over four decades of teaching and publishing.

After a few obsequious emails and phone calls in which I had insisted on addressing him as Dr. Rockwell, he finally sent me an email telling me that his preferred name wasn't Robert, Dr. Rockwell, Robert Rockwell, or any other permutation like that. "It really is 'Rocky,'" he said. And from then on I never called him anything else. Many of his students addressed him simply as Rock. At a point in his career when many tenured professors are either flogging their graduate students to death or avoiding heavy scientific lifting by devoting themselves to the circular firing squads known as academic committee meetings, Rocky was eating canned beans in a bug-infested research camp, with a band of students forty years his junior to keep him company. And not only was he loving it, but he was also publishing at a fever pitch and making plans for new long-term projects. "Until they fly me out of here in a body bag," Rocky answered when I asked him how long he planned to continue working.

If the Heavy Hitters had their way, Rocky would spend a lot more time talking about birds, and a lot less time on polar bears. When you're a polar bear apostate, your friends in the upper echelons of the environmental movement have a way of evaporating fairly rapidly. To be fair, Rocky isn't a one-note polar bear specialist like Amstrup and his tiny group of intimates. When he first came to the region, Rocky worked with fruit flies, then built his career studying the exploding population of snow geese that was wreaking havoc on the landscape. "But the bottom line is that I'm a population biologist," Rocky said, when I joined him in the kitchen building. "And I've been out here working with bears and around bears for forty years, so I like to think that maybe I've got a tiny little bit of insight into how they behave." Rocky's voice was heavy with sarcasm. He'd been kissed off by the Heavy Hitters one time too many, and he didn't seem inclined to roll over for them any longer.

THE MAIN KITCHEN BUILDING was a single, dim room that smelled of mildew and fish. Every spring the river overflows the island, inundating the buildings. The researchers' first job is often to chip out their frozen living quarters and bleach the entire camp top to bottom. One entire wall of the shed was covered with haphazard shelves where towers of peanut butter competed for space with cans of tuna, jugs of corn oil, and enough Ramen noodles to sustain a fraternity house for several semesters. "We might have to let those go this year," Rocky said sadly, eyeing thirty pounds of instant mashed potatoes that looked untouched since the mid-1980s.

A gun rack hung on the wall, and people took up and deposited weaponry as they came and went. Every available surface, from doors to walls to ceiling, was covered with graffiti from the dozens of research assistants who had killed time at this table. Although some of the writing was of the "Marlon was here" variety, most was testament to long nights of drinking and lots of pheromone-laden young people cooped up far from home. "I might suck on 'em for a while, but I won't eat 'em—Barb, 1999" read one. "It rose all night but never got hard—Tanya" said another.

The pièce de résistance, over the long central table, was a gnarled, dried goose foot hanging limp on the end of a string, a metal identification band snapped neatly around the ankle. I tried to imagine how many peanut butter sandwiches and shots of whiskey had been consumed beneath that grim little specimen. If you were a director of low-budget horror movies, Nestor Two camp would be irresistible. If, on the other hand, you were an anchor for *Good Morning America* or CNN, or some other newsy show that regularly featured people like Steven Amstrup, you'd take one look at Rocky's secret hideout and get on the satellite phone to demand an immediate rescue chopper or a hefty chunk of hardship pay.

Rocky wiped his forehead with the back of his hand and took a long drink from a bottle of beer. It looked more like he was rehydrating after a long workout than having a sip before dinner.

"Hey," yelled one of his grad students, a lanky woman who'd been flipping through a bird-identification book while half listening to our conversation. "That was totally my beer you drank and you totally know it!"

"Did I?" Rocky grinned. "Well, there have to be some privileges connected to being your thesis adviser."

"You're dead to me," the woman said brightly.

"Ditto, sweetie." Everyone in the camp, from Rocky on down to the maintenance guy—who happened to be married to a PhD candidate with a specialty in potato bugs—was an inveterate New Yorker, and being there sometimes felt like an extended foray among the bleacher bums on a happy Bronx afternoon.

The beerless grad student slammed her book closed in mock indignation and stalked out the door, returning moments later with a fresh round of semi-cold Labatt's, which was the hors d'oeuvres of choice for the evening. Dinner was being prepared, but only in a very theoretical way; it's hard to gin up enthusiasm for cooking, much less bedtime, when the sun never really sets.

"Look, it could be birds or bees or bears," Rocky said, continuing our previous conversation as if we'd never stopped. "It doesn't really matter what animal you're working with because the math and the principles of forecasting population size are pretty universal. And in this case, the evidence just isn't there to say that polar bears are declining at the rate everybody says they are."

"So if it's not true, then why are they saying it?" I asked.

"Because they've built their careers on it. Because that's the story that gets attention. Because if they backtrack now, it will invalidate everything they've done up to this point."

Rocky and I looked at each other for a long minute. He leaned back in his chair at the head of the table, and the back legs squealed. His forehead was bright red, he breathed noisily through his mouth, and his intertwined fingers rested on his stomach. In this dingy shack with its shotguns on the wall and its hundreds of pounds of canned food, Rocky could be mistaken for a survivalist, holed up in the midst of a bloody standoff. Were these haphazard buildings really just a base camp for the revisionist science crowd? Was this whole place on the payroll of Big Oil? What was he going to tell me next—that cigarettes cure cancer and seals who get clubbed are probably just asking for it?

And yet, there was nothing about Rocky that screamed wing nut to me. He was a well-respected faculty member of the City University of New York and the American Museum of Natural History. He talked about the scientific method like the concept alone was more important to him than any of his individual projects. He *did* like to rant, but no more so than a lot of academics I've known who get revved up about their own obscure corners of the world. Most important, I never heard him make any objection to the idea of global warming in general. In fact, he'd been around Hudson Bay long enough to witness it with his own

eyes in the timing of the seasons and the increasingly common appearance of unusual southern birds.

So just what kind of guy was this? I'd met plenty of people who
thought that the polar bears were doing fine, but they also universally
belonged to the crowd that thought global warming was an elaborate
sham. They tended to get their research knowledge from world-
renowned scientists like Rush Limbaugh. To them, our national obses-
sion with polar bears was further evidence of our corroding, liberal,
sissified society. The polar bear scam was, to them, just the public relations wing of the larger global-warming hoax.

But Rocky was different, and frankly, it made me uncomfortable. I
like my heroes and villains clean and uncomplicated. I like to be able to
drop people neatly into categories: smart, good-looking, open-minded
lefties on one side, and greedy, disfigured, willfully ignorant fascist ditto-
head kleptocrats on the other. Rocky—with his reasoned objections, his
years of experience, and his infuriating ability to simultaneously consider
two seemingly opposed schools of thought—was damnably difficult to
pigeonhole. I could see why the Heavy Hitters kept him at arm's length.

Still, it seemed unlikely that Amstrup and his colleagues were con-
vening secret tribunals in remote igloos where they plotted to deceive
the animal-loving American public. Everything I'd read in the scientific
literature and the popular press pointed to the fact that polar bears were
in precipitous decline. Bears ate seals, seals lived under the ice, and the
ice was melting. If that wasn't the case, then what the hell was I doing in
Churchill? No ice, no seals, no bears, no question. "Why would they lie?"
I asked.

"No, no, no," Rocky answered. "I don't want you to get the idea that
they're lying, or even that they're necessarily wrong. But they've crossed
the line from science into advocacy. Whenever they have a choice between A or B in their assumptions, they always choose B, which is the
Chicken Little scenario, the worst possible outcome. They realize that
polar bears are a gloom and doom story that's become the defining environmental issue of the day."

"And the truth is . . ."

"The truth is that we just don't know!" Rocky exploded. "All this certainty that's being thrown around, and all of these firm dates about when exactly the last polar bear is going to die . . . it's ridiculous. Science doesn't work that way." He didn't have a polar bear count of his own to counter Amstrup's, but he'd worked with the available numbers—and the bears—enough to believe that dire future predictions didn't match the facts on the ground. Rocky was getting worked up now, his evangelical fervor building, and he smacked the table for emphasis. The dried goose foot swayed gently back and forth as wind rocked the rafters. Whereas the Heavy Hitters complained about being inundated with media requests, Rocky's public profile was much lower. The media love apocalypse, and Rocky wasn't offering that.

He took another long pull on his beer—or maybe it was mine; it was difficult to tell with all the empties littering the tabletop. Then he heaved himself out of his chair to prepare dinner. I offered to help but he turned me away, suggesting that I go up onto the roof and do a thorough scan for any bears in the area.

"How old are you?" Rocky asked abruptly as I headed out the door.

"Thirty-four," I replied.

He considered that for a moment and then said, "Did you know that there are more bears alive today than when you were born?"

"Excuse me?"

"That's right. In 1973, the entire worldwide polar bear population had been hunted down to around 5,000." And now, as it turned out, there were between 20,000 and 25,000 bears spread across the Arctic. "Everybody agrees on that," Rocky said. "Amstrup, the World Wildlife Fund, everybody."

Twenty thousand? That sure sounded like an awful lot of bears. Global warming catastrophists were fond of saying that two-thirds of the polar bear population could be wiped out. But even if that dismal number were true, it still meant that there would be more polar bears on earth than there had been thirty years ago, back when nobody ever mentioned polar bears at all. My first thought as I clambered onto the roof was that it was a great and welcome surprise that these endangered animals were doing so well. And my second thought was that if I told anybody what I was thinking, then I must be a giant climate-change-denying asshole.

CHAPTER 7

Polar Bears Need
Crime Labs, Too

*It's an absolutely bizarre construct that people have. For no
other species anywhere in the world have we predicted that
major habitat loss would cause an animal to change its behavior
fundamentally. If animals were able to do that, we should have
lots of ivory-billed woodpeckers these days because just about
the time they were going extinct we were putting up telephone
poles all over the county, so why didn't they move to use the
telephone poles? It's the same sort of stupid logic. We've got
woodpeckers on telephone poles in Edmonton all the time, but
ivory-bills didn't do that. That idea that they're going to
somehow do something magical that no other bear has done or
will do. I mean, why didn't giant pandas just start eating rice in
the fields and frolicking in the city? It's nonsensical.*

—DR. ANDREW DEROCHER, UNIVERSITY OF
ALBERTA (ONE OF THE HEAVY HITTERS)

WHAT ROCKY WAS SAYING all made sense in a vague and
theoretical way—after all, some animals do have the ability
to change their tactics when particular resources get scarce.
Like grizzlies, for example—the polar bear's closest relative—which can
eat fish or berries or small mammals or pretty much anything else. But
a lot of animals can't switch so easily. Pandas, for instance, eat bamboo

and bamboo only, even if that means starving to death in a forest full of everything but. The fossil record is a tribute to failure: 99 percent of the species that have ever walked the earth are now extinct. And beyond our desire to have it be so, there didn't seem to be any glaring reason that polar bears should be any different. Still, a jawbone found in Svalbard had recently been identified as coming from a polar bear. Scientific dating indicated that it was 130,000 years old, meaning the polar bears had existed both before and after the Eemian period, an epoch that was significantly warmer than the earth is currently experiencing.

To put it mildly, I was confused. Maybe polar bears would be fine and maybe they wouldn't, but up to this point Rocky had done a lot of talking while showing me very little. He would have to do a lot better than this if he wanted me to cast aside three decades of environmentalist indoctrination, not to mention the schoolboy crush I'd developed on Steven Amstrup, the high priest of my own personal church of gloom and doom.

Rocky seemed to be in a pugilistic mood, but he wasn't going to take on the Heavy Hitters by himself. Instead, his allies included two other individuals: a PhD candidate named Linda Gormezano, and Quinoa, her Dutch shepherd.

UNLIKE MOST DOG OWNERS, Linda Gormezano won't tell you how friendly her puppy is. She won't invite you to tickle him and she won't wax on about how good he is with children. Before I arrived at Nestor Two, Linda emailed me a list of rules. Don't pet Quinoa, she told me. Don't talk to him and don't play with him without permission. Don't feed him, don't give him affection, and don't interact with him if you've been drinking. Don't make eye contact. By the time I arrived at Nestor Two, I had so built up Quinoa's ferocity in my mind that I was surprised when he presented himself as something other than a red-eyed slavering wolf-beast with a forked tail and bits of human flesh clinging to his lips. First and foremost, Quinoa was a working dog, and the point was that he didn't need me bumbling around trying to be his pal.

Despite all the stern warnings, Linda was a typically loving and effusive pet owner. She used silly voices when she talked to Quinoa, she gave him booties and earmuffs, and she fixed him meals that were more nutritionally balanced than what I usually feed myself. But she also had a little something extra riding on her relationship with her dog—namely, a big chunk of her academic success. Because even though Quinoa might look like just any other black shepherd, he has a skill that he shares with no other pooch on the planet: he can sniff out a polar bear turd at a hundred paces.

So this was the plan? This was how conventional wisdom was going to be turned on its head? A tenured professor, a smart grad student, and a dog would gather up as much polar bear excrement as possible, which they would then use to do . . . well, what exactly?

"There's just so much to learn from their scat," Linda said. "It's hard to even know where to begin." No wonder Steven Amstrup, King of the Polar Bears, wasn't looking for a new endangered species on which to hang his hat.

Linda trained Quinoa back home, using polar bear scat that she'd been given by benevolent zookeepers. She would hide samples in parks, teaching the dog to distinguish polar bear shit from all of the other delicious urban odors. Training a normal dog isn't easy, but training a dog to do a job this unusual is even harder. Linda put in long hours, huge effort, and no small amount of her own money. And, when it was all said and done, the two of them became a unique and specialized scientific team.

The general idea was that Linda would scoop up the samples and poke around to see what was inside. If it was full of goose feathers and fish heads then—voilà!—so much for the theory that polar bears are picky eaters, capable of subsisting on seal meat alone. Back in the lab she'd do a second pass, a detailed DNA analysis using all sorts of expensive lab equipment that an average TV-watcher might imagine was mostly reserved for catching serial killers instead.

But polar bears need crime labs, too. In the course of grooming themselves, bears ingest a lot of hair, the roots of which contain genetic material. Also, a bit of the gut lining is excreted with every bowel movement, and there's DNA there as well. After hearing Linda's study protocols, these few facts comprised the sum total of my knowledge about scat analysis, as well as being 100 percent more information about the subject than I wanted to have floating around in my head. This was hardly the intimate polar bear experience I'd had in mind when I first started cold-calling researchers and begging to tag along.

Nonetheless, Nestor Two was where I was going to be for the next week, and it didn't seem likely that Amstrup was ever going to come to me, hat in hand, begging me to immerse myself in his life and write the shining chronicles of his noble quest.

I FOLLOWED ROCKY AND LINDA to the low building they used as a laboratory. It also had the camp's only refrigeration unit, an essential piece of equipment not only for science, but also for keeping beer cold. Linda went first; Rocky and I hung back. Quinoa was in there, and we had to show him the proper deference before entering. I could hear Linda inside speaking softly to him.

"Is it clear?" Rocky asked. Linda didn't answer for a long time.

"You can come in now," she said at last. "He should be okay . . . I think." Quinoa came from a long line of police dogs, and he'd been intended for "bite work" until it was determined that he was generally too mild and good-natured to be successful as a badass police dog.

I pushed aside a makeshift screen door and stepped inside. Quinoa was curled up on a blanket near the front door. I looked him in the eyes. Quite by accident, but I couldn't help it; he was sitting right there and happened to be looking up when I was looking down. His ferocious reputation aside, I was having trouble getting any sense at all of Quinoa's personality. He wasn't mean or warmhearted or playful or . . . anything really. He just seemed kind of present, quiet and doggish and inscrutable.

Rocky expounded on his plans for Quinoa with his customary gusto while Linda hung back, making commentary around the edges. Although Linda was friendly, and even forceful when we were talking one on one, in groups she got smaller. The other people at the camp seemed to be in various good-natured stages of midseason burnout, homesickness, and cabin fever. The result was a constant barrage of trash talk and innuendo, the kind you might expect to find on a forward military base. But Linda always rose above the fray, fussing with her dog in a corner while the rest of the crew killed the endless hours until the next meal or potential bear attack.

It seems, at times, that Linda and Rocky are two halves of a comedy team, one loud and full of guffaws, the other a skittish, nervy counterpoint. Linda is small and slight; she looks as though she could be knocked off her feet by a swift snap from a rolled-up towel, which is perhaps why she kept to the fringes of the constant kitchen melee. She has long, unruly curls that spill over her shoulders and a splash of freckles across her nose. She was perennially tapping her fingers, looking behind her, or jumping up to do some just-remembered task. If she were in kindergarten, her teacher would yell at her for fidgeting during quiet hour. One thing was abundantly clear, however: Linda was careful, intent, and utterly focused on the project at hand.

Like most people in the Far North, Linda arrived via a circuitous path. As an undergrad at CUNY–Queens, she majored in music. But the world only needs so many musicians, and any symphony dreams she may have had eventually evaporated. She made an abrupt turnaround and decided on a career with wildlife, though the grad schools that rejected her tended to think music was a weak springboard for a career in applied ecology. She threw herself into unpaid internships, veterinary jobs, and the literature of her intended field. As it turned out, the rigid hierarchies and thought patterns of classical music weren't so different from the complex equations required for population ecology. Once it was clear that she was masterful with numbers—and that she had a penchant for working herself beyond the point of exhaustion—she became a lot more attractive as a graduate student. A master's degree at the SUNY College of Environmental Science and Forestry led to a biologist job at Fire Island Seashore National Park. "But I was just doing a beach renourishment project so rich friggin' New York people could have nice beaches even though the natural succession says the beaches should be going away. It was ridiculous." So she doubled down on graduate school and from there it wasn't long until one woodsy stats nerd found another and Linda joined Rocky's lab.

"You must love polar bears," I said. This kind of PhD program was the kind of thing most wildlife biologists would kill for.

"Eh," Linda shrugged, wrinkling her nose. "They're OK, I guess. But I'll be ready to be done with my PhD."

CHAPTER 8

Sniff Away

When a male polar bear and a human are face to face
there occurs a brief kind of magic, an intense, visceral
connection between man and beast whose poignancy
and import cannot be expressed in mere words.
Then he rips your arms off.

—GRAFFITI ON THE GUN RACK IN
THE KITCHEN OF NESTOR TWO

T HE NEXT DAY DAWNED warm and buggy, like all days in the short, brutal Manitoba summer. I'd slept poorly in the communal dorm. Midnight light streamed through the windows, and a chorus of snores and squeaky bedsprings penetrated the towel that I had wrapped around my head to ward off an unkillable mosquito. Rocky had instructed me that if I needed to pee in the night I was to use a bucket in the mudroom rather than step outside, lest a bear gobble me up while everyone else was sleeping.

But now it was finally time to head into the field. The chopper was inbound, and Linda skittered around making breakfast for Quinoa, and as an afterthought, for herself. Quinoa watched the bacon greedily but settled for a foul-looking slurry that Linda called "Canine Superfood."

"It's human grade," Linda said, as I eyed the bowl with suspicion.

"Is it good?" I asked.

"I've never tried it," she said.

Linda clearly treated Quinoa better than I treat my own children, so I thought I'd see what the Superfood was all about. Maybe I could start giving it to my kids in their lunch boxes.

I grabbed a spoon and took a bite. It was like watery grits made with rancid chicken broth, then sprinkled with brewer's yeast and infused with fish sauce.

"It's horrible," I said. "Your poor dog." I would have made it my mission to slip Quinoa a proper snack, like a tin of tuna fish or a honey nut chocolate chip granola bar. But I'd seen Linda reading food labels like a Waldorf teacher from Berkeley, clucking about additives, preservatives, and sodium. Quinoa lapped at his bowl. *Sorry, pup,* I thought, as I tucked into two fried eggs and a bowl of leftover Rice-A-Roni. Sucks being a dog.

The pilot radioed that he was five minutes out, and we scrambled to the landing pad. Linda knelt next to Quinoa and fitted a pair of noise-protection earmuffs over his head, then punched a few keys on her hand-held GPS unit while also rearranging her fanny pack. I laid down a blanket for Quinoa and strapped myself into a rear seat. Quinoa followed and laid his head in my lap. Apparently, riding in a spinning, bumping, loud-as-hell death machine was no big excitement for him. While Linda was busy strapping in, I even permitted myself a quick pat on the top of the dog's head. The pilot revved the engine, and off we went.

We made it all of two feet off the ground.

"These machines either work, or else they don't," the pilot explained unhelpfully. "And if it's going to fail in the first minute, this is right where I want to be." A good enough tactic, to be sure, but not one designed to inspire maximum confidence in the general enterprise of helicopter travel. At dinner the night before, Rocky had regaled me with stories about helicopters that had gone down. He'd been in two crashes himself. "More like really hard landings," he'd amended, seeing my concern. "And that's over forty years, so really it's a pretty good track record." All things being equal, I would have preferred if it had been fewer.

After the pilot assured himself that the helicopter wasn't coming apart, he pulled us upward and we banked hard, heading for the rocky coast of Hudson Bay. The ground beneath us was lifeless and barren, as if it had been baked and dried a hundred times, then assaulted by an army of Boy Scouts with weed whackers, then carpet bombed with Agent Orange for good measure. Ugly rings of salt and dirt swirled in every direction like angry scars. Even the ponds looked wrong. With no greenery at the edges, the water was heavy and gelid, like puddles of oil rippling under our prop wash as we passed over. All in all, it looked like a really easy place to die a really miserable death.

This was the goose-borne destruction that Rocky had made his career studying. This area around La Perouse Bay had been home to 2,500 nesting pairs of geese back in the 1960s. But nowadays, upward of 50,000 pairs are in residence, each pair capable of producing four goslings annually, and all of them ravenous for the sedges and grasses that used to abound. Snow geese are migratory, wintering in the South in the United States and coming to the Churchill area in early summer. Over the years, Southern farmers plowed ever increasing acreages into high-calorie crops such as corn and soy, which the geese then plundered. Fat and happy, the geese turned to sex, and the population exploded. At about this same time, nature lovers from north to south established a network of bird sanctuaries, making the geese's easy life even easier. Which was all fine, except for the fact that the vegetation around Hudson Bay didn't get the message that it needed to ramp up production. Soon the marauding army of geese had grubbed out every single blade of grass on the tidal plains.

Normally, exploding populations have the graciousness to die en masse when they overuse their resources. Instead, these geese displayed a near-human level of rapaciousness and simply expanded their foraging grounds. Every year the swath of destruction got bigger, like an expanding doughnut with the Nestor Two camp at its center. Some of Rocky's study plots had been monitored for forty years, and they showed no sign of ever coming back.

Still, no matter how scarred the landscape, there's never a bad day to be riding in a helicopter. We sliced through the sky like the Angel of Death on his way to repossess a soul or two, scanning the ground for polar bears and just generally feeling an acute, deity-like ownership of all that we surveyed. Even Quinoa perked up and eyed the world with interest. Apparently, the dog didn't mind riding in the helicopter one bit. Early in his training Linda called up the airborne unit of the New York City Police Department, explained her project, and asked if they'd mind if she brought her dog down to get him accustomed to helicopters. The guys were willing, and soon Quinoa was jumping in and out of helicopters as easily as farm dogs jump into pickup trucks.

The bay shimmered with heat waves, and lost-looking little bands of geese wandered back and forth over the desolate ground searching for some last shred of living material that hadn't already been devoured. A lone caribou, spooked by our noise, bolted from a pond-side wallow and then resumed wandering aimlessly in search of shade or food or momentary relief from the choking mosquitoes, none of which would be found around here. House-sized chunks of ice floated in the bay like abandoned battleships; a few more 80°F days and the water would be ice free as far as you could see. For the bears, this was the end of the gravy train. It was still too early in the year for them to come into Churchill proper, but they'd stay out here by the coast all summer, cooling themselves in ponds and trying to conserve calories. Geese, caribou, polar bears, even people—it was hard to understand why such an unpleasant corner of the earth attracted such a passionately devoted multispecies group of repeat customers. Imagine how popular this place would be if it had a shade tree.

"That's the spot," Linda said, leaning over the pilot's shoulder to point to a spit of land jutting into the bay like a hooked finger. The coastline of Hudson Bay is made up of a series of beach ridges, miles-long sandy strips that trace the contours of the water's edge. The beach ridges mark the spots where the water's edge used to be located—one hundred years ago, or five hundred, or ten thousand. It's not that the bay is receding; instead, the land is rising, rebounding slowly from the weight of an ancient glacier. Caribou like to migrate along the beach ridges because the ground is firm and well-packed and free of obstructions. The Natives liked the beach ridges for the same reason, and so do helicopter pilots, who prefer not to dip their treads into wet sand.

"That's exactly the spot," Linda said again.

There was just one problem. A polar bear the size of a small elephant sat on the tip of the promontory, right where Linda was directing us to touch down. He was stretched out with his forepaws in front of him and his head up like a sphinx. Even from the air I could tell this guy was a bruiser. Old wounds and bits of matted hair crisscrossed his back, and the black pad of his nose was mashed and scabrous. A long scar ran off his snout and down the side of his face.

He was the most enormous animal I had ever seen. It was as though he had expanded to fit the size of the peninsula, a solid wall of muscle and inertia, as immobile as a boulder and ten times as mean. I may have felt like the Angel of Death a minute ago, but now, even with our rotors screaming and a mini-maelstrom in our wake, I felt as insignificant as a man can feel. As we spun in a circle above his head, he glanced up with regal disinterest, yawning demonstratively.

"How about someplace else then?" Linda chirped.

"Copy that," the pilot replied.

Unfortunately, by "someplace else" Linda had in mind a spot not nearly far enough away from the bear to satisfy my own cowardice.

"You guys sure don't mind working close, eh?" the pilot said.

"This isn't close," she said. "This is perfect." As the machine settled down in a semi-flat patch of lyme grass, I lost sight of the bear behind a low hillock. Were he so inclined, he could cover the distance between us in no time. I could only hope he'd stuffed himself with one last fat seal before swimming off the sea ice. We piled out of the helicopter, grabbed our gear, and huddled up just beyond the rotor's danger zone. Quinoa hugged the ground and swatted at his head with a paw, probably to dislodge a mosquito. With a wave and a half-smile that seemed to say,

"Better you than me, you crazy bastards," the pilot lifted off, leaving us not quite alone in the vastness of the barrens.

Because Linda was going to have her head down while she did her work, and because I was more likely to shoot my own knee rather than an onrushing polar bear, we needed an experienced bear guard. The man for the job was Kevin Burke, who had grown up in Churchill and was now a ranger for Wapusk National Park. Over the years he'd worked as a research assistant, a tour guide, a Tundra Buggy driver, and a go-to guy for the many film projects undertaken in Churchill. If there was a way to be employed in the polar bear business, Kevin had done it. He wore camouflage knee boots, a Parks Department parka, and an ammunition belt with dozens of slugs lined up and ready for action. With his shotgun, overstuffed backpack, and mirrored sunglasses, he looked like a tundra Terminator, ready to handle any emergency from a summer snowstorm to a caribou stampede.

THE MISSION FOR THE DAY was to collect as many samples of polar bear scat as possible. In Rocky and Linda's grand scheme, this sort of collection could replace, or at least vastly augment, what Amstrup and his colleagues were doing with tranquilizer darts and radio collars. The DNA extracted from the scat would be enough to identify individual animals, to the point where you could say "Joe the Bear was here" as surely as if you'd spent the money to shoot him from the sky and check his gums for a permanent tattoo from an earlier capture.

The point of this was to test a new method for counting polar bears. This was the most closely monitored polar bear population on earth, the one that every politician and environmentalist and global warming skeptic focused on. And because the local population was only about 1,000 animals, a miscount of a few dozen bears could be enough to vastly embolden or chastise one or another side of the debate over how bears are doing. A more accurate count could be a potentially huge finding.

When they're doing a census, scientists like Steven Amstrup don't count every single animal. Instead, they catch a portion of a population and use that to estimate the whole. Imagine a colony of a million ants, and then imagine that there is some way to reliably mark individual bugs. Even if you laid a thousand traps, in a population of that size, odds are that you wouldn't trap the same ant twice. But if the population is smaller—say, 1,000 polar bears—you can reasonably expect to catch the same bear over and over again. The greater the absolute number of animals caught and recaught, the closer you get to coming up with an accurate count of the entire population.

It's not that simple, of course—for every population estimate there are pages of scribbled equations and rows of graduate students chained to their desks, but that's the gist of it. Amstrup's helicopter-based "mark-recapture" studies are the standard, but it's expensive and time consuming. What Linda had in mind was that each piece of poop represented a kind of "captured" polar bear. Whereas Amstrup and the Heavy Hitters could handle maybe five bears a day, Linda and Quinoa could collect upward of 1,000 samples in a single field season.

"Buscalo!" Linda yelled, as soon as the helicopter disappeared from view. Quinoa leapt forward at a dead run, pulling his leash with such ferocity that I worried he'd dislocate Linda's skinny arm.

The Spanish was a surprise. I had always thought that you were supposed to speak to working dogs in German, because bystanders are unlikely to call out instructions by accident in that language, and also because nothing commands respect like a snarling dog reacting to someone who sounds like a Nazi.

I asked Linda about how she spoke to her dog. She ran down a list of additional commands for me: *venga* for come, the Spanglicized *despach* for walk slowly, and "sniff away" when she wanted to give Quinoa free time to wander around.

Linda released Quinoa from his leash and he set off with a purposeful lope, his nose low to the ground and his whipsaw tail spiraling in a happy circle. Thirty seconds later, he sat down abruptly, his ears pricked and an expectant look on his face. At his feet was a brown pile of goo the size of a dinner plate.

"Did you find a poop?" Linda gushed, patting Quinoa vigorously. "Did you find a poop? Good boy, gooooood good boy, you're just such a good boy, such a good good good boy." Later, Rocky told me that this sort of overwhelming positive reinforcement was crucial to the strong bond that dogs and owners must have when working under such difficult conditions.

Quinoa didn't seem to let the praise go to his head, but when Linda pulled a red ball from her pack, he leaped straight into the air; a few rounds of fetch was his reward for a successful find. Linda threw the ball high in the air and he caught it on the fly, then ran twenty yards and dropped it into a puddle. Linda ran, retrieved the ball, and threw it again. They continued like this until it seemed to me that Quinoa's reward wasn't fetching balls, but instead lay in watching Linda run herself ragged as he led her into one puddle after another. Smart dog.

"Don't go over that way," Kevin admonished, as Linda plunged into some high reeds alongside a large pond. He stood with his feet apart like a prison guard, gun cradled in his arms. "I can't see in there too well." By which he meant that a polar bear could easily be hiding in the willows ten feet away and we'd have no way of knowing until it reared up on its hind legs Godzilla-style and started chewing on somebody's skull.

"This is a nice one," Linda said, panting, as she finished her game of fetch and knelt down next to the sample. "Really nice. And it's got a good polar bear poop smell to it, too."

She dropped the sample into a Ziploc bag and passed it over. I put my head down like a horse eating from an oat bag. It wasn't an unpleasant odor exactly, though not one I'd make an air freshener out of. It was wet and meaty, distinctly marine, like a clump of seaweed. It didn't look like anything I would have picked out as a bowel movement. It was more like a pile of grass that had been mixed with dirt and trampled on for a while. On closer inspection, in fact, it really *was* just grass that had passed through the bear so completely undigested as to retain individual blades and root balls.

Linda explained to me that when bears come off the ice, they'll eat whatever they come to first, even if it happens to be kelp or lyme grass.

"I didn't know they could eat plants," I said.

Linda gave a derisive snort, as if I'd just suggested that polar bear dens have sofa beds and flat screens. But I was just parroting what every polar bear expert said every time they opened their mouths.

"How's that for fasting?" said Linda, sounding combative to me. Quinoa had alerted on another pile of scat, and this one was full of feathers and tiny bones. "Snow geese. Bears love 'em. About a quarter of the samples have some kind of waterfowl in them. And I'm not even talking about all the other stuff like eggs and berries and lemmings. Even caribou sometimes."

"I thought their diet was supposed to be all seals," I said.

"Supposed to be? I don't know about 'supposed to be,' but I do know that when I do my diet analysis, I find all kinds of stuff that isn't seal."

"But Amstrup says . . ."

"I know what Amstrup says," Linda said sharply. "I've tried to talk to him, but he doesn't want to have anything to do with me." Apparently, the Heavy Hitters just didn't want to even entertain the notion that bears might be eating something other than seals.

I asked Linda why she thought Amstrup and the others were so resistant, but she wouldn't say anything, though it seemed clear to me that she had some pretty good ideas. If I'd been thinking that Linda was some kind of shrinking violet, she was rapidly proving me wrong. Her caustic inner New Yorker was rising to the surface, and just the mention of the Heavy Hitters set her bullshit detector clicking into high gear.

"*Buscalo!*" she yelled, and Quinoa set off like a rocket, lifting Linda off the ground at the end of the leash. She tumbled after him in an out-of-control stagger, half walking, half being dragged until the dog stopped at the next pile.

The bugs intensified, and it became claustrophobic and damp inside my bug jacket and mesh hood. Sweat ran down my head and chest, pooling at my belt line and inside my boots. I felt a little ridiculous watching Linda bagging sample after sample. Was this really how the seminal environmental battle of the twenty-first century was going to play out? The shooters versus the shitters? Did Rachel Carson ever find herself in a spot like this? Did John Muir? Poking through poop might be one way to discover the truth, but getting anybody in the popular press to take you seriously was a more difficult battle.

If I'd thought that polar bear research was going to be all glamour and gunplay, a day with Quinoa and Linda set me straight. The sun was high and immobile in the sky; the first promise of shade was two months away. *The Arctic is bullshit,* I thought, sweating underneath my layers of sunscreen and mesh. Heat waves shimmered over the gray rocks and the bay was full of mirages. Some trick of light made it appear as if an immense wave, as broad as the horizon and a thousand feet tall, was bearing down upon us. I could look at the water once, then look at it again ten seconds later and the fake tsunami would take me by surprise every time.

The bugs were relentless, nibbling at the corners of my mouth and squirming into my boots, up my pant legs. My fingernails were caked with dried blood and the crushed carcasses of my tormentors. Linda had been rubbing Quinoa's fur with Deet but was trying an organic, holistic, and completely ineffective bug repellent on his face. He rolled and thrashed on the ground as if in the grip of demonic possession until Linda finally relented and splashed a little of the blessed poison onto his neck. I tried to adopt a Zen mindset: the heat is my friend, the bites only itch if you scratch them. But within thirty seconds of my spiritual conversion, a blackfly tore a hunk from inside my left nostril and I was back to sweating, scratching, and cursing like a heathen.

As Linda and the dog worked, bagging sample after sample, I joined Kevin Burke on the top of a beach ridge. He stood like a statue, his eyes hidden behind mirrored sunglasses. I took a long swig from my Nalgene water bottle. It tasted like hot plastic and stale bleach. I unwrapped a peanut butter sandwich; it tasted like sunscreen and Deet. I licked the jelly off my fingers. They tasted like polar bear shit.

"I don't know what it is about bugs and blood," Kevin said, smashing a mosquito against the side of his face. "Why can't they just drink beer like the rest of us?" He lifted his binoculars to his eyes, a half-eaten chocolate bar hanging out of his mouth like an oversized cigar. "Gone," he said, looking at the spot where we'd almost landed atop that polar bear.

"Where'd he go?" I asked.

"I didn't ask him and he didn't tell me," Kevin said. He had the air of someone who had elevated suffering fools gladly into an art form. Scientists came and went, the overeager tourists did their thing, and the prominence of polar bears ebbed and flowed. But no matter what, Kevin was staying put in Churchill; he'd seen it all and he'd see it all again. The rest of us were a pleasant-enough distraction, but he knew better than to take short-timers like me too seriously.

"He could be in those willows over there"—Kevin pointed to a stand of bushes about eighteen inches tall—"or he could be two clicks away by now. Or he could be in the water right next to us." Kevin indicated two suspicious white blobs just offshore and suggested that I keep an eye on them. Seeing imaginary polar bears was becoming a habit, and as I stood there, every bush and rock did its customary transformational dance before my eyes.

Watching the water's edge was remarkable. Hudson Bay is shallow, and in places the tidal flats extend for miles. In the space of less than an hour of lowering tides, the bay disappeared in front of me until the water's edge was half a mile away. What had been an ocean became a pitted moonscape of jagged ledges and slimy, kelp-covered pools. If the bear had slid into the water, he had to be far away to have found enough water to submerge. Or else he was nearby, "rugged out" as Kevin termed it, lying flat in some rivulet of mud trying to escape the heat and the incessant bugs.

"Those big males are usually okay," Kevin said. "It's the subadults you gotta watch out for. They're curious, but they're not very good hunters yet. And let's face it—we're pretty easy pickings out here." He paused a moment to let that sink it, and then said, "They're too old to suck, too young to fuck, and all they do is run around and get into trouble. They're kind of like the teenagers in town, come to think of it."

I MADE MY WAY BACK TOWARD LINDA, who had an enormous bag slung over her shoulder, stuffed with Ziploc baggies full of bear shit. She looked like some weird facsimile of one of Santa's elves, scampering around, discovering tiny treasures inside each new pile of crap. Her freckled face was hatched with scratch marks, and little flecks of dried blood dotted her skin. Her hair was knotted and bedraggled, and basically she looked a mess, albeit a completely exhilarated one. When she found a half-digested starfish, she let out a whoop. "I've never seen this before!" Finding a new item on the polar bear menu was a major triumph, and I could imagine her adding it to her running catalog of things the Heavy Hitters would tell her are impossible.

There was too much work for her to do alone, so we fell into a rhythm where Linda would catalog the shit, and I would collect hairs from the so-called "daybeds." When polar bears come in from the last ice, they are exhausted from the swim, so they haul themselves ashore and collapse into pits that they excavate in the gravel.

I shrugged off my pack and nestled into a large daybed. There was bear hair everywhere, from the lip of the pit down into the very bottom, and I stuffed as much as I could find into a brown envelope. Polar bear hair isn't actually white. It's clear. And polar bear skin isn't white, either. It's black. When you look at it under a microscope you can see that each individual hair isn't really a strand at all, but a hollow tube. The theory is that the hair actually reflects visible light while also serving as an ultra-efficient channel for collecting ultraviolet light, which is gathered up by the polar bear's black skin.

There was no way for me to know whether this daybed had been vacated last year, or just an hour ago. The gravel was warm, heated by the sun or the backside of whomever had deposited all of that silky fur.

From up close, the tundra was less monotonous than it appeared from the sky. Minuscule red and yellow flowers bloomed on scattered patches of dirt. Eagle feathers and tufts of caribou hair lay abandoned behind spiny willows. There were fossils everywhere, some embedded in the rock and some, shaped like tightly coiled springs, scattered over the ground. Quinoa often suffered from cuts to his footpads, and I could see why. Rocks that had been worn smooth by the water were split apart by years of freezing and thawing, leaving razor edges poking out of the earth like scrap metal. There was no shortage of human detritus, either, from bits of old weather balloons to a rusted, three-foot-long test rocket, a relic of cold war days. Linda had booties to protect Quinoa's feet, but convincing him to wear them was difficult.

As I pawed through the dirt, I noticed Kevin standing over me. "Must be a nice feeling, eh?" he said.

"What's that?"

"Sitting back in a spot like this and knowing that if you want to, you can kill and eat absolutely anything that comes along."

Having never had any desire to kill and eat anything that came along, I tried to consider this spot from a bear's perspective. The rocks were cool and moist, a refreshing break from the unrelenting heat of the barrens. This particular hole was located at the top of a low dune, where I could look out over the bay and enjoy the breezes blowing off the water. The scattered clouds in the sky were high and harmless, just large enough to cast the occasional blessed shadow. The waters of Hudson Bay were as still as glass, unthreatening and serene. It was impossible to tell if the icebergs floating on the horizon were real or a reflection of the low-hanging clouds. Sure enough, I felt like a lazy king, splayed out in an enveloping throne, secure in the knowledge that I was the master of all I surveyed. No predators, no responsibilities, nothing to do but lie low and wait out the summer. It was an ursine paradise . . . save for the oppressive heat, the kamikaze insects, and the threat of imminent starvation.

"I've got a fresh one here," Linda shouted, the excitement in her voice breaking apart my little reverie. "It's got maggots and everything. It's so cool!" Most of the samples so far had been deposited the previous season, and they were brittle and degraded. Finding a recently laid turd was a treasure of no small consequence. From what I'd seen, the Heavy Hitters wouldn't believe this stuff if you handed it to them on a silver platter. Linda pointed to a pile that was so full of feathers that it looked like the inside of a down comforter. "And they only eat seals, huh?" she said.

"I always wondered how those birds managed to crawl up a bear's ass," Kevin said.

CHAPTER 9

Going Nuclear

Some circumstantial evidence is very strong,
as when you find a trout in the milk.
—HENRY DAVID THOREAU, FROM *THE JOURNAL*
OF HENRY DAVID THOREAU, 1837–1861

A S I GOT BACK IN THE HELICOPTER, with the sacks of shit stowed carefully in a compartment alongside some survival gear, I began to wonder if this entire experience at Nestor Two had been a colossal failure. What exactly did I have to show for my time and expense after the better part of a week in camp? That was hard to say, but I knew what I didn't have. I didn't have an audience with the Heavy Hitters. I didn't have the macho, gritty bear-science experience I'd been hoping for, the chance to manhandle a drugged bear so I could make earnest proclamations about how it felt to nestle down next to the savage beast at rest. I hadn't been attacked and hadn't fired a gun; I hadn't seen anyone get mauled or had the opportunity to smell a bear's briny breath from two feet away. Instead, I'd filled gallon bags with bear poop and drunk a lot of powdered milk.

Moreover, the few bears that I'd seen from the air didn't appear to be in all that much distress. I wasn't an expert, but fat is fat. And these bears weren't showing a lot of bony ribcages. More distressing—to my project, if not to the bears—was that I had a lot less certainty than I'd had going in. It had been my intention to tidily dismiss the "bears are OK" cranks and then get down to some serious eulogizing for *Ursus maritimus*. Maybe geese and starfish would be enough to tide the bears over and maybe they wouldn't; I had no way of knowing. But one thing was clear: the story line that bears eat seals and only seals was not holding up. What other gospel truths had I been wrong about?

Rocky was waiting by the helicopter pad when we landed at Nestor Two. He was casually munching a snack, and he seemed to relish the mad whirlwind of dust and pebbles kicked up by the rotors. "How many samples did you get?" he shouted over the roar.

Kevin rolled his eyes, as if the answer was too obvious to have to say: "A *shitload*!" We unloaded the gear and Quinoa rolled in the dirt, happy to be home. Linda dumped her samples into the lab building and then we all went off in search of snacks and beer. The cool darkness and mosquito-free air of the kitchen felt like heaven. Quinoa stretched out atop an old sleeping bag and dutifully ate a bowl of Canine Super-food. Two warm beers and a kippered herring sandwich later, I felt much restored.

Linda and Rocky couldn't stop talking about how excited they were by the bags of poop sequestered in the deep freezer. In a few weeks Linda would place them in coolers full of dry ice, fly to Winnipeg, and then race home across the country before her precious samples could thaw. The biggest hurdle of the trip was always the border crossing back into the United States. In this age of dirty bombs, you can never be too careful about a curly-headed PhD candidate bound for the Big Apple with a bunch of ice chests full of polar bear shit.

This was going to be a big new break in the field, and—not trivially— a thumb in the eye of any polar bear bigwig who had ever dismissed Rocky for being just a goose biologist. Proving that polar bears had a large and varied land-based diet would challenge the commonly held as-sumptions about the summer starvation period. And if the genetic sam-pling worked as well as they hoped, Linda and Rocky would have gone a long way toward an accurate population count that they could easily re-create year after year without the cost and risk of darting hundreds of bears.

"So how do your data compare to Amstrup and Stirling's?" I asked. Ian Stirling is a charter member of the Heavy Hitters, a colleague of Amstrup's, and, in my experience, a generally cantankerous character.

"Jury's still out," Rocky said. "And it's going to stay out forever, because they'll never share their data with us."

He stepped to the sink, where an immense Arctic char was thawing in a metal bowl, head and tail fins dangling over the sides. As he spoke, Rocky chopped onions, garlic, and potatoes, then built an elaborate tinfoil tent in which to bake the fish. The subject of collaboration with the Heavy Hitters was a sore point. When rival academics bicker over minutiae, it's best just to stand back and try to avoid the shrapnel. Then again, this wasn't some subtle disagreement about British maritime art or the sociology of human love. Polar bears are either on the verge of extinction or else they're not, and there's a pretty good amount of daylight between those two camps. As well as a hell of a lot of worldwide attention and public policy consequences.

"I just want to get this straight," I said, wanting to give Rocky a chance to prove he wasn't a kook, a conservative-movement-based pseudo-scientist looking to bend his data to fit his politics. "Are you telling me that you don't think global warming is a problem for the bears? Are you saying that what they lose in seals they can make up for by eating geese and caribou and plants? Are you telling me that everything is going to be fine?"

"I have no idea!" Rocky exploded. "That's just it! But we have to be willing to ask that question. Which is exactly what Stirling won't do. We submitted a paper once about polar bears eating goose eggs, and when Stirling read it he went absolutely nuts, saying, 'Why don't they come ashore earlier if the eggs are so good?' and 'Eggs aren't going to save the bears.' Well, that wasn't what we were saying. We were saying that it's *possible* that bears *may* be able to derive *some* nutritional benefit from eating something other than seals. And Stirling couldn't accept even that limited hypothesis."

"Why not?"

"Because it challenges his thesis that everything is hopeless."

Rocky jabbed the fish like an assassin gutting his victim in an alleyway. Quinoa never even lifted his ears.

Linda had had much the same experience with the Heavy Hitters. One fall she'd attended a dinner where Amstrup held court. As Linda tells it, she sat down next to him to talk about her work, and he brushed her off rudely. Later, when she called to ask him if he'd look over a portion of her thesis, he declined, citing overwork; when she pushed, he said, "I wouldn't hold your breath." At one point he even told Linda that he didn't "think her stuff was going to work." I had my share of doubts, too, but you don't make too many new discoveries by trying things that you know are going to work before you do them.

"So now I'm just concentrating on getting papers out," Linda said. She would let the data do the talking. She'd tried the collaborative route and had been rebuffed. Negative comments from anonymous peer reviewers were the norm; getting blown off at conferences and informal gatherings was something she could learn to take in stride.

"Let's just say that if Linda were named Larry, she'd be having a much easier time," Rocky chimed in. "You have to understand, these are guys who still walk around with .44s strapped to their hips. It's a very macho culture." That might have been true, but it was also just as likely that her failure to connect with the Heavy Hitters had as much to do with the fact that she was young, new on the scene, lived in New York, and (to be fair) used a method that was easy to make fun of. If you're a guy like Amstrup who rides helicopters and shoots rifles, it's no mystery why you'll resist the idea that you might be replaced by a pack of shit-sniffing dogs.

THE FISH WAS IN ITS FOIL, covered with garlic, onions, and lemon slices, and Rocky was ready to slide it into the ancient oven. But first he asked if I'd go up on the roof to have a look around. "I've never cooked a char without bringing in a bear," he said. Topside, everything looked clear. After a week at La Perouse Bay, I'd stopped being afraid of every little rock or polar bear-esque hump of grass. It was nine in the evening and the sun was beginning its half-hearted dip toward a horizon it wouldn't reach for months. The river shimmered, whispering softly as it braided its way around the thousand islands that dotted its path. A steady breeze calmed the mosquitoes as the call of an Arctic loon echoed off lowering clouds.

So this was Rocky's grand theory, I thought, as I looked out toward the distant expanse of Hudson Bay. In a nutshell, he thought that as the Arctic warmed and the sea ice shrank, the bears would somehow manage to adapt. They'd learn to take advantage of the abundant food on land. Rocky's ideas were engaging, and he was a good salesman for them, but I wasn't entirely buying it. Compared to a one-hundred-pound, blubber-laden seal carcass, the occasional bony goose or puffball mushroom didn't seem like an adequate meal. It seemed a tenuous bit of evidence on which to pin a wholesale revolution in the conventional wisdom re-garding polar bears and global warming.

I sat on the roof in silence, scanning the barrens. Nothing. The scarcity of bears this year was a sign that they were doing well, Rocky had told me. If they were hungrier, they'd be piling up along the fence line like tumbleweeds, drawn in by the sweet smell of garbage.

I've been to a lot of remote places in my life but never had I felt any-thing like this emptiness. The camp was an outpost on the surface of the moon, surrounded by monotony, but with the threat of death at every turn. In a place this desolate it was hard to remember that the polar bears of Hudson Bay were the center of a maelstrom, a jumping-off point for all sorts of overheated rhetoric and carefully calibrated outrage. I strad-dled the peak of the roof, dangling a leg over each side.

Later I found Rocky in the dorm, sitting heavily on his bunk as the rusty springs groaned in protest. A tiny box hanging from the rafters spit out a puff of bug repellent every minute, and the fine poison mist filtered down over us. Rocky exchanged his filthy shirt for a marginally cleaner one and covered himself all over with Deet. He looked tired and a little sad, and I wondered whether immersing himself in this controversy was the best way to finish out an illustrious career spent mostly with birds. Was he really the lone voice speaking out against groupthink or was he just a graying scientist fighting against the inevitable downslope of his academic relevance?

"Look," he said, "I don't want you to come away from your time here thinking that we're against these people. But there are things going on that affect polar bears that are not getting a full hearing. The polar bear is really special to me, but the Endangered Species Act and the commission of proper science are more important."

Rocky rattled off a long line of statistical jargon, pointing out the ways he believed that the Heavy Hitters had played fast and loose with the rules of population dynamics and scientific methodology. The more we talked, the clearer it became that he didn't really care about polar bears at all, at least not in the cuddly, cutesy way that advertisers are always trying to make us feel. Sure, he had affection for them, thought they were impressive and beautiful, and he liked the cachet of being the gun-toting mountain man in contrast to his lab-coated Manhattan colleagues. But, like Linda, what really turned his crank was the math, the numbers and equations and computerized statistics programs.

"Take the 2050 thing, for example," he said. "That's just a huge problem." Rocky was referring to a series of reports, sprawling over nearly 1,000 pages, that Amstrup had written for the US Geological Survey. Despite the minutiae in his work, one single factoid had been catnip to the press, reported and rereported in every media outlet on earth. One typical headline read, "Scientists: Most Polar Bears Dead by 2050." The rigid specificity and the closeness of the drop-dead date had propelled Amstrup to gloomy stardom.

Rocky reiterated the ways in which he thought the Heavy Hitters had botched their methodology, the ways they'd made all sorts of assumptions that biased their results in the most pessimistic way possible.

I had no way of knowing if Rocky was right or wrong, but I had faith in the scientific process to do the heavy lifting that I couldn't do myself. Surely some journal would weed out flimsy numbers and peer reviewers would reject shoddy work.

"That's just it!" Rocky thundered. "Those USGS papers aren't science. They're junk! And they should be thrown out. There were a lot of places where the assumptions could have been A or B and it was always A, always coming down on the side of the bear needing help. That's not science, that's being an advocate. If this had been a bird or a fish, I guarantee you it would not have happened this quickly."

This was news to me. When the stakes were this high—as they had been years ago in the battle between the spotted owl and the timber industry—the science had to be beyond reproach or the whole enterprise would devolve into an orgy of finger-pointing and name-calling. (Sometimes it would anyway, but you had to do your best.) The right way to go forward in these situations was with lots of peer review by top-notch scientists who had no personal stake in the crisis du jour. The wrong way was manufacturing a rush job to satisfy antsy politicians, with no time to call in outside experts to do the slow, thoughtful analysis that good science demands.

Then again . . . big fucking deal.

Part of me felt that this was all just a lot of inside-baseball nonsense. The group of people who lost sleep over Amstrup's research methods pretty much extended only as far as the electric fence surrounding Nestor Two. On the day the sun explodes, you can guarantee that a bunch of academics will be squabbling over who was the first one to predict the earth's annihilation.

But it doesn't take a genius to see that if the ice goes away, then the ice bear is going to be in trouble. If anything, I think most people would say that science is too damned slow, and that once something is obvious—like the coming extinction of the polar bear—you ought to quit pissing away grant money and get out there and do something about the problem.

And so what if Amstrup was "becoming an advocate," as Rocky put it? It wasn't like he was being secretive about it. In his curriculum vitae for the USGS, he'd included a blurb entitled, "Life Mission": "Engage science to reconcile the ever enlarging human footprint on our environment with the needs of other species for that same environment— thereby assuring that prosperous people can live sustainably on healthy productive landscapes that provide their food, fiber, aesthetic, and recreational needs." I'd never seen anything so nonspecific and loosey-goosey on a scientist's CV, but at least he wasn't shy about having crossed over from science to cheerleading.

And sure, maybe he was playing a little loose with the numbers, and maybe he was spending too much time on a soapbox rather than at a lab bench, but was anybody really being harmed? Polar bears could use a good advocate, and it seemed unlikely that Exxon or Halliburton would step up. At least Amstrup was good-looking and blond and articulate and carried a gun. If Americans were going to pay attention to anybody, it was going to be this guy.

Rocky was becoming increasingly agitated. He'd spent a lot of years cooped up on this little patch of dirt in the blazing sun, and he'd had a lot of time to mull over how things ought to work if he ran the world. Good science was more important to him than the specifics of any one particular issue. "A scientist's first commitment needs to be to science, not to the end result," he said. "A single-minded scientist leads us to the Dr. Mengele problem," Rocky went on, referring to the Third Reich doctor who performed unspeakable human experiments under the cloak of scientific inquiry.

"Sure, but the opposite extreme is just as bad," I said. "A scientist can't throw up his hands and say, 'I'm just splitting the atom here and I don't have any idea what the military might use it for.'" This was getting ridiculous. I'd gone nuclear and he'd gone Nazi, which is the universal symbol that any conversation has come unhinged. But polar bears have a way of doing that to people. We looked at each other, realized that we were heading toward the brink of ridiculousness and made a silent pact to tone it down.

"But to say that they're all going to be extinct in 2050?" Rocky said. "Come on. No scientist would believe that. There will come a day when Amstrup will regret having said that. His credibility will be gone." Rocky took off his glasses and rubbed his eyes while the bug machine spritzed out another deadly dose. "And what happens if the bears in the Beaufort Sea are not extirpated by 2050?" he continued. "And then what if something else goes wrong and some other species is more at risk. Will people listen to any of us then?"

Rocky massaged his feet and pulled on a fresh pair of socks. This lifestyle was starting to take its toll, but he never complained, and you have to admire a tenured professor who sleeps in a bunk bed and eats powdered mashed potatoes in the name of science. He shouldered his gun and I followed him outside. Before he reached the door, he turned toward me and gave his final word on the subject. "We all understand that there are changes coming," he said. "I'm not disputing that. But the question is: What is this big, charismatic species going to do about that change? Will they all die? Sit around town with a sign begging for a meal? We don't know. But it's the height of hubris to say with certainty that polar bears are an evolutionary dead end and that they can't adapt. I think that's as bad as arguing for intelligent design."

As promised, the Arctic char was delicious. It was light and flaky, and not even a little bit rancid, which is often my impression of novel seafood. I pushed my chair back from the table, savoring a tiny square of the carefully apportioned chocolate that remained, when I saw a flash bearing down on me from behind.

It took me a few seconds to realize what was happening. Quinoa stared up at me with calm, expressionless black eyes. His teeth, on the other hand, were full of life, and at the moment they were firmly planted in the meat of my thigh. Apparently, Quinoa's police-dog lineage hadn't been entirely replaced by a new job in the sciences, and he was, in his own unassuming way, doing what came naturally. Something in the way I'd scraped my chair had spooked him, and instinct caused him to lash out.

My first instinct, being the hypermasculine, Davy Crockett–style hero that I am, was to punch the little bastard in the face. My second instinct, being the eminently good houseguest that my mother raised me to be, was to downplay the situation and try not to inconvenience anybody with my personal issues. *I can't punch this dog,* I thought. *He cost $2,000.* I wrapped my hands around his snout, hoping to keep him from thrashing his head back and dislodging a big chunk of me.

Fortunately, Linda didn't have the same deference to decorum. She hollered and grabbed him. Rocky and the rest of the students watched in rapt silence. Instantly, Quinoa relaxed his grip and looked up at Linda with an expectant expression. Easy for him to pretend nothing special was going on; he wasn't the one with a row of vampire bites all over his leg.

"Oh my God," Linda said, looking mortified. "I am so sorry. I can't believe he did that. I'm sorry, I'm so sorry." She grabbed Quinoa and led him out of the kitchen. The rest of us sat in stunned silence.

"Well, that certainly puts a damper on the evening," Rocky said at last. "But the fish was good, wouldn't you say?" He grabbed a metal cup and poured me several fingers of whiskey—the good stuff that he'd been hiding in reserve for a special occasion. "Drop your pants," he said. Six ragged bite marks stood out on my thigh like glowing cigarette tips. Rocky applied some Betadine and a few ceremonial Band-Aids. Not the most thorough emergency medicine I'd ever seen, but it looked like I was going to live. I'd come into the tundra to face down one of the most vicious wild beasts known to man, and instead I'd been taken out by a shit-sniffing shepherd from New York.

THE NEXT DAY I STOOD by the helicopter pad, waiting for the Bell Ranger helicopter that would take me back to Churchill. From there I'd fly to Winnipeg, then to Minneapolis, on to Denver, and finally, many hours later, to my home in Oakland, where all the produce was organic, the thought of owning a gun was abhorrent, and absolutely everybody knew with complete certainty exactly what was happening with the polar bears way up north.

Quinoa stood beside me, as placid and happy as if we had no history together. Apparently, I wasn't delicious enough to tempt him toward another bite. (Then again, I'd tasted his Canine Superfood—could I really be less palatable than that?) Even if you didn't count the dog bite, the trip hadn't been anything like I'd expected. Linda's poop-detection method was both more ridiculous and more promising than I thought it would be. And Rocky—a marginalized figure as far as the Heavy Hitters were concerned—had the most reasoned, rational take on polar bears I'd ever heard. While the treehuggers and the global warming deniers wailed in outrage, Rocky was quietly riding the middle ground.

And he had managed to infect me with a kernel of doubt. I wasn't ready to buy into the idea that polar bears could meet their nutritional needs with plants and geese, but I'd also seen with my own eyes that seals most certainly weren't the only item on the buffet table. More important, Rocky had knocked the Heavy Hitters off their pedestal a little. Amstrup wasn't an unassailable avatar of pure scientific truth; he was just an academic like any other, who sometimes got it right and sometimes didn't. An inconvenient truth, to be sure. Suddenly polar bears weren't on the knife edge of extinction, the ice wasn't everything, and most disturbing, I wasn't quite the evangelist I had been one week earlier.

The helicopter made its final approach, taking its customary low circle to scout for bears. When the pilot landed he kept the rotors going—$30 a minute is a lot to pay for a long good-bye. Rocky leaned in close to be heard above the prop wash.

"This world would be a very sad place without polar bears," he said to me. "And I'm glad I won't be around to see it."

CHAPTER 10

I Think We Should Move to Churchill

*More and more Americans are coming to conclude,
after the record cold temperatures in many cities this
winter, that global warming is a crock—that there is no
conclusive proof it is happening, no conclusive proof
man is the cause, no conclusive proof it would be a
calamity for us or the polar bears.*

—PATRICK BUCHANAN, CONSERVATIVE
COMMENTATOR, MAY 13, 2009

O OOOH MAN . . . I GOT A BONE TO PICK with you. I am not happy with you!"

A few days after coming home from Nestor Two, I picked up my son Mac at preschool. His teacher, a pretty, young Trinidadian woman, met me at the gate. Normally, she was the sunniest person, always giggling for no apparent reason. But today she was stone-faced. She thrust Mac's lunch box into my hands, glaring at me all the while.

"Macky told me where you've been," she said. "He told me you've been hunting polar bears. How could you do such a thing? They're just poor happy little creatures who don't mean any harm to anybody and you go up and kill them? Haven't they got enough to worry about already?"

Mac looked at me innocently, blinking his big brown eyes. "What did you tell her?" I asked him.

"I told her that you were hunting polars," he said, using the shorthand that he developed because saying the entire phrase "polar bears" was apparently too onerous. "I told her that you went to Canada and that everybody there had lots of guns and that you were hunting polars." He held his hands out at his sides, palms up, in a classic "Who, me?" pose. Some of the other parents had gathered around, pretending not to eavesdrop, though their faces showed their newfound loathing of me. An environmental criminal in their midst!

"No, no, no, that's not right at all," I said, envisioning an angry mob of well-heeled, Sierra Clubbing moms, expressing their disapproval in the strictest possible terms.

"I wasn't hunting polar bears," I said. "I was hunting *for* polar bears. I was looking for them. To see them, not to kill them, get it?" The moms reluctantly tucked their pitchforks and torches back into their double strollers. The teacher softened a bit, though it was clear I was still on her probation list.

I turned to Mac. "You knew what I meant, didn't you?" I said, looking down at the little instigator, who was serenely excavating both nostrils at once with twin index fingers. "You knew I wasn't trying to kill them, right?"

Mac shrugged. "I dunno. I'm just saying what you said. And you said you were hunting for them." He flipped up the kickstand on his bike and started off, but not without one last parting scold in full earshot of the assembled crowd. "You know, Dad, there's not very many of those polars left anymore." Devious little bastard.

IT WAS AT ABOUT THIS TIME that polar bears transitioned from being merely interesting to being the subject of an outright frenzy. Al Gore's movie, a re-creation of his favorite moments on PowerPoint, had its most dramatic moment with an animation about a drowning polar bear. Steven Amstrup's projection of near extinction by 2050 was getting huge press. His observations of polar bear cannibalism were even bigger. Paramount made a wretched pseudo-documentary about a polar bear family, narrated by the noted Arctic researcher Queen Latifah.

Moreover, polar bears had ceased to be merely furry animals and had become pawns in a new front of the culture wars. Tell me how you feel about the future of the polar bears, and I'll bet I can guess exactly where you stand on abortion and gay marriage. Reading all of the available science was a huge pain in the ass; it always is. And so people took sides in the global warming debate based on how Fox News or the Sierra Club told them how to feel. Then we all slipped into our cozy ideological bubbles of self-satisfaction and moral righteousness.

The explosion in interest wasn't random, and it wasn't solely driven by Amstrup's dire predictions. In January 2007, scientists at the US Fish and Wildlife Service suggested that polar bears might need protection under the Endangered Species Act. By law, the political appointees at the head of the agency had one year to make the decision. The battle for the polar bear was going to be fought in Washington, DC.

The deadline came and went. George Bush's interior secretary, Dirk Kempthorne, delayed and deferred while the environmental community fumed. The world looked to the United States for guidance; Canada, home to the vast majority of the polar bears, put off its "special status" decision, waiting to see what the Americans would do. Democratic senator Barbara Boxer, criticizing Kempthorne's refusal to testify on the issue, said that his absence was "a slap at this committee and a slap at the American people who care about this." Republican senator John Warner committed a minor act of apostasy, scandalizing his colleagues by essentially agreeing with Boxer. "I think we have an obligation toward this extraordinary animal," he said. "It's America's panda bear, and all Americans are in love with it." Apparently, "all" didn't include conservative columnist George Will, who wrote relentlessly snide pieces calling polar bears "wards of the government."

As far as the listing decision went, there were two issues at play, one regional and one global. The first was a proposed oil and gas lease in the Chukchi Sea, the icy waters off the Alaskan coast where most American polar bears live. Oil companies had their eyes on a 29 million-acre bit of ocean said to contain 15 billion barrels of oil and 75 trillion cubic feet of natural gas. Just how much is that? Well, nobody without a geological engineering degree really cared, but it sure sounded like a hell of a lot, especially because this was the year of $4.50 gasoline and endless "Pain at the Pumps" reports on the nightly news.

The Bush administration desperately wanted the leases to go through. Listing the polar bear as threatened would cause endless rounds of litigation. Delaying the decision by a few months would allow the leases to be sold before the pesky bears got their paws all over the paperwork.

The second issue was more far-reaching. Up to this point, no species had ever been put on the Endangered Species List as a result of climate change. It's possible to help most endangered animals, for example, by stopping logging in a particular region or by scuttling a proposed dam project. Resetting the thermostat of the entire earth is a bit trickier. A lawsuit from a group called the Center for Biological Diversity (CBD) argued that polar bears could be used as a roundabout way to enact climate change legislation, concluding that any of the industries that produced carbon or contributed to global warming would have to consider how their business model affected the polar bears. It was an unprecedented legal theory.

Republicans went bonkers. Alaska senator Ted Stevens—who would later be indicted for accepting illegal gifts from an oil executive—said that the listing "would establish a dangerous precedent based on mathematical models." (No great lover of the whole math-and-science thing, Stevens famously declared that the Internet is not a big truck, but instead a series of tubes.) Alaska's governor, Sarah Palin—who would remain irrelevant outside of her home state for only a few more months—penned an op-ed in the *New York Times,* citing her extreme love of polar bears and her abhorrence at the thought of protecting them. And George Will, ever reliable, wrote: "Want to build a power plant in Arizona? A building in Florida? Do you want to drive an SUV? Or leave your cellphone charger plugged in overnight? Some judge might construe federal policy as proscribing these activities." With no intelligible segue, he finished that paragraph on polar bears by saying "and no authors of the Constitution or the 14th Amendment intended to create a 'fundamental' right to abortion, but there it is." He may have been nonsensically off-topic, but at least you knew which camp he was in.

Delay, delay, delay. Fight, fight, fight. Had any of these people on either side ever actually seen a polar bear? It didn't matter; they were all landing heavy political blows.

The deadline passed, the months wore on. In the interim, the oil and gas leases in the Chukchi Sea sailed through, including a record-breaking $105 million offer from Shell Oil, an amount nearly twice as high as any previous bid for an offshore tract. In all, the sale raised a staggering $2.6 billion. The delay had worked, and supporters of the polar bear were apoplectic. The Center for Biological Diversity prepared more lawsuits. The bears remained oblivious to their newfound celebrity. Life went on.

Until finally in May 2008, Dirk Kempthorne—a square-jawed Idaho Republican straight out of central casting—stood before the cameras and announced his decision. During his time in the Senate, Kempthorne had received a 1 percent rating from the League of Conservation Voters. Six hundred days into his tenure as secretary of the interior, he held the record for placing the fewest number of plants or animals on the Endangered Species List. To be specific, that number was zero. But he hadn't been completely idle: the *Washington Post* reported that he spent $235,000 to renovate the bathroom in his office, installing a shower, a wood-paneled refrigerator, and a set of monogrammed towels. Needless to say, environmentalists weren't expecting much.

Standing beside a giant picture of a polar bear, Kempthorne launched into his press conference. "Today I am listing the polar bear as a 'Threatened' species under the Endangered Species Act." He even showed satellite images of declining sea ice and talked about taking the advice of scientific experts. What a shock! This was actually going to go the right way! It was clear that Kempthorne wasn't happy about this, complaining that his hands were tied, and that the Endangered Species Act was "perhaps the least flexible law Congress has ever enacted." Nonetheless, this was the first time that climate change had ever been cited as a causative factor in an endangered species listing. Finally, the US government had been forced to sit up and pay attention.

But any elation that environmentalists might have felt was short-lived. As hopeful bear lovers around the world looked on slack-jawed, Kempthorne sliced the guts out of the regulation he had just announced. "While the legal standards under the ESA compel me to list the polar bear as threatened, I want to make clear that this listing will not stop global climate change or prevent any sea ice from melting. . . . That is why I am taking administrative and regulatory action to make certain the ESA isn't abused to make global warming policies." He went on to state that "no polar bears have been killed due to encounters associated with oil and gas operations," and therefore the listing could not be used to limit drilling or prospecting in any way.

In short, the much-touted listing meant next to nothing. Polar bears would be protected . . . just not from the things that were actually threatening them. It was like your dad saying he would buy you a new car for your birthday, and then mentioning that his offer didn't include a steering wheel, seats, a drive train, or a motor. The Center for Biological Diversity issued a press release saying that "the administration's attempts to reduce protection to the polar bear from greenhouse gas emissions are illegal and won't hold up in court." Sarah Palin announced her intention to sue as well; she wanted the federal government to reverse itself and de-list the polar bear once and for all. The CBD fired back, saying Palin was either "grossly misinformed or intentionally misleading, and both are unbecoming."

The decision was in, but the war of words was just beginning. Years of litigation and thousands of pages of testimony had helped the United States to arrive at exactly the same place it had started out. Polar bears were dying, or maybe they weren't. Greenhouses gases were the cause, or maybe they weren't. The government would do something about it, or maybe it wouldn't. And far up in the North, a million miles from

Washington, DC, and the nearest federal courthouse, the polar bears sat on shore, waiting for the ice.

As THE HARANGUES MOUNTED, one thing was becoming increasingly clear to me: polar bears were essentially irrelevant to the drama that surrounded them. Oh sure, a picture of a polar bear mom playing with her cubs was pure gold, and a picture of a skin-and-bones bear starving to death was even better, as far as public relations was concerned. But time and again people glossed over what was happening with the polar bears in order to talk about what *could* happen, provided that certain ideological conditions were met. Corporate lobbyists hollered that polar bears would bankrupt America, and movie stars made mournful photo-op "reporting" trips to the Far North. But with the exception of Steven Amstrup and a few other scientists, it seemed that nobody talking about polar bears actually knew anything that they hadn't read in a press release. Throughout it all, Amstrup was there in measured tones, calm and good-looking as ever, appearing before Congress, on the evening news, and in the pages of newspapers everywhere.

Nonetheless, people always spoke as if the problem—increased carbon emissions—was in the cities, and the effect—dying bears—was on another planet. True, there weren't a lot of places where people and polar bears were neighbors, but I suspected the interaction between people and bears was much more substantial than the theoretical connection between mass extinction and our everyday decisions about where to set our thermostats. The disconnect held for me as well; despite my intense interest in the subject, I was probably just as likely to be spouting a bunch of nonsense as everyone else.

"I THINK WE SHOULD MOVE to Churchill," I said to my wife one warm, summer California day, as we ate dinner at the picnic table in our backyard.

"I'm not sure what you mean by 'we,'" she said, eyeing me with suspicion. "I'm from Canada, remember? I don't really enjoy negative twenty anymore." At home we bought sunscreen by the gallon; our kids spent every waking moment in the backyard, covered with a coarse external layer of watermelon juice, lawn clippings, and SPF 50. We'd recently bought a cheap swing set, and the kids had discovered the joys of riding bikes; they'd never been happier. Shona had a point.

"We won't stay there forever," I said. "I'm just thinking about a couple of months in fall and winter. You know, the entire bear season." I understood that it wasn't the offer of a lifetime. Shona had started work at a new law firm, my job as a fireman was as stable as ever, and our daughter, Percy, our oldest, was set to begin her first year of school. It wasn't the most auspicious time to pull up stakes.

"So let's see here," she said, after I explained my desire to get to the bottom of the whole polar bear thing. "You'll be running around town, interviewing people, having adventures, and I'll be doing what?"

"I don't know. You could go skating a lot, do arts-and-crafts projects, take care of the kids, and . . ."

"And make sure nobody gets eaten by a polar bear?"

"Yeah, pretty much." This wasn't the best sales pitch I'd ever given.

Shona thought about it for a minute, weighing the pros and cons of leaving our comfortable life for an unfurnished apartment surrounded by subzero temperatures and vicious wild animals.

"Sure," she said. "It sounds great."

"Really?" I don't know why I should have been so surprised. Shona is a hundred gallons of sunshine packed into a three-ounce teacup. She's five feet tall on a good day—snow boots help—but she's a whirring little buzz saw of energy and grit. You might not pick her first for your basketball team, but if you had to be marooned on an island with someone, she'd be the right choice.

"You'll really go up there with me?" I repeated.

"Why not? I love the North. And it will be good for the kids to learn how to wear long johns and mitts. You don't really think they'll get eaten, do you?"

"No," I answered. "Well, probably not all of them anyway. That's why we have three."

CHAPTER 11

A Perfect Place
for a Bear Attack

*My number one goal is to be able to have
people travel through town without fear.*

—ALBERT MEIJERING, CHIEF ADMINISTRATIVE
OFFICER, TOWN OF CHURCHILL

W E DECIDED THAT I WOULD GO to Churchill in advance of Shona and the kids. This was so I could get things ready and scope out the scene. Also, not incidentally, the thought of a thirty-six-hour family trip with three plane transfers and a night at a Winnipeg airport hotel didn't strike me as entirely pleasant. Much better to make the trip alone with a stack of novels and the chance to watch the in-flight romantic comedy without interruption.

"You're going to go there when?" my mom asked when I informed her of our travel plans.

"October and November," I said.

"Isn't that, um, right in the middle of the school year?" she asked. True enough, we'd have to pull Percy out of school for this polar adventure, short-circuiting her kindergarten year just as she was establishing the academic and social skills that would inevitably propel her onward to the Ivy League, and from there to the White House.

Basic math and reading skills be damned: high adventure awaited us up north. Bears! Frostbite! Conventionally grown produce! I knew this wasn't the equivalent of trekking in the Himalayas with your newborn, but I was excited about the looming shake-up in our lives. I arranged with the fire chief for a leave of absence, and then tried not to second-guess myself when his jaw dropped at the prospect of me using several years' worth of accumulated vacation time for an extended homestay in northern Manitoba. "Why can't you just go on a cruise like everyone else?" he asked.

The other firefighters were similarly nonplussed. "You know it's all a hoax, don't you?" one of them asked. "The picture of the polar bears stranded on that melting ice thing was completely Photoshopped." Now, this was the sort of ignorance I'd set out to stop. When you accuse Al Gore of digital camera crimes, well, that's just going too far.

Unlike your typical polar death march, we'd be traveling both light and in relative comfort. I'd arranged for us to rent an apartment in Churchill; most of the housing in town is owned by the government of Manitoba, and getting a place was as easy as showing them Shona's Canadian passport and promising not to park my snowmobile on the carpeting. The rent—$930 a month—seemed a little high for an edge-of-nowhere town with a wild animal problem. But heat was included, so I could run the furnace with abandon, global warming be damned.

I packed five plates and five forks, a frying pan, and a Swiss Army knife. Our place in Oakland was stuffed with the accumulated detritus that modern life deems necessary, ridiculous luxuries like pillows and laundry baskets and measuring spoons. In Churchill we'd have no car, no furniture, precious little in the way of clean clothes. We'd also have no friends. But Shona is the kind of person who can make nice at a mercenaries' convention, so I figured we'd be all right.

All of the arrangements were made. We stopped the mail and canceled the newspapers, emptied the fridge and made peace with the fact that all of our houseplants were going to die. The kids were instructed to ruthlessly choose favorites among their stuffed animals: Brown Doggie was in, but I convinced Mac that Pink Bear had been plotting against him and didn't deserve to make the voyage. We might have been setting ourselves up for an uncomfortable life up there, but I'd be damned if I was going to pay $50 to check a second bag on the airplane.

IT WAS 72°F AND CLEAR, the rare fogless early fall day that makes every smug San Franciscan believe that people who live elsewhere must be lunatics or shut-ins. The Transamerica Building rose from the water's edge in its perfect pyramid, the Golden Gate shimmered in the distance, and a thousand bespandexed fitness freaks jogged along footpaths and contorted themselves into transcendent yoga poses under fragrant eucalyptus trees.

In the security line at the airport, however, my feet were sweating uncontrollably inside my ski-lift operator's boots. I tried to relax, shifting my weight back and forth as I finished the dregs of a frozen banana-berry smoothie. But it's hard to do anything gracefully when you're wearing an expedition-weight, Arctic-lined goose-down North Face parka with attached hood and what I hoped was a fake-fur lining. By the time I reached the metal detector I was dripping wet, and the Transportation Security Administration screener eyed me dubiously as I extracted my boarding pass from one of the seventeen survival pockets located strategically throughout my coat.

"Is that what you're wearing?" she asked.

"It's not cold here," I said, fumbling for an explanation.

"I know that."

"I mean, it's colder where I'm going."

"You're going to have to take off the whole . . . costume. Boots, too," she said.

The rest of the travelers behind me, day-trippers in business suits and climate-appropriate khakis, cursed themselves for having chosen my line. Did I really look that suspicious? Since when did jihadists start wearing mukluks?

Strip search completed, I settled into my seat, parka stowed in the overhead bin and boots occupying 90 percent of the scant legroom.

The last time I'd flown out of San Francisco, the normally blasé attitude of the frequent flier had been punctuated by a woman beside me gasping, "My God, would you look at that." We all craned our necks to look out the window, and indeed, on that day the bay was covered with something other than sailboats and whitecaps. An oily sheen spread out from the second tower of the San Francisco Bay Bridge, giving the low swells an ugly, iridescent hue. Two days earlier, the tanker *Cosco Busan* had plowed into the bridge, and despite the pilot's initial report of 140 gallons of fuel oil in the water, the spill eventually blossomed to 58,000 gallons. Somewhere down below us, earnest volunteers in Tyvek jumpsuits were busy scrubbing rocks and shampooing shorebirds.

"Put another mark in the global warming column," said the man seated next to me.

"What a waste. Total disaster," said his wife, and then we all opened our magazines and forgot about the whole thing as the force of 20,000 gallons of burning jet fuel pressed us backward into our seats.

But today was different. The ocean was clean and calm, the skies were blue, and I was leaving the Bay Area behind, about to replace the urban grime with the wide open vistas of the Great White North.

I'd been hoping my foul weather outfit might come in handy, but when we touched down in Winnipeg, the temperature turned out to be as balmy as it had been in San Francisco. I asked if there was anyplace to get something to eat, and a gate agent in shorts directed me to a vending machine that sold ice cream. *Weather isn't climate,* I kept telling myself, repeating an old meteorologist's mantra. A day of Frisbee-playing warmth in winter doesn't signal global warming; a freak snowstorm in early June isn't evidence for the idea that the earth has corrected itself and we should all return to the carefree days of burning tires and hacking down rain forests. Still, it was hard not to have global warming on the brain as I kicked off my snow boots, folded my parka into a pillow, and curled up on the industrial rug of the airport floor to catch a few hours of sleep before my early morning flight to Churchill.

An hour before departure, the gate was packed. Half of the people sitting on the hard plastic chairs were the usual customers for a regional flight to a frontier town: stony-faced young men in Carhartt jackets, grease beneath their fingernails and plugs of tobacco in their lips; tradesmen and skilled laborers shuttling between jobs, or coming home after a hard-partying, quest-for-girls-type weekend in what passes for the big city; exhausted senior citizens returning from visits to their cardiologists at the urban medical center. And off to one side sat a single Native woman, no more than a teenager, wearing a handmade coat with a pink-cheeked baby poking out from a pouch sewn into the back.

But in among these regulars was an odd scrum of foreigners. A Frenchwoman with perfect hair and boots that reached to mid-thigh tapped anxiously at a pack of cigarettes that she knew she wasn't allowed to smoke; half a dozen Korean men and women did stretching exercises outside the doughnut shop, their high-dollar camera equipment in a pile at their feet.

An American who looked as though he had just stepped out of an L.L. Bean catalog—neon-green fleece hat, fleece tights, fleece gloves, and an elaborate jacket with armpit vents and a tiny thermometer on the zipper—stepped up to the gate attendant and asked, "Has it been a good bear year?"

"It's a little early yet, but if you see even one bear you're ahead of most people," she equivocated. The man scowled. In his day job, he probably wasn't subject to the vagaries of weather and animal behavior. Seeing just one bear, as the gate attendant had suggested, would cause this guy to deem the trip an unmitigated disaster. The attendant shrugged; issuing bear guarantees was outside of her job description. She smiled and said, "Churchill's always nice even if you don't . . ."

She was interrupted by a red-faced man who swaggered up to the counter. He addressed his traveling companion in a voice loud enough so that it couldn't be missed by the assembled tourists. "Who in hell would want to see a polar bear, anyhow?" he asked.

"Everybody," said his friend, a big guy with curly hair in such tight ringlets that it could pass for an albino's afro. "That's why they're dying."

Red and Curly bantered for a few minutes, holding court on the ridiculousness of the polar bear tour industry. For the most part the travelers ignored the men, possibly because their English was too weak to fully absorb the condescension, but more likely because they'd been looking forward to this trip for years, because they were already thousands of dollars out of pocket and halfway across the earth, and because nothing, absolutely nothing, would spoil the trip of their dreams.

"Polar bears *kill* people," said Curly, the more amiable of the two men. "That's basically their job. They kill things for a living."

"Going to Churchill to see bears is like going to Iraq because you want to see what a roadside bomb looks like," Red said with a snort, as several dozen smiling tourists shouldered their gear and headed onto the tarmac to board the plane.

ONCE ON THE GROUND in Churchill, my luggage emerged on its carousel before I could go to the bathroom and get my bearings. The Churchill airport is little more than an oversized waiting room with a few rows of chairs bolted to the floor. However, the mood is quite a bit better than you'll find in most airports that have ten times the number of so-called conveniences. People come and go as if the terminal were housing a church social; gate attendants pass out coffee and granola bars; and women rush behind the ticket counter to give their pilot husbands the brown-bag lunches forgotten on the kitchen counter. You can watch the airplanes out on the tarmac getting fueled and loaded. And on one wall, there's a giant polar bear skin rug—head still firmly attached—in a beautifully ornate wooden case. It may not be much of an airport if you're accustomed to the whole Star Alliance Premier Lounge thing, but what it lacks in Chili's Express kiosks and $12 chewing gum, it more than makes up for in pure soul.

I threw my luggage into a battered taxi-van. A long crack ran the length of the windshield, and despite a sad-looking pine-tree freshener on the rearview mirror, the interior smelled of cheeseburgers. The driver, a man of very few teeth, filled the gaps in his dental work with one cigarette after another as he drove.

The airport is fifteen minutes from town, and the fact that there exists a wide, well-paved highway between the two feels somewhat unnecessary.

Even though gasoline is dispensed from a single pump at usurious rates, nobody in town is without a vehicle. The ride of choice is an American-made monster truck with tractor-sized tires and enough seating for an entire hockey team. I would estimate that there are ten times as many seatbelts in town as there are people, which is not to say that any of them are ever clicked into place.

"That's gonna be the new RCMP building there," my driver said, pointing to a half-built structure surrounded by five men in various stages of lunch break. RCMP refers to the Royal Canadian Mounted Police, who are neither royal nor mounted, though on ceremonial occasions they do still wear spurs, flat-brimmed cowboy hats, and blood-red uniforms that add a high degree of difficulty to a surreptitious stakeout.

"Why do they need a new building?" I asked.

"It's gonna have more jail cells."

"Do they need more jail cells?"

"You always need more jail cells," he said, lighting yet another cigarette. I resolved to be on my best behavior. I looked out the window to see that we were being passed by a pickup truck with a painting on the door of a snarling bear ripping apart the sheet metal in his desperation to get out of the vehicle.

I was sharing the taxi-van with Curly and Red, along with a handful of Swiss tourists. The Swiss peered anxiously out of the windows, chattering to one another as they tried to catch their first-ever glimpse of the big white beast. But the only thing on the horizon was the gray water of Hudson Bay, which surged against the rocks without breaking, rising and falling rhythmically as if being massaged by an immense pump hidden beneath the depths. Accustomed to much grander vistas, the Swiss were underwhelmed. Being a smug California coastal boy, I should have felt the same way, but the empty coastline was growing on me. It was so . . . unassuming. What it lacked in postcard-worthy spectacularity, it more than made up for in sheer, plodding presence. There was nothing here to suggest beach blankets or margaritas beneath thatched huts. Instead, the endless arc of the coastline offered a workmanlike stolidity. The sloped and timeworn boulders that reached all the way from the road's edge to well past the high-tide line said that this was an ocean for real men only.

The Swiss, however, were disappointed by not having seen a bear in the first three minutes after deplaning. Much to their delight, Curly pulled out a batch of glossy photographs of bears. It seemed odd that someone who had so loudly professed his disdain would be carrying around bear pictures, so I asked the pair what they were doing in Churchill. As it turned out, neither one of them had ever seen a polar bear before. "We're from the North, though," said Red gruffly. "So seeing a bear wouldn't be all that much of a big deal to us." I noticed that they scanned the countryside as closely as the rest of us. And exactly how indifferent can a guy really be if he brings polar bear pictures to the Polar Bear Capital of the World, like a kid bringing a bat and mitt to his first big-league game?

Curly and Red weren't locals, but they did follow in the tradition of people who expected the North Country to make them immensely rich. They represented a corporate conglomerate with big designs on Hudson Bay's mineral wealth. The plan involved shipping 5 million pounds of gear and 4 million gallons of fuel through the Port of Churchill and up to the gold fields. Estimates were that the proposed mine would produce 350,000 ounces of gold a year and be productive for ten full years. If the mine paid off as intended, it would bring its backers $250 million a year, and $2.5 billion over the life of the mine. And this was in the pre-bailout era, back when $2 billion still sounded like a lot of money.

The guys were in Churchill to check on their gear. They'd been madly shipping steel and fuel and tractors in an attempt to beat the freeze, but the window had slammed shut. Now, thousands of pounds of gear sat on the ice-encrusted docks gathering rust. Even worse, one of the boats hauling gear up through Rankin Inlet had been outrun by the weather. Now it sat paralyzed, frozen into Hudson Bay, listing dangerously to one side and taking on water. It was a bad beginning, but Curly was unconcerned. "You have to understand," he said, "doing business up north is different. You've got to really want it bad. Everything costs huge money, absolutely huge."

"And sometimes the rewards are even worth it," Red added.

The taxi-van dropped us off in what passes for downtown. We each forked over $20 to the driver; apparently there's no such thing as sharing a ride in Churchill. Somewhat reluctantly, the men agreed to let me follow them to the port.

The Port of Churchill was a fantastic concept that suffered mightily in its execution. The basic idea is sound: Churchill is a shortish rail journey from the Midwest in the United States; Hudson Bay connects to the North Atlantic; and from there it's just a modest transatlantic hop to Europe, or even to the rail lines of Russia. Churchill is 800 kilometers closer to Europe than Halifax is, and 500 kilometers closer to China. Shipping companies have the option to go directly over the top of the world rather than going the long way around, across the wide Atlantic.

That's the theory, at any rate, though actual results have been anemic. The thing about Hudson Bay, as any polar bear could tell you, is that it's choked with ice for a good portion of the year. And ice—or even just the threat of it—is a ship captain's worst enemy. Not being idiots, maritime insurance companies charge exorbitant rates to cover boats making their way through Hudson Strait, which pretty much eliminates any cost savings that could be had by going to Churchill in the first place. For most of the year, the port sits idle.

Of course, this is one of those instances where climate change could be a huge net positive on a local scale. Nobody really likes to talk about it, but it's hard to make the case that global warming is going to be bad for Canada; a lengthened growing season, more navigable waterways, and milder temperatures all around don't sound entirely terrible. If Hudson Bay were to be reliably ice free for long periods every summer, then Arctic shipping could become the reality that the Port of Churchill's architects dreamed of when they built the place in 1931. In 1997, an astute Denver businessman named Pat Broe saw the writing on the wall and bought the dilapidated port for $7 from the government of Canada, which was desperate to get rid of it. Since then, he has managed to cajole the government into giving him tens of millions of dollars to repair the port and improve the railway. Not a bad deal, all told, especially if global warming manages to live up to its enormous promise. If the polar bears *do* all die as a result of global warming, at least Churchillians who've been laid off from the tourism industry might be able to get jobs as longshoremen.

EVEN BY THE STANDARDS of a town where dilapidation can be considered an architectural style, the Port of Churchill looks frighteningly bad. As we walked toward it, I got the same sort of foreboding sense in my gut that you might feel in a horror movie as the happy-go-lucky backpackers decide to investigate the abandoned castle.

The Port of Churchill looms at the end of Kelsey Boulevard, a series of immense brick and concrete granaries stacked along a narrow quay. A long conveyor belt, held up by spindly metal struts, rises precipitously from the storehouses in order to deliver grain to the cargo ships. Wherever there is a window, you can count on it being broken; if there is a ladder or a catwalk, you can count on it being rusted and looking unlikely to support the weight of a human being. I can only assume that Canada has an occupational safety agency; I also have to wonder what its agents do all day.

Train tracks run through the heart of the port and reach their end exactly where the land does. This is the northernmost spot in North America accessible by rail. There is a small but dedicated community of train junkies who make the long trek, touch a toe on Churchill's soil just to say they've done it, then turn right around and head home, where I imagine they tinker with their scale models and go to sleep wearing man-sized footie pajamas with Thomas the Tank Engine logos.

We breezed past green signs warning of imminent bear attacks and escorted ourselves onto the docks. With the exception of a guy in a fork-lift shuttling cargo from one pile to another, the port was a ghost town. Nobody flagged us as we explored the various warehouses, boxcars, and dark old buildings dotted along the disintegrating wharf. Inside one drafty building were hundreds of bags marked "Ammonium Nitrate."

"Isn't ammonium nitrate what they used to blow up the federal building in Oklahoma City?" I asked.

"Yeah, it's basically the same stuff," Red said. I must have looked concerned because he quickly played down the terrorist threat. "If this was Vancouver or San Francisco, you'd never be able to walk right into a port like this. But what's al Qaeda gonna do . . . bring two tons of fertilizer onto the plane as a carry-on?"

The men soon found their gear, dozens of boxcars full of steel, eventually to be used to build a dam for the mining operation. The equipment was stacked in odd-sized piles, marooned well short of its destination. Curly clambered up onto one of the boxes to inspect an ugly gash in the metal, the result of violent manhandling somewhere along the journey. He dropped to his knees and peered inside, reaching down to see if he could wedge open the barricaded doors.

With Curly and Red in their element—checking loads, scrawling down serial numbers, kicking at tractor tires—I wandered off to the edge of the yard. I cleared away some dirt under one of the cranes and sat at the water's edge, my feet dangling in free air like a kid fishing from the end of the pier. This is the spot where the Churchill River meets Hudson Bay at long last, and it is a large part of the reason polar bears have chosen this place for their annual muster. The fresh river water dumps into the salty bay, and the diluted mixture freezes more easily, so ice forms here much sooner than it does in other spots. Year after year, hungry bears return to the place they know will offer the earliest jump-off for their return to the hunting grounds.

I peered across the river to the far shore, where the town itself had once been located. All I could see was a low rise, studded with bushes. The river rushed furiously by, carrying bits of driftwood and hillocks of foam. In the summertime, the river is full of beluga whales in pods so thick that tour operators gush that you can walk across the river on their backs and never get wet. It suddenly occurred to me that I had no idea what a bear in the water looked like. Did they swim with their heads erect like dogs? Or did they linger just below the surface like alligators, ready to pounce and kill without warning? Surely the two eyes that I saw peering out of the water at me were just an old rusty portion of the dock, right? And all of those white furry heads bobbing in front of me were just whitecaps, weren't they?

I dusted off the seat of my pants and rejoined Red; Curly was off by himself somewhere, happily immersed in logistics. A pickup truck approached as we stood beneath the grain elevator, admiring the onrushing river. The driver, a man about my age wearing well-seasoned overalls over a thick sweatshirt, rolled down his window. "Can I help you guys?" he asked. It wasn't the threatening fake politesse of a security guard, but rather the bemused voice of someone who is used to running off gawky tourists on a semi-regular basis. Red explained his business and we shook hands all around.

The man in the truck was Marc Cool, president of Kivalliq Marine, the company in charge of handling whatever small amount of cargo made its way through the Port of Churchill. "At least I think I'm the president," he said. "It's basically just me and my brother. He's the CEO. Or maybe I'm the CEO and he's the president. I can never really keep it straight." He handed me a business card on which he'd scratched out his brother's first name and written in his own. He motioned to the empty seats in the truck. "Wanna get in?"

"Nah," said Red. "We're just poking around trying to find all our crap. If you don't mind, that is."

"That's fine with me, but you're a brave man standing out there like that. It's polar bear season."

Red looked astonished. "Right now?" he asked. "You mean right here?"

"Of course. Why do you think your plane was full this morning?" Cool gave his goatee a slow, early-morning scratch. "There's bears everywhere."

Red had too much invested in his Man of the North persona to let me see that he was taken aback for long. "If a bear wants me, it'll have to come and get me right here," he said with a swagger.

"Suit yourself," said Cool, with all of the nonchalance that Red wished he possessed for himself. "But don't even think you're gonna be able to climb one of those shipping boxes faster than a bear can." Red's machismo started to fall away and he listened intently. "If you ask me, this is the perfect place for a bear attack. Dead-end wharf with water on both sides, lots of dark corners to hide behind. . . ." As the image of his entrapment sank in, Red ran off, shouting Curly's name and repeating, "There's bears here! There's bears here! Get in the truck!"

I wedged myself into the back seat of the truck, pushing aside a box of tools, a collapsible crib, and a couple of stuffed animals. Cool shook his head. "Those guys are nuts," he muttered. "I always take the truck on a lap around the yard in the morning before I set foot on the ground. You never know who's going to be lurking." I nodded sagely, as if to reassure him that I always did the same thing myself.

"Some animals will hunt you and stalk you," Cool continued. "But not polar bears."

"Really?" I said, with no small measure of surprise. The hunting-and-stalking bit is the bread-and-butter of polar bear stories. Usually it starts with a stranded motorist, or sometimes a kid who wanders into the bush looking for bottle caps. But the bear side of the equation is pretty constant; with wretched cunning the bear sniffs out his human prey, sneaks up like an assassin, then pounces at the exact second the hapless youngster is least expecting it.

"Nah, it's nothing personal. They won't stalk you," Cool said. "They'll just jump up out of nowhere and flat out eat you." Which seemed like a distinction without a difference to me.

It being all of about 10:15 in the morning, Cool agreed to knock off work for the day and show us around. With the impending freeze-up, he'd be leaving town soon, and it was clear that he was far past ready to be done for the season. His wife and kids had already gone, and now he was just killing time until he could join them. A lot of people in Churchill spend a lot of their lives getting away from Churchill. Everybody seems to have a part-time job somewhere south, or a cousin they visit in Florida every couple of months. People think of Winnipeg, 600 miles to the south, as a place to go for the weekend in order to buy underpants and see the latest movie.

The two miners would be heading out on the afternoon flight, but they had a few hours to kill and they'd given up pretending that they didn't care about seeing polar bears. We all squeezed into the truck, and when I asked, "Is there a seat belt back here?" the men all looked at me as though I had requested caviar blintzes and a flute of champagne.

Cool's satellite radio was tuned to a station that seemed to play all Duran Duran, all the time, and we drove away from the port to the strains of early 1980s Europop.

"Let's take you boys out to see some bears," he said, as he hit cruising speed and headed out of town.

Beartopia

UNLIKE SOME SMALL TOWNS that gradually peter out into the wilderness, a farmhouse here, a woodsman's shed over there, Churchill just ends. On the western edge of town sits the Iceberg Tavern; behind it there's a steel-mesh garbage cage, rusted by the salt air and battered by the bears. And beyond that . . . there's nothing. If you were to stand on the roof of the bar and throw a rock, it would land in bear country. There's a signpost planted in the ground, with a picture of a bear and an admonition not to go any farther. One step backward and you're inside enjoying caribou steaks and Canadian whiskey. One step forward and you're in the wild—over 1 million square kilometers of frozen sea ice, dotted with blood stains where bears have dragged hapless seals from the water. Walk down Laverendrye Avenue on the back end of town and you'll see the stark contrast: movie theater, school, hospital, and then . . . badlands. All Churchillians have a sixth sense, like an internal compass, that tells them exactly where they are in relation to the invisible line. The line moves, too; it's different for different people, depending on the season, the time of day, the wind, and how immortal you're feeling at any given moment. If you respect the line, you can live your whole life in bear country without incident.

And in a big American-built pickup, the poor man's Sherman tank, it's easy to feel bulletproof. Cool steered his rig away from the main drag and along a series of narrow paths that picked their way down to the water's edge. The no-man's-land between the hospital and the edge of the bay was a jumble of boulders and glacial upheavals, everything dusted with the same dirty snow. We parked with the front wheels a few feet from the lapping waves of Hudson Bay, in the shadow of an *inukshuk* that towered over the beach. Inukshuks are giant rock piles, often twice as tall as a man, that the First Nations people built in order to mark territory. There's no specific shape required, but silhouetted in the distance, they tend to look like a man with arms outstretched. Churchill has a few of them; like polar bears, inukshuks have become as much a symbol of the North as an actual part of the North. You can buy inukshuk-shaped key chains, refrigerator magnets, and maple sugar candies to show how rugged you are for having gone to the Far North.

It had snowed lightly a few days before, and a dirty sheen of brown ice clung to the ground like some fungal disease. "Those are pretty fresh," Cool said, letting the truck drift to a stop.

"What are?" the other three of us said in unison.

"Those footprints." Cool bent over the steering wheel and wiped condensation off the window with the sleeve of his sweatshirt. In front of us was a set of polar bear prints, widely spaced in the crusty snow. To be honest, I wouldn't have been able to identify them as footprints if somebody hadn't told me they were, and even with an expert in the driver's seat, it was still hard to say for sure. Whatever we were looking at was comically large, too big to be real, each indentation the size of a hubcap. The unexpected sound of gunfire at close range was another bit of information that my mind didn't know quite how to process.

"Good," Cool said as he goosed the gas pedal to bring us out of a gully. "That means that there's one nearby."

Like many cities, Churchill does what it can to protect its citizens from indiscriminate slaughter. This being a small town, gang warfare is pretty far from the fore, but polar bears can pose a real threat to public safety. In response, the town created the Polar Bear Alert program, scientifically designed and engineered to keep bears from eating people.

The Alert program uses a variety of methods to accomplish its mission, but the main line of attack is to seat a couple of conservation officers in a big pickup truck, give them some guns, and task them with driving around the town and chasing bears back into the bush.

The gunfire we'd heard came from one such truck, visible over the next hill. It disappeared into a ditch, and then we did the same, bobbing through the landscape like two boats in the ocean. Using the sound of the shotgun blasts, Cool triangulated his position relative to the conservation officers. "There's just *got* to be one around here," he said, craning his neck as we bumped through the boulders. He turned sharply toward the shore on the theory that if he got between the rangers and the water there would be no way to avoid stumbling directly onto the bear. Although my natural inclination would be to avoid both gunfire and cornered polar bears, I was sitting in what is generally referred to as "the bitch seat" in the back of the truck and so I kept my suggestions to myself.

"Let's see if we can stealth up on him," Cool said. Unless the bear reared up on its hind legs in a taxidermized parody of ferociousness, we would have basically no chance of seeing it. We were surrounded by boulders bigger than the truck, not to mention gullies, alleys, valleys, and any other kind of secret lair a bear could want. The whole enterprise seemed incredibly unwise. I'd once had my windshield shattered by a tiny pebble; any bear worth his salt ought to be able to do the same with a flick of his paw, after which extracting the four of us would be as easy as sliding pickles from a jar.

At last we found ourselves nose to nose with the wildlife officer in the other truck. He wore a fur-lined hat and a pained expression. As if trying to chase a polar bear away from the good citizens of Churchill wasn't headache enough, now he had a truckload of yahoos working at perfect cross-purposes to him. He didn't bother to ask what we were doing, or even suggest that maybe we ought to quit it. Anybody who has ever said that Canada is an overprotective quasi-Socialist nanny state clearly hasn't been to Churchill. Apparently, all Canadians have the God-given right to go cowboying around polar bear country whenever they choose.

"We're trying to scare him away from town," the ranger said. The barrel of a shotgun poked above the dashboard. "So if you could, you know, maybe try not to drive him *toward* this direction . . ." He jerked his thumb over his shoulder, pointing to a church.

We drove around aimlessly for a while, making big loops on dirt roads that meandered through the bush. None of the roads seemed to go anywhere, or to have any purpose, though the sight of broken bottles suggested that quite a bit of partying went on out here. In bear country. Thank God for alcohol, I suppose.

I peered out at the gray rocks, any one of which could easily have been a bear that just wanted to be left alone, a solitude that we were determined to shatter at any cost. At least there hadn't been any more gunfire in the past few minutes.

"You can find them on these roads a lot of times," Cool said. "You'll come around a corner and they'll just be sitting there right in front of you. It's easier walking for them than on the rocks."

"So what are the roads for, anyway?" I asked.

"For the Alert guys to chase the bears on."

AFTER ANOTHER TWENTY MINUTES of nothing, Curly and Red were getting restless, and I was nearly asleep in the back seat. Dirt roads and Duran Duran have that effect on me. Cool leaned out the window and tested the air, like a hunter on the verge of firing a kill shot. "I can always tell when there's a polar bear nearby," he said.

"You can just sort of feel it, huh?" asked Curly, a note of appreciative mysticism in his voice.

"Nah. Because it's surrounded by tour buses, that's how." Cool gunned the engine and we were back onto Kelsey Boulevard, speeding away from our fruitless search. "I want to take you guys someplace where we're guaranteed to see a bear."

We drove out of town, parallel to the rocky coastline. At one point we stopped to take a picture next to one of the ubiquitous Polar Bear Alert signs. The signs are green with a soft silhouette of a polar bear; on the sign it looks fluffy and cute, more like a stuffed animal than like something to avoid. If I were in charge of the Alert program, every warning sign would have an actual photograph of a man with a bloody arm stump and half his gonads torn away.

Red took his place next to the sign for a photograph, arms crossed and jaw set in open defiance.

"That's a great shot," Curly said, squinting into the eyepiece. "You with that sign, the bay in the background, and that big bear off to the side . . ."

I never got a chance to see the developed picture, but Red was running so fast that he must have looked like little more than a smudge. Curly doubled over laughing, and Cool regarded us with weary indulgence. The "hey-there's-a-bear-behind-you" trick is classic junior-high material. If I'd had any idea how many more times I would hear that gag during my time in Churchill, I might have adopted the same pained expression as Cool.

We turned off the main road just beyond two immense geodesic balls covered with tattered fabric. Cool referred to them as the Golf Balls and said that they had had something to do with satellite communication. Churchill is filled with things like this, decaying remnants of big ideas long dead. We bumped up a rutted path, twisting between omnipresent gray rocks, which the miners reverently described as belonging to the Canadian Shield, as if the earth alone was all the national defense that the mighty Canucks would ever need.

We rolled to a stop when we came to a long metal chain strung between two piled rock cairns on either side of the road. It seemed a little whimsical to string a blockade between two posts that are themselves anchored in the middle of nowhere. But a road is a road, and when there's a chain across it you stop, even if walking around seems to be the obvious move. Canadians are a rule-abiding bunch, and even more than that, they're reluctant to exit their cars if there's a chill in the air. Which means that a string of dental floss across a frozen road is as effective as a moat full of alligators.

A long-haired man with a greasy headband and bib overalls dozed in a truck on the other side of the barrier. "That's Brian," Cool said, turning down the radio and lowering his voice as though we were in the presence of something that might attack if startled. Brian, he explained, was Brian Ladoon, sole owner and proprietor of what is likely the only non-zoo location on earth where you can be absolutely certain of scoring a face-to-face encounter with a polar bear.

"Put away your cameras," Cool said. "He won't usually charge locals but if he thinks you're tourists it'll be expensive." Cool tooted his horn. Ladoon awoke and strolled over, eyeing me and the miners the entire time. But Cool didn't introduce us and Ladoon didn't ask. I tried to make myself look rough and uneager, though the odds of being mistaken for a local in a town of 900 seemed pretty low. Eventually, Ladoon waved us through and we bumped down to where three school buses full of tourists idled on a strip of bare dirt. We were on a peninsula jutting out into the bay, one of those typical Hudson lowland spots where the line between land and water is hazy.

Dozens of dogs sat limply on either side of the road, attached to metal stakes by lengths of chain. A few of the dogs were off-leash and trotted back and forth without enthusiasm among their compatriots.

"That's fantastic," said Curly. "It doesn't bother them a bit to be out there in the cold like that."

Cool mulled this and then said, "Well, they are *dogs* after all. I mean, if it does bother them, what the hell are they going to do about it?"

But the main attraction lay beyond the end of the leash. An enormous male polar bear, easily as long as our truck, was napping on the snow ten feet beyond the front tire of the lead school bus. He had cradled his head on his outstretched front paws, and his rear haunches were elevated, his backside into the wind.

Tourists leaned precariously out of the tiny windows, snapping photographs and pounding on the sides of the bus to get the bear's attention. Standing up, the bear swayed and lumbered forward three steps, yawned, sat, walked some more. The tourists hooted and yammered, wriggling around for the best view. Somebody dropped a hat onto the ground. The bear blinked in boredom.

"It would be great if one of them fell out," Red said.

"It would be awesome," I said.

"The best," Curly agreed.

As the bear began to move, the buses gunned their engines and jockeyed for position, black smoke spewing from their tailpipes. In no hurry, the bear ambled along as if leading a royal procession, while the vehicles crawled dutifully behind. A hundred sets of eyes watched his every twitch. When the dogs began to howl—perhaps it was feeding time, or maybe they were just jealous of all the attention the bear was receiving—Cool rolled up his window and switched the satellite tuner to a bubblegum pop station. The air smelled of diesel fumes. The bear scratched his genitals contemplatively. Not exactly the noble "Lords of the Arctic" experience.

The bear looked at the assembled crowd, making no attempt to disguise his disinterest. Red snapped a picture whenever the bear opened his mouth; it seemed like mostly yawning to me, but with teeth like that who can tell the difference between fatigue and menace? Red needed some shots of the saber-toothed savage to show to friends and family back home.

Despite the circumstances, it was impossible not to be impressed by the bear's enormousness, the muscles that rippled through his haunches as he picked his way through the traffic jam. He was less white than I would have expected, more of a dingy cream color. His underside was a mess of dirty dreadlocks, twigs, and urine stains. But what struck me most was his simple presence, the calm authority he bore without any apparent effort. I had never seen a wild animal as unconcerned with the presence of screaming people as this bear was; even a fat old domesticated tabby couldn't remain indifferent to a scene like this. The bear knew that we were all in awe of him. And he knew that he deserved it.

Whenever he stretched his foreleg or lifted a paw to scratch, three dozen telephoto lenses swiveled in unison like gun turrets on a tank. He lowered his head, scanning the earth for trace food scents. The shutters clicked again. He sniffed the air, the shutters clicked. Dogs howled, cameras snapped, Justin Timberlake busied himself bringing sexy back on the car stereo.

Eventually, the animal veered away from our little parking lot, sniffing his way out toward the water's edge. And once you've seen a bear from five feet away, a bear at a hundred yards is barely worth mentioning, so we joined the parade of departing buses and made for town in hopes of greasy food and hot coffee.

"That was incredible, absolutely unbelievable," Red jabbered. "Did you see the size of that thing? Did you see how close we got?"

"I thought you didn't care about polar bears," I said.

He paused for a moment, then looked up from the screen of his digital camera. "I thought I didn't either."

CHAPTER 13

This Is a Disaster

Mr. Carl Johnson arrived in town Wednesday,
December 24, from his trapline in the Churchill River
area and reported that a polar bear broke into a shack
situated on Churchill Creek, and belonging to
Mr. Angus McIvor, and gave birth to twin cubs, and to
date they are still there, making themselves very much
at home, to the great discomfiture of the owner.

—THE *NORTHERN MAIL* NEWSPAPER, JANUARY 15, 1942

S O WHO DID YOU SAY you were going to be working for?"

"Nobody," I said. "I'm not working for anybody. I'm just going to be here." I had arrived at the Manitoba Housing Authority office, and the scowling middle-aged woman who handled my paperwork made no attempt to hide her mistrust of me. I didn't see much point in telling her I was coming to town to save the polar bears. She probably got that all the time.

"Your wife and two kids are coming up tomorrow?" she asked as she drove me over to my new digs.

"*Three* kids. But the little guy's small. He won't take up much space."

"And they'll be doing nothing, too?"

"That's the plan."

"For the entire fall. Doing nothing." She raised an eyebrow. I didn't see why she should be confused; from everything I'd heard, doing nothing was the dominant occupation in Churchill. When you apply for an apartment, you are asked your salary and then charged a percentage of it; in the nontourist months when it's either very hot or very cold, there's not a lot of incentive to increase your rent by doing something radical like getting a job. Maybe it was the thought of me doing nothing during the gold rush of tourist season that confused her, or maybe she just didn't understand why somebody would move an entire family of happy Californians to the sub-Arctic for the express purpose of doing nothing in the middle of nowhere.

She turned the key in the lock and then handed it to me. "If you lose these keys, we'll charge you for them," she said, stepping into an expansive mudroom. "If this room is dirty when you leave, we'll charge you for it." Beginning at the front door, she went through an exhaustive checklist to detail every single scuff and ding in the entire apartment. We'd repeat this process upon my departure, she told me, and if anything was different in even the most minuscule of ways . . . they'd charge me for it. I thought about my own house in Oakland, which has a stately Craftsman-style exterior and, thanks to my kids, an interior-decorating scheme that is reminiscent of London during the Blitz. Doing nothing was going to be very expensive.

I followed the woman from room to room, suggesting bits of imaginary damage she might want to add to her checklist. "The bathroom mirror is a little chipped, don't you think?" I'd say. Or "Does that carpeting in the rear of the closet look a little unraveled?" Mostly though, the apartment was in excellent shape; Mac would have a lovely time destroying it.

As we moved into the living room, she looked as if something had just occurred to her and said, "Somebody *did* tell you this apartment was unfurnished, right?"

"Yes, yes, of course," I answered. "No problem."

"I mean, it's not totally unfurnished," she added. "It's got a fridge and a stove and stuff. And a toilet, so that's nice."

"Very nice," I said, feeling genuinely thankful. I hadn't realized that the presence of a toilet was an open question.

"The garbage and utilities are all paid for, and I guess you won't be needing cable TV," she said, eyeing the bag that contained everything I owned in Canada.

"No, no TV, but I did want to ask you about the garbage. Is there some big locked dumpster somewhere that we're supposed to use?"

"Nah, you just leave it outside your door on garbage day. They'll come pick it up." The garbage can she pointed to was the size of something you might fit under the kitchen counter. My little army would fill it in half a day. "If you have more garbage you can just put it in bags and leave it outside next to the can," she suggested.

"Leaving your garbage outside like that . . . don't you ever have problems with bears?"

"Sometimes. But it's garbage, right? So who cares if they get into it," she said. Was this a joke? A Northern version of "Waiter, there's a fly in my soup"?

I have to admit that I appreciated the fact that utilities were covered with the rent. The first thing I did after she left was set the needle to 72°F, where it remained untouched until the day I had to turn over my keys.

As the sun began to dip, however, I realized that when it came to overhead lights, I was not quite so lucky. I'm not just talking about light *bulbs* here, I mean the actual *lights.* Specifically, there were none; not in the living room, not in any of the bedrooms. Which might seem like a small point, except that it's almost always dark in Churchill, and the nearest place to buy a cheap lamp is 600 miles away.

I hustled to the hardware store and came home with an extension cord, a cheap light fixture, and a box of bulbs. I hooked them all together, stole a screw from the bathroom door hinge, and poked a hole in the ceiling of the living room, security deposit be damned. Sitting down with a can of soup heated directly on the stove, hobo style, I leaned back and admired my home improvement skills. The bare bulb lit the room like an interrogation chamber, and every passing truck slowed down, drivers staring at their new, freakish neighbor through the curtainless front window. What a perfect spot to bring my entire family to!

Outside the wind was just picking up, and it shook the house like a passing freight train. Dogs howled and the smell of cigarette smoke leaked through the walls from an adjoining apartment. What the hell was I doing here? This wasn't the frontier; I wasn't about to confront Nature in all its toothy glory; I wasn't a great mammalogist or an intrepid explorer. I was just a guy with an apartment in a tourist town.

"This is a disaster," I said to Shona on the phone, which, miraculously enough, worked perfectly as soon as I plugged it into the wall. "It's dark and there's nothing here and I can tell that nobody wants us around. And we don't even have a shower curtain. I should never have decided to drag you guys up here. I can already tell it's going to be a huge failure."

But true to her optimistic and altogether infuriating Canadian roots, Shona was unfazed. "Why don't we just come up there and see how it goes," she said. In retrospect, it seems like the obvious decision. After all, she *was* already in the Winnipeg airport with a gaggle of children in tow.

I stood outside on the porch as the last rays of sun filtered through the dark October clouds. Our place was on Simpson Street, the very last row of houses on the edge of town. Out our front door was a hill, several hundred yards of rock, and then the vast chilly waters of Hudson Bay. Stepping down from the porch, I crossed the street and walked off the road, into the dirt that divided the civilized world from the great unknown. The woman from the housing authority had warned me that this was a major thoroughfare for polar bears and suggested that we might be making a poor choice in not having secured a vehicle, "especially with all those little ones of yours." After spending the summer in the coastal daybeds and boggy wallows near Nestor Two, this was the time the bears would begin to use the rocky strip just outside my door as a highway to the mouth of the Churchill River, where the first ice of winter would form. Having no real schedule to follow, sometimes the bears would step away from the rocks and drop into town for a bite from one of the local garbage cans. No place in Churchill is entirely safe, but some places are more risky than others. And our house was one of them.

A FEW HOURS LATER, the same ancient taxi-van pulled up in front of my new castle, disgorging its contents of kids, cribs, strollers, and princess-themed carry-on bags. The polar bears stayed away long enough for me to hustle the family inside and introduce them to the industrial carpeting that would be their new beds, chairs, kitchen tables, and everything else.

"I'm sorry," I said to Shona. "This is a disaster."

"It's not so bad," she replied. "This place is way nicer than the trailer I grew up in." The kids seemed to agree. Mac, who has pure testosterone flowing where normal children have blood, had stripped down to his underpants and was racing across the open floor, doing barrel rolls in the air and punching the walls. He looked like a hairless monkey escaped from a laboratory experiment on the effects of PCP. The near total lack of amenities was perfect for my semi-feral boy. I love him immensely, of course, but it must be said that this is a kid who keeps an extensive dirt collection underneath his mattress and considers Wheaties with milk to be a finger food.

Zeke, the two-year-old, dragged a backpack from window to window to give himself the height he needed to mark his territory with long snot trails on the chilly glass. And Percy, the five-year-old, is the kind of person who can be blissfully oblivious of location and circumstance provided she has a comb, barrettes, and a mirror in which she can ad-mire her skills as a hairdresser. The polar assault team was assembled and ready.

After a makeshift dinner, we set up the porta-crib for Zeke and un-rolled sleeping bags on the floor for everyone else. "Don't go outside without a grown-up, no matter what," I said. Percy and Mac had reached the terrifying age at which they no longer needed assistance to operate deadbolts and doorknobs in the middle of the night.

"We *know* that dad," Mac said, with the exaggerated annoyance that I hadn't thought he would bestow upon me until he was at least thirteen.

"I mean it," I said. "Don't go outside for any reason."

"Even if there's a fire?" Mac asked innocently; the kid has a gift for loopholes. "Is it better to be stuck in a fire or eaten by a polar?" he asked.

"Just come get me, that's all I'm saying." I plugged in the night-light and kissed him good night. When I checked on him twenty minutes later, he was standing on his tiptoes, face pressed to the window.

"I'm checking for polars," he whispered when he saw me in the doorway.

"That's fine, buddy. Let me know if you see one."

"I really wanna see one. I mean I really *really* wanna see one."

"Don't worry, buddy," I said. "They're all over this town. I promise you'll see one before we leave." The next time I checked on him, he was in the exact same spot, collapsed in sleep just below the window. I nudged him away from the floor heater and covered him with a sleeping bag.

DOWNSTAIRS, SHONA WAS SUITING UP, extracting mittens and long johns from the depths of her duffel bag. "I want to go outside," she said. "I want to see the sky. Maybe there'll be some northern lights." We stepped cautiously onto the porch, looking to the left and right like kids crossing the street on their own for the first time. The sight of a coatless drunk staggering home without so much as a glance over his shoulder spoke well of the current safety situation. Given a choice, we reasoned, a bear would investigate this well-marinated individual before turning to us.

The Aurora Borealis was quiet tonight, but the stars were shimmering brilliance, jagged crystals of ice suspended in frozen air. At home in California, I never see the night sky. Most nights, the fog rolls in before the darkness does, and even when it's clear, the all-consuming lightwash of a million streetlamps drowns out all but the most persistent stars. There's something about the North that makes it seem like the sky is closer to the earth. You can feel the clouds as they race past your head; a sliver of moon is as wide as the horizon. The smell of the sea was on the air, and I imagined I could hear waves breaking on the rocks of Hudson Bay. The clouds were few but the winds were frenzied, and we huddled together for warmth and to keep from falling over.

Shona and I had been here before, many times. Not literally in Manitoba, of course, but elsewhere in Canada, all over the North, standing outside of various homes and tents and trailers, staring up at the enveloping night sky. I'd gone to the Yukon with her one winter, just a few months after we'd met, to introduce myself to her family. I remember standing in the snow outside her cousin's cabin as the northern lights dripped over us like rainbow-colored rain. *I could marry this girl,* I'd thought. *I could really live like this.* Now, twelve years and three kids later, here we were, standing in the cold with our arms around each other, scanning the sky for impossible things.

But it's the nature of parenthood that such romantic flights of fancy never last for long. Case in point: when we came inside, I noticed that Mac, still fast asleep, was lying in an enormous pool of his own vomit.

"We don't even have a washing machine," I said, holding up Mac's soiled sleeping bag. "We're screwed."

Shona was already peeling Mac out of his clothes, calmly getting down to business rather than declaring our entire lives a failure, which was my preferred tack. Mac stood unsteadily in the bathtub as Shona washed him down with one of those tiny, stolen hotel soaps that had been kicking around the bottom of my luggage.

"This is a disaster," I repeated, just in case Shona hadn't heard me the first time. I looked down at the rug, which was discolored and stinking where Mac had made his mess. The closest thing I had to cleaning supplies was a roll of toilet paper and a tube of organic, fennel-flavored toothpaste. "My security deposit," I wailed. "They're going to have to charge me for that. This is a complete catastrophe."

"You know what?" Shona chirped. "You're right. We should just pack up right this second and walk home."

Point taken. As Shona put Mac back to sleep, I knelt in front of the tub and washed out his pajamas and bedclothes frontier-style, scrubbing them into a lather over and over again and twisting them around a stick I found in the backyard. Clean enough for a four-year-old, I figured. I would have made a lousy pioneer woman.

Because Shona had given Mac her own sleeping bag, we huddled on the floor together inside mine. A few hours later, I was jolted awake by a powerful earthquake. If there had been a chair or a table, I would have been underneath it in a second. Instead, I sat bolt upright against the wall and hoped that the shattering glass wouldn't get into my eyes. Shona rolled over lazily. "Wind," she said. "That's the thing I really hate about Canada. The fucking wind." And then she went back to sleep. I sat awake for a while longer, listening to the creak of the floorboards. The windows rattled in their casements and our five forks jangled in the drawer. How could people live like this without going absolutely insane?

Fortunately, I had a decent enough reason to be awake. A certain odor came drifting along the hallway. There on the floor, across the room from the wet spot, lay little Mac, dreams of polar bears in his head and a fresh pile of sick dripping from his hair. He hadn't even had the decency to discolor the same spot of carpet. After engaging in my frontier laundryman routine for a second time, I lay back down again to give sleep one last shot. The wind hammered the apartment, a dog howled like it was being skinned alive, and Shona and I were now both making do with bath towels in place of blankets. My fingers smelled like puke.

"Don't say I never take you anyplace nice," I said, and we drifted off to sleep.

CHAPTER 14

Bedeviled
from the Start

A miserable poor place of it. York fort is badd,
but this is tenn times worse.

—JAMES KNIGHT, HUDSON'S BAY COMPANY
EMPLOYEE, DESCRIBING CHURCHILL, 1717

T HE NEXT MORNING, Mac appeared to be much restored—
which was more than I could say for his sleeping bag, which
would take three days to dry and would smell sour and unpleasant
forevermore. And so we headed into town for a bit of an exploration. A
few tourists made their way about, but for the most part the town was
in an anticipatory frenzy. In another two weeks, the tourists would arrive
en masse, and there was a lot to get done before then. People zipped around
in pickup trucks, hauling lumber and supplies, getting the town ready
for the onslaught. Not only did everything need to be prepared for the
increased population, but there was also the feeling that if you had anything in the world that you needed to do for yourself, you had better do
it now. There wouldn't be time to start any projects—let alone sleep or
rest or catch your breath—for the next two months. And after that would
come the brutality of winter, so this was the window where everything
needed to be accomplished, or else held over again for yet another year.

"Dog!" screamed Zeke, as we walked past a particularly vicious painting of a polar bear.

"No, it's not," said Mac. "It's a polar bear, because this is Churchill, and what they have here is polars."

"Is dog," replied Zeke, pouting and burying his face in his sleeve. "*Is* dog."

Mac looked up at me and sighed. "Zekey already doesn't know anything. And now I have to teach him about polars, too."

One thing that Mac didn't yet know was the potential for unsurpassed awesomeness in a town that is a combination construction zone/industrial wasteland/extreme tourism theme park. It is an enduring tragedy that he has to grow up in a comfortable urban household. At heart he'd like nothing more than to be the child of a caveman or a lumberjack or a highway bandit. I feel like a criminal every time he brings an arts-and-crafts project home from preschool; this kid should spend his life slaying orcs, or at the very least living on a farm where he can operate dangerous machinery and break wild horses. Until I had boys, I never really understood how Third World militias could conscript child soldiers, but now it's a mystery to me why the American army lets so much pure destructive talent go to waste.

"You know what's different about this town?" Mac asked me.

"What's that?"

"Everybody drives everywhere even though there's no place to go. And what are those little cars that everybody is riding on?"

I looked to see what he was pointing at. Half a dozen kids, the oldest maybe fourteen, were perched precariously on the back of a muddy all-terrain vehicle. "They're ATVs," I said. "They're good for driving on dirt and snow and rough roads."

"OK," he said as he watched one after another fly past, their drivers bouncing happily in the saddles. "I think I should probably get one of those."

"You think?"

"Yeah, probably. I could use it to help Zeke when a bear is chasing him." This wasn't a bad point. I told him I'd take it under advisement.

Later, I overheard Shona telling him to call it a "quad" instead of an ATV. God forbid the kid should talk dorky Americanese like his dad.

"They don't have those at home," Mac said, breathing in the sweet bouquet of exhaust fumes. "This place is way better than Oakland."

THE NORTHERN EDGE OF CHURCHILL consists of a single enormous building, known as the Complex, which contains just about everything else in town that is neither a private residence nor church. Starting at the northern corner and working south, you have a nursing home and a full-service hospital, an impressive indoor playground with multiple slides and jungle gyms, the city offices and council chambers, a library, a 300-seat movie theater, a workout room, a basketball court, a swimming pool, ice skating rink, half a dozen pool and foosball tables, and, almost as an afterthought, complete educational facilities for all the kids in town, from day care through grade twelve. I was told there was also a bowling alley and a curling rink somewhere, though I was never able to locate them. The school is new; on the opposite end there's another entire school building, but it was infested with some sort of lethal mold, and now it just sits there boarded up, a useless and toxic appendage to the rest of the building. It's an impressive structure, with multistory floor-to-ceiling windows that overlook the bay and a heating bill that must consume most of the municipal budget.

The few houses in town that are not owned by the government have a fairly consistent outdoor aesthetic, a scheme that relies on rusted-out car bodies, stacks of mildewed lumber, and twisted piles of scrap metal as the lawn ornaments of choice. Down by the river, the distinction between what is a house and what is a pile of construction materials becomes pretty vague. This area, known as the Flats, is where you would go to live if the idea of indoor plumbing and central heating strikes you as a burden imposed by The Man. Many of the houses have couches out in front, though who would sit on them in this weather I could not imagine. One structure appeared to be a bombed-out old bus with one or two makeshift bedrooms added haphazardly onto the end of it.

The way to build a house in Churchill is to go ahead and build it. At some point afterward, you might hear complaints that you don't actually own the land, or that you've never acquired any permits. But at that point you'll already have your house, and there's plenty of land to go around for anybody else who wants to do the same thing. The Flats, more than anywhere else in town, has a lawless, squatters' village feeling to it. The great advantage of living there is that every shack has a view of the river; the disadvantage is that the riverbank is often crawling with polar bears. As a result, many residents of the Flats lay down doormats with dozens of nails sticking straight up. Some windows and doors are similarly boarded, with a forest of nails pointing outward. Any bear trying to get inside will get a snoutful of spikes as a reward for his troubles. Unfortunately, many of the free spirits who choose to live in the Flats also tend to be heavy drinkers, and the fortifications of home are only effective if you can manage to get there. The paths to the nearest bar lead either through waist-high brush or along the darkened railroad tracks that run along the river. As in most places, you're only as safe as your sobriety allows.

Churchill looks as though it's in the middle of a rebuilding process that has no beginning and no end. You work at a project until it becomes too cold, too complicated, or too expensive, and then you move on to the next one. Maybe you'll return to what you started and maybe you won't, but these constantly shifting priorities make the mounds of detritus seem more like works in progress than symbols of decay.

"You know what's different about this town than about Oakland?" Mac asked me, as we walked past the building that housed the town's only bank, post office, and (perhaps most crucially) liquor store.

"What's that?"

"At home they wouldn't have this big empty space here. They'd want to build something on it." About the size of a football field, the dirt lot we stood on appeared to have no functional purpose. "At least they'd park cars here or something," Mac said, growing increasingly alarmed by the idea of a patch of bare earth that wasn't in the process of being actively developed. "What does it do?" He tugged at my sleeve. "What's it *for*?"

MAC WAS NOT THE FIRST PERSON to notice that Churchill and the shores of Hudson Bay had an attractive level of emptiness that was itching to be exploited. For years before white people settled in this area, Europe was filled with rumors of great treasure to be found in the northern reaches of the New World. And it was true: despite being barren, cold, and hostile to agriculture, the area around Hudson Bay was far from unproductive. Ringed seals filled the bay and beluga whales swam in the river. Vast herds of caribou blanketed the land, and valuable fur-bearing animals like fox and marten skittered around in the undergrowth. There were even rumors of priceless deposits of copper and gold. With the promise of riches like that, conquest was inevitable.

In 1610, while exploring for the British East India Company, Henry Hudson sailed his ship the *Discovery* into the bay that later came to bear his name. Searching for the Northwest Passage, that holy grail of American exploration, Hudson and his crew picked their way along the coastline, looking for an opening that didn't exist. Winter came on fast, and the *Discovery* froze solid into the ice of James Bay, south of where modern-day Churchill sits. The crew members left their boat and trudged ashore, doubtless cursing themselves for not having had the foresight to have signed on to a Polynesian expedition instead.

At the end of a brutal winter, Hudson suggested that he might like to have another go at it and continue the exploration for another year. His men took the idea under advisement and decided instead to mutiny. Hudson, his young son, and half a dozen loyalists were set adrift in a small, open boat. Four of the mutineers were later killed in an altercation with an Inuit tribe, but the rest successfully returned to England. Hudson and his loyalists were never heard from again. When you look out over the bay, it's not difficult to imagine a dozen horrible ways in which eight men in an open boat could have met a gruesome end.

Henry Hudson went to his death believing that he had, in fact, discovered the Northwest Passage. Never having made it as far as the western shore of Hudson Bay, he assumed that he had been sailing in the waters of the Pacific, rather than this unmapped inland sea. Under normal circumstances, the mutineers would surely have been hanged upon their return to England, but on this occasion—much to their surprise—they were allowed to live. After all, as far as anyone knew, they were the only people on earth who knew the route through the Northwest Passage. And that knowledge was far too valuable to extinguish on a gallows platform.

Subsequent explorations proved that Hudson was wrong, and that there was still a fairly significant patch of dry land between Hudson Bay and the California coast. But even with this failure, the temptations of an inland waterway were too great to ignore for long. In 1619, the Norwegian explorer Jens Munk, in the employment of Denmark's King Christian IV, set out to find what Hudson had failed to discover. The expedition was bedeviled from the start. Immediately after setting sail, one of the boats sprang a leak. One of the crew members killed himself shortly thereafter. Other seafarers might have taken such things as omens, but Munk was not so easily deterred. The Atlantic crossing proved uneventful, but as soon as they reached Hudson Bay, the expedition became hopelessly lost in the endless backwaters. Before the first snowfall of winter, the men were miserable, cold, skinny, and beset with scurvy.

Munk decided to lay up for the winter near Churchill. One boat, the *Lamprey*, was hauled out of the water, and the other, the *Unicorn*, was tied down and made ready to be frozen into the inevitable ice. The first few months of fall were tolerable; by Christmas, only two of the original sixty-five men had died. Hardly more than a rounding error as far as Arctic expeditions go. In his journals, Munk seemed more distressed by what to do with the bodies than with the fact that the men had died in the first place. He wrote: "We had to keep his body on the ship for two days because the frost was so severe that no one could get ashore to bury him until the fourteenth, and even then the cold was of such intensity that many of the men had their faces frostbitten."

The men went ashore to hunt for hare, ptarmigan, and fox; they ate gooseberries and cloudberries in an unsuccessful attempt to beat back scurvy. On occasion, they even ate polar bear. "A large white bear came down to the water's edge," noted Munk. "I shot the bear and gave the meat to the crew with orders that it was to be just slightly boiled, then kept in vinegar overnight. I even had two or three pieces of the flesh roasted for the cabin. It was of good taste and quite agreeable."

Perhaps they should have boiled the meat a little more thoroughly. Unbeknownst to Munk, polar bear meat is highly toxic if not prepared correctly. And really, how could they have known? It's every explorer's God-given right to kill and eat whatever comes within the range of his musket. But polar bear liver contains vitamin A in such great concentrations that it can lead to headaches, bone pain, and uncontrollable vomiting. In addition, the meat is often infected with the nasty Trichinella roundworm. Gastrointestinal symptoms and general body aches result from ingesting this parasite, and Munk's crewmen were horribly afflicted.

Whether it was toxic meat, scurvy, starvation, or exposure to the elements, the alien environment soon took its toll on the unhappy crew. The men fell ill and were confined to their bunks for weeks on end with what Munk referred to simply as "the sickness." The ship's surgeon told Munk that "he had already used every medicine he had with him and that without God's assistance he was helpless." There being nothing else he could do for his crew, the surgeon promptly died himself rather than go on being completely useless.

During their time near Churchill, Munk and his men did not encounter any of the local inhabitants. They did find bits of recently broken campsites, however, the outlines of which caused Munk to "conclude that these places had been used for idolatrous worship, and if that is so, then it is to be wished that these poor blinded pagans might be led to accept the true Christian faith." Godless or not, the idolators at least had the good sense to cook their meat thoroughly and head inland to avoid the ravages of a coastal winter.

As the winter dragged on, the men began to die in quick succession. By mid-February, twenty men were gone, and the rest were confined to their bunks, beset with dysentery. Disposing of the dead was a monumental chore, and bodies often lay where they fell for days until the living could muster the strength to throw them overboard. Describing their illness, Munk wrote that the "limbs and joints were painfully drawn together, and there were great pains in the loins as if a thousand knives had been thrust there."

By the time the fierce winter broke in early June, only three of the sixty-five men remained alive. Munk named the accursed spot "Jens Munk's Bay" and the exhausted men began the brutal work of digging themselves out of the ice and sailing for home. With three men doing the work of dozens of able-bodied sailors, they picked feebly through the ice, taking more than a month to find their way out of Hudson Bay. The survivors fought their way across the stormy Atlantic, finally mooring at some anonymous fjord along the rocky Norwegian coast-line. "Then, with the ship properly looked after and ourselves in a Christian country once again, our joy was so great we could not hold back our tears, and we thanked God that He had graciously granted us such happiness."

MUNK'S TRAVAILS WERE ENOUGH to dissuade future explorers for several decades. But the promise of profit has a way of obscuring memories of the suffering of others. By the early eighteenth century, the British and the French were hard at work extracting fur and fish from the coasts of Hudson Bay. Looking to expand its empire, the Hudson's Bay Company sent a man north from its post at York Fort in 1717. He ended up near the site of Munk's hellacious winter, within view of modern-day Churchill.

The company decided to make a major effort at the mouth of the river there, and work began on Prince of Wales Fort, a stone stronghold with walls forty feet thick. Here the British would trade with the natives and hunker down for protection from the harsh winters. Additionally, a fort of this size—with forty cannons—would be an insurmountable obstacle to any Frenchmen looking to encroach on the company's trapping territory. The fort was built in the shape of a four-pointed star, with walls angled so that attackers from any direction could be shot at with at least two cannon. Young boys from the Orkney Islands, hardworking and accustomed to misery, were imported to build the fort, and a backbreaking quarrying effort was soon under way. It was a difficult life; the boys would curl up around heated cannonballs in order to sleep. One man reported awakening with his hair frozen to the wall. In addition to the elements, the boys often lost life and limb in accidents with gunpowder and drilling equipment. The ones who survived were rewarded with alcohol and unremitting loneliness. Mac would have loved it there.

In 1766, a young man named Samuel Hearne arrived at the fort. Hearne had joined the British navy at eleven, and by the time he reached Churchill at the age of twenty-four, he was a promising amateur naturalist, shipbuilder, and astronomer. He would soon add exploring and anthropology to his résumé.

The natives in the area—a mixture of Cree, Chippewa, Inuit, and Dene—had long told the settlers about a copper deposit far to the north of Churchill. Dreams of an inland passage to Asia were still very much alive at the time, though the thought of attempting such a journey had proved too daunting. Into the breach stepped Hearne, who was brave (and foolish) enough to be thrilled by such a challenge. Unlike many of his contemporaries, Hearne decided to trust the natives, and he even endeavored to learn their languages. He realized that if he had any chance of reaching the legendary copper mines, he would have to learn to work the land like a Native trapper rather than a British naval officer.

With high spirits, Hearne set out from Churchill in November 1769. He returned less than a week later, after his native guide abandoned him. Undaunted, he set out again with a new guide. After eight months of aimless rambling in the tundra, he was once again forced back to the fort. With less than two weeks' rest, he reprovisioned and set out one more time, now with the aid of a native man named Matonabbee, an expert guide who would later become Hearne's close friend.

The journey was enormously difficult; the prospect of starvation and death by exposure was always close at hand. Unlike his predecessors, Matonabbee insisted that the expedition include several women, in this case his half dozen wives. "Women . . . were made for labor," Hearne wrote. "One of them can carry, or haul, as much as two men can do. They also pitch our tents, make and mend our clothing, keep us warm at night; and in fact, there is no such thing as traveling any considerable distance, or for any length of time, in this country, without their assistance. Women . . . though they do every thing, are maintained at a trifling expense; for as they always stand cook, the very licking of their fingers in scarce times, is sufficient for their subsistence." How very handy!

Political correctness aside, something Matonabbee was doing seemed to work. By summer, the party had reached the Coppermine River. But apart from a few interesting bits of rock, Hearne found nothing of commercial value. Still, he became the first European to reach the Arctic Ocean on foot, no small feat. He looked over the vast Northern sea and took possession of the entire area in the name of the Hudson's Bay Company. Then he turned around and walked back to Churchill. In all, two and a half years of toil and nearly 5,000 hard miles of famine and frostbite had yielded no copper, no passage to Asia, and very little glory. Hearne doubtless realized what generations of seekers still feel compelled to discover afresh: in the Arctic, everything is infinitely more difficult than it seems, and infinitely less profitable.

Following his endless round-trip to nowhere, Hearne threw himself into life along the Churchill River. He continued his explorations and his botany, and deepened his relationships with the local population, even marrying a half Native woman named Mary Norton. Eventually, Hearne rose to the position of governor of the fort.

But despite this seeming success, all was not well with the world. The smallpox epidemic that Europeans had brought to the New World was sweeping northward, and by 1781, Hearne estimated that 90 percent of the local Chippewa population had been killed. In addition, tensions were heating up between the British and the French. Not only did fur mean big money, but the two nations were full of animosity in the wake of the American Revolution. Hudson Bay was a convenient place to engage in fits of pique.

On August 8, 1782, three French warships appeared on the horizon, flying the Union Jack for disguise. Hearne had fewer than forty men, many of whom were out hunting. Firing a cannon was no simple task; it required a dozen trained soldiers, and the occupants of the fort were carpenters and stonemasons, not hardened warriors.

The French warships contained hundreds of soldiers and far more firepower than Hearne could hope to compete with. At dawn the next morning, he surrendered to the French captain, Jean-François de Galaup, comte de La Pérouse. The mighty Prince of Wales Fort, forty years in the making, was defeated without a single shot fired. The Frenchmen streamed over the walls, raising their flag, destroying the British cannon, and looting everything they could find.

Hearne and some of his men were taken as captives, and they watched helplessly as La Pérouse sailed south to capture and destroy York Fort. As the days passed and the ice began its inevitable entrance into Hudson Bay, La Pérouse became increasingly nervous about his lack of local knowledge. He and Hearne struck a deal. If Hearne and his men would guide the French through the treacherous Hudson Strait and into open waters, La Pérouse would release the British and allow them to take their chances across the Atlantic in a small, rat-infested sloop.

Hearne did his part, then somehow managed to captain his way back to England with thirty-one of his men. It had been sixteen years since he had seen the British Isles, but all he wanted was to return to Hudson Bay. Less than a year after his easterly crossing of the Atlantic, he crossed back westward. Prince of Wales Fort lay in ruins, crumbling and abandoned. But the news was worse than that. It had been a difficult winter, like so many in the North. Mary Norton, Hearne's beloved Native wife, had refused to take another husband after Hearne's departure. Without a man to hunt for her, she had slowly starved to death.

OF COURSE, TO SPEAK OF THE HISTORY of a place and only mention the ways in which the indigenous people helped out the whites is as common as it is inappropriate. Archaeological study of this area is not nearly as advanced as it is in other areas of the world. Fortunately, the extreme cold and unyielding permafrost have done an excellent job of preserving artifacts of an earlier time. Sometimes researchers find remnants of human hair and perfectly preserved tools, as if camp had just been struck a few weeks earlier. (Polar bear fossils, by contrast, are extremely rare. The bears typically die out on the ice and are interred at the bottom of the ocean.)

The first people entered this Arctic region around 5,000 years ago, spilling into North America from eastern Siberia and Labrador. Very little is known about them, but it is safe to say that their lives would not have been easy. Around 500 BC, this "paleo-Eskimo" group gave way to the Dorset culture. The Dorset roamed over thousands of square miles, occupying a vast geographic range that encompassed most of the Canadian Arctic as well as Greenland. You could say that the sun never set on the Dorset Empire. At least in the summertime.

To call the Dorset an empire would be misleading, though. There was no central control, no grand schemes of conquest. The Dorset probably existed as small bands of nomadic hunters who would come into contact with each other on a regular basis. Their environment simply wouldn't allow for permanence. In the Arctic, building materials are scarce and agriculture is impossible. The simple act of gathering enough food and clothing to survive was all-consuming.

The Dorset made their living hunting seals. They would wait next to breathing holes and spear the animals when they surfaced. They would camouflage themselves behind blocks of ice, flatten themselves against the ground in order to sneak up on seals that were resting on the snow. One Native man told me that everything the Dorset knew about hunting seals they learned from watching polar bears.

Hunting for polar bears themselves certainly happened, but it probably wasn't common; top predators tend to avoid each other. Any bears these people killed would have been brought down at spear point, a particularly dangerous way to attack a 1,500-pound animal with teeth and claws like knives. Where remains are found in Dorset sites, polar bear bones show distinct signs of butchery. Polar bear hunting might have been rare, but the meat did not go to waste.

About 1,000 years ago, a gradual warming period began. Suddenly, Native groups from the boreal forests to the south moved into the area formerly occupied by the Dorset. This new culture was known as the Thule, and its members are the ancestors of the modern Inuit. It seems unlikely that there was a mighty clash of civilizations; instead, the Dorset were pushed onto smaller and smaller bits of land, and by 1,000 AD, they disappeared from their last remaining settlements in northern Quebec and Labrador.

OVER THE PAST FEW HUNDRED YEARS, Canada's policies toward Natives have not exactly mirrored those in the United States, but that doesn't mean that the First Nations people in the North fared any better. In the area around Churchill, one of the most prominent groups was the Sayisi Dene, and one cold afternoon I met up with a woman named Ila Bussidor, who had been their chief for a time. "I'm an urban Indian now," Ila said, laughing and hugging herself against the wind. "I used to be able to live out here, but now I like my car and my supermarket and my central heating." Stylish and well-spoken, with designer sunglasses and a little purse, Ila lives in Winnipeg now but makes occasional trips back to see friends and check in on the remnants of the Sayisi Dene. I'd stupidly expected leather clothing and maybe some feathers and beads. Instead, she looked like a businesswoman on her way to catch the 8:43 train into downtown.

Ila agreed to drive with me out to Dene Village, the spot a few miles outside of Churchill where she lived as a child. We rode in silence until she directed us onto a dirt road that was overgrown with brush. Maneuvering around blackwater bogs, we scraped past gnarled willow bushes and the occasional stunted spruce tree. Mosquitoes and blackflies beat themselves to death against the car windows as if they could smell our blood through the glass. Soon a few low walls came into view, crumbling cement foundations ringed by moats of broken glass.

"That was the house where my parents lived," Ila said, pressing her finger to the window. "They were inside when it burned down."

Ila got out of the car as it idled next to the ruins of her house. A cloud of mosquitoes descended, invading our nostrils and nibbling at the wet corners of our eyes. The assault was intolerable; I couldn't last ten minutes here, let alone an entire childhood. We stepped over a cement barrier and into what was once the center of the tiny house. Ila reached into the dirt and dredged out a couple of green glass bottles that she set along the wall like sentinels.

When they first arrived in Churchill, the Dene had been housed closer to town, at a spot near the cemetery. Each family was given a tent cabin measuring less than 150 square feet, with no heat or running water. They were accustomed to the cold and the lack of amenities, but the lack of purpose was devastating. In the past they had hunted caribou, fished in the bay, and pursued a migratory life that, though difficult, gave people a reason to get up in the morning. The government had decided that the way the Dene hunted caribou was wasteful, and that their nomadic lifestyle was unhealthy. Without their customs, the Dene had nothing: no jobs, no income, no connection to their history. Even their children were taken away by force, shipped off to distant "residential schools" to be civilized, whether their parents wanted it or not.

Predictably, the culture degraded quickly. Illness and depression set in; violence was epidemic and despair was palpable. Anthropologist Virginia Petch described the scene: "You move into an area where your house is on skids, you're facing the crosses of the cemetery, and you've got the North wind blowing off the Bay. You've got the polar bears marching by your house. You have nothing to do. Your kids are cold, they don't have enough to eat. They're being teased and beaten up at school. Your women are being raped. Just at that time, alcohol is legalized."

It was hoped that a move from one side of town to the other, to a new spot called Dene Village, would be an improvement. Nothing changed; the community was too deeply beset by alcoholism and hopelessness. "I used to babysit for four or five days at a time and no one would check on me," Ila said, remembering her preteen years. "They'd be off partying and they'd just leave me out there with their kids." The Dene died in staggering numbers. They drank themselves to death, and they murdered each other over petty grievances. They drowned, and they died in car wrecks. They froze to death when they were too drunk to find their way inside. Ila's own parents were too incapacitated by alcohol to get outside when their house caught fire.

Out in the bush, interactions with polar bears were all too common. Few people had cars, so the walk into Churchill was fraught with danger. "I have nightmares about polar bears," Ila said. "I dream that they're chasing me off a cliff." Ila remembers nights when the adults would be drunk, or gone, and the children huddled inside beating pots together to scare away the bears.

"One time there was a guy walking to town and all of a sudden he got hit from behind and he just went flying," Ila said as we stood in the ruins. The man thought he was about to be beaten and robbed, a common occurrence in those dark days. Instead, he found himself looking up at one large polar bear. Very carefully, the bear lowered itself until it was sitting squarely on top of him. "He could have panicked," Ila said. But instead he spoke to the bear in the Dene language and said, "Why are you bothering me? I don't bother you. If you're going to kill me, kill me now and make it quick." Instead, the bear got up and walked off down the road, leaving the man to stumble home.

"I don't think they were after humans, but if they smell something or if you're in their way . . . ," Ila continued. The old people taught her that the biggest danger with polar bears came after you had disrespected them. "They'll hear you," Ila recalled the elders saying. "And they don't like being joked about. I remember one time this guy said to his wife, 'There's so many polar bears around here, I should use them instead of dog teams.'" According to Ila, the man's wife was attacked by a bear the next day.

But the place where bears and people came into contact most often was at the dump. "Kids used to get drunk and go to the dump," Ila told me. "This one time we were all there, and these five bears jumped out of the incinerator. Everyone was all laughing and pointing, but I was the only one sober enough to be scared, and I just started yelling that we had to leave."

The worst part of the story is that the bears and the Dene kids were at the dump for the same reason. They had both become scavengers. With their parents absent and the government turning a blind eye, the kids discovered that picking through the garbage was their only means of subsistence. There must have been a wary daily standoff between the bears and the teenagers, both of them hustling for resources that neither of them really wanted. "If it hadn't been for the dump, I don't think my people would have survived," Ila said. But living like that extracted a heavy toll. "My father used to be so strong, such a proud man. But when he saw us eating from the dump, it destroyed him. He knew he was too drunk to provide for us any more, and seeing us live like that. . . ," Ila's voice trailed off.

It hadn't always been like this. When the Dene were warring with the Cree, back in the early 1700s, a Dene woman named Thandelthur saved the day. Captured by the Cree, she learned their language before she escaped in 1714, after a year of captivity. She arrived at the Hudson's Bay Company post half-starved, begging to be taken in. At the time the enmity between the two tribes was so great that it threatened to put a halt to all trading. But because she was able to speak both languages, Thandelthur—the Slave Woman, as she came to be known—brokered a tenuous peace. Without her, there would have been no trading post. There would have been no Churchill. All that's left of her now is a small rock monument. The Churchill Dene have been destroyed.

Standing there in the ring of rubble that had once been her home, Ila reached into her purse and pulled out a pack of cigarettes. "These aren't for me. They're for them." She shook out two smokes and placed them in the crook of a little tree growing in the middle of the house. "You can't come by here and not leave something," she said. She hunted in the bushes and found a few more weathered bottles to stand along the walls. Broken bottles were all that was left of this village now. Broken bottles of alcohol.

We retreated into the car and drove off, threading our way past one foundation after another, each one recalling some horrific story. "That one over there burned up with three little kids inside. There was one brother who lived there, and he grew up to be a policeman," she said. "But I guess the memories were too much for him because he came back out here to Dene Village one day and shot himself."

One after another, the stories flowed, and none of them were good. "I remember where every family lived," she said. The subtext hung in the air: *I remember where my community died.* Where the dirt road headed back out toward the highway, we parked next to a stone monument. Etched in the rock were the names of the dead. Ila traced the letters with her fingers and spoke the names aloud. She put another cigarette in the dirt at the base of the monument, covering it with gravel so it wouldn't blow away. I picked up a rock and placed it on top of the memorial stone, a Jewish tradition to show that the dead have not been forgotten. But the monument was too rounded, too beaten down by the years. The rock slid off into the dirt.

"DAD, COULD YOU FIGHT A POLAR?" Mac asked me as we scouted out the town on one of our early days there. He had been uncharacteristically quiet for the past few minutes, his hands thrust deep into his coat pockets. Headed to a coffee shop for hot chocolate and doughnuts, Mac had been carefully peering behind every shed and carport, more eager than terrified.

"Are you asking if *I* could fight a polar bear or if *somebody* could fight a polar bear," I stalled, realizing that this was one of those inflection points in a young boy's life where he has to decide if his father is a true hero or a total pussy.

"Could you, I mean."

"No, not really." Better to be honest than to create a situation in which I had to fight a bear in order to impress a four-year-old.

He looked disappointed. "But I've seen you fight a dog," he said with a glimmer of hope. He was, I think, referring to the time he saw me stare down a dachshund that was urinating on our rosemary bush.

"It's just not safe, Macky. They're way bigger and stronger and tougher than people. Nobody can fight a bear."

"I could," he said under his breath.

"What's that?"

"I could fight a bear."

"I don't think you could," I said, mustering as much fatherly sternness as I was able. "Even if you think you could, you're not allowed to. Do you understand?"

"I won't," he said, sighing as if I'd just taken away his birthday. "I won't . . . but I could." And with that, he pronounced the conversation over by stuffing the lapel of his down coat into his mouth and gnawing away on it happily. I needed to get that boy a cruller before he ate himself out of warm clothes.

Welcome mat, Churchill-style. *Zac Unger*

Main drag—yes, Churchill-style. (This is the summer view; to imagine the winter view, use the identical photo but reduce visibility to six inches and add 1,000 tourists.) *Eugene Reimer, 2004, ereimer.net*

If you can read this sign, you're too close. *Kelsey Eliasson, www.polarbearalley.com*

Smart bear trap, not-so-smart writer. *Zac Unger*

Author and children on intrepid quest for hot chocolate. From back to front, that's Mac, Percy, and Zeke. *Zac Unger*

Actually, it's a good idea to always leave one child in safety to carry on the family name. That's Percy and Mac and my wife, Shona. *Richard Unger*

The Polar Bear Capital of the World is a great place for families to live . . . *Travel Manitoba*

. . . or visit. *Richard Unger*

Polar bears against the somewhat surreal backdrop of the wreck of the *Ithaka*—a ship that may or may not have once been part of Mussolini's navy and that either ran aground in a gale or was purposefully scuttled for insurance money in 1959 (or 1960, or 1961, depending on whom you believe). One of the wonderful things about a town as remote as Churchill is that actual events become myths in no time flat.
Kelsey Eliasson, www.polarbearalley.com

CHAPTER 15

Polar Bear
Pitchman

YOURS FREE! POLAR BEAR TOTE BAG. AVAILABLE ONLY TO NRDC MEMBERS. Show the world you're playing a personal role in saving the polar bear!

—FUND-RAISING LETTER, NATURAL
RESOURCES DEFENSE COUNCIL

Get two FREE World Wildlife Fund Polar Bear Totes when you support WWF today! You can help save endangered species and their habitats! And one of the most important things you can do is send a gift to WWF today of $16 or more, and receive two FREE WWF Polar Bear Tote Bags as your special gift.

—FUND-RAISING LETTER,
WORLD WILDLIFE FUND

Help Protect America's Arctic. Climate change threatens to drown Arctic nesting areas for millions of migratory birds and birthing sites for polar bears and caribou. YES! It is time to say "NO!" to Big Oil and "YES!" to protecting The Polar Bear Seas. Get your own polar bear cub stuffed animal when you give $50 or more.

—FUND-RAISING LETTER,
ALASKA WILDERNESS LEAGUE

B ECAUSE EVERYONE AGREES that polar bears are celebrities, it seems only fair that they should have agents. And in the North American market, the prime mover and shaker is a scruffy-bearded former advertising executive named Robert Buchanan. If all you want to do is see bears the way everyone else sees bears—on TV specials, in magazine articles, and even on Tundra Buggies in Churchill—then you will never make his acquaintance. But if you want to *make* the movies or write the articles or see inside the guts of the tourist operation, then all roads lead straight to him. To put it bluntly, if you want to kiss a polar bear, you're going to have to make love to Robert Buchanan first.

Buchanan is the president and CEO of Polar Bears International, a once-sleepy nonprofit that has grown into a multi-million-dollar clearinghouse for all things *Ursus maritimus.* Although many organizations lay claim to the polar bears' best interest, it is PBI that they all turn to for access, advice, and logistical support. PBI gives financial support to much of the polar bear research that takes place in North America. It's like a mini National Science Foundation with a one-track mind.

Time and again, I was told that if I wanted to do anything regarding polar bears, I would have to clear it through Robert Buchanan. Scientists, government officials, and tour operators had learned to say, "You should talk to PBI," instead of saying, "No comment." Once I was paying attention, I started to see PBI's logo everywhere: it had co-branding and cross-marketing agreements with everyone from the World Wildlife Fund to the San Diego Zoo to British Petroleum. In Churchill, just about every business was a sponsor of—and in turn promoted by—PBI; Mac and I watched a pilot clean dirt from a PBI logo placed directly on the side of his helicopter.

For a man so adept at working the media, Buchanan keeps a surprisingly low profile. PBI has no published phone number, and Buchanan himself isn't just unlisted, he also has no fixed home address. When he's not in Churchill managing the bears, he drives circles around the United States in a specially customized eco-RV that he's dubbed the Tin Kan. And Buchanan does nothing to dispel his aura as the Great and Powerful

Oz of the Arctic. Before my family and I arrived in Churchill, I caught Buchanan on the phone and he told me that he could take me "from zero to Mach Ten in no time flat." I started to thank him, but he cut me off, saying that he wouldn't do that for just anyone.

"I just have to be careful. I'm sure you understand," he said, as if we were spies about to trade nuclear launch codes in a parking garage. "PBI isn't political. . . . I just want to make sure you understand that. Polar bears aren't a right issue or a left issue. They're a human being issue. Got it?" He then proceeded to grill me for thirty minutes regarding my background, my writing style, my academic bona fides.

Evidently, I passed Buchanan's test, because hours after we hung up, I got an email from a tour operator who had been ducking my advances. "Any friend of PBI is a friend of mine," it said. Later, I called Buchanan to thank him and then asked whether he could get me an audience with the Heavy Hitters just as easily. "They're extremely busy, and they usually don't like to talk to the press much," he said. "But if I vouch for you and ask them to give you a little of their time, they'll usually do it." This was the golden ticket I'd been waiting for!

Although Buchanan is from the United States, he and his predominantly American team descend on Churchill every fall. They lease and furnish a couple of apartments and immediately set to work coordinating the media onslaught that surrounds the fall migration. Drop into the PBI house at any time of day or night and you'll find Robert holding court over Korean newscasters, Canadian government officials, top-tier international zoologists, and B-list American celebrities. At night Buchanan plays host to a raucous, ongoing party: dinner at Gypsy's Restaurant and Bakery, drinks at the Seaport Lounge, more drinks around the kitchen table at the PBI house. There's good food, better wine, and a seemingly inexhaustible supply of Crown Royal whiskey, Robert's favorite. Every day, Buchanan or one of his assistants runs to the airport to pick up some new arrival; every night brings a welcome party or a going-away feast. I quickly learned that the only time to talk with Robert was first thing in the morning; by 10:00 AM he'd be buried in telephone calls and already late for a videoconference with London or LA. More important, I could usually count on him having his cook whip me up a tidy plate of steak and eggs with fresh tomatoes and a blueberry Danish on the side.

I'd call Buchanan a big fish in a small pond except that I'm not sure that anybody else in town knows that they're supposed to be swimming. Especially in Churchill, where everything is so slapdash and last minute, Buchanan's professionalism makes him stand out like Michael Jordan at a local Tuesday night pickup game. You can't help but like Robert Buchanan: he pours drinks and picks up tabs and slips you little asides that are just off-message enough to make you feel like you've pierced the inner sanctum. He's the kind of guy who will ask a waiter his name at the beginning of lunch, then clasp his shoulder and bid farewell like an old friend after the check has been paid. It's only after you've trailed him for a couple of days that you realize he's quietly sucked all the oxygen out of the room and that if want to catch your breath in Churchill, you need Buchanan's key to unlock your lungs for you.

"Here they come!"

"Who?"

"The Greatest Conservation Generation the world has ever seen!"

"The what?" I screamed, trying to be heard over the wind.

"The Greatest Generation for Conservation in history. That's the future of the polar bear, right there. Right there!"

Shivering in the cold on the back deck of a Tundra Buggy, I scanned the receding shoreline of Hudson Bay for what Robert Buchanan could possibly be talking about. Soon five helicopters came into view, low and jittery in the distance like a line of gnats. They landed in front of us with military precision, closer to each other than seemed wise, given the madly gusting winds. As the prop wash blew frigid air and tiny pebbles into my face, I peeked at the scene through splayed fingers. Buchanan held his ground, reviewing his troops like a Soviet general in Red Square. Feet firmly planted shoulder width apart, chest out, shotgun cradled in his arms. Hell, he was even wearing a thick fur hat with a hammer and sickle on the front.

The roar of the blades dampened to a steadily murderous *chop-chop-chop*, and a stream of teenagers spilled out of the machines. Soon they assembled into groups, hugging and bouncing and posing giddily for photographs. The weary helicopter pilots darted back and forth, shepherding the little cliques away from the spinning tail blades.

"High five!" Buchanan yelled, and each of the passing boys punched at his outstretched hand. The girls hugged him as they piled past, and Buchanan beamed the Cheshire grin of an indulgent grandfather. Unlike most people in Churchill, he held his shotgun awkwardly, as if he were worried it might go off in his face. Still, a man with a gun is a man with a gun, and the kids regarded him with something close to awe as he racked the weapon over and over to clear it of any shells before going inside.

Name tags dangled from the ends of lanyards around the kids' necks. They were from everywhere: Alaska, Kentucky, Ohio, Australia, Denmark. There was even one from Churchill. I followed them inside, where they were rapidly shedding clothing. The buggy looked like a garage sale, with hats and parkas and mitts in a pile on the floor. A few minutes earlier, we'd been completely alone on the tundra save for a few ptarmigan pecking at the earth. Now the buggy vibrated with the pure, clean kinetic energy of sixteen teenagers having the best day of their lives. This, I could only assume, was what Buchanan was referring to as the Greatest Conservation Generation the world had ever seen.

THE INNER SANCTUM OF THE POLAR BEAR media machine is located wherever Robert Buchanan happens to be at the moment. Today his surroundings looked less like a media war-room and more like the mosh pit at a Justin Bieber concert. Steven Amstrup was nowhere in evidence, so I'd have to make do with a pack of teenagers in various stages of undress.

At the beginning of every bear season, before the tourist and media circus gets into full swing, Buchanan hosts two "Leadership Camps" in which kids from all over the world receive an all-expenses paid trip to

Churchill, free high-end Canada Goose–brand parkas, and a mandate to do . . . something. Just what that something was, I hadn't yet been able to figure out. Which is why Buchanan had invited me out to the Tundra Buggy Lodge to see for myself.

The Tundra Buggy Lodge is more like an Amtrak train than a bed and breakfast. In both cases you tether a few square boxes together, put snack food in one and call it the dining car, put pillows in another and call it a sleeper, then slam all the doors for days on end and tell everyone that sticking any body part out of a window will result in certain dismemberment. The kids were here for free, but later in the season, well-heeled travelers would fork over $10,000 for the privilege of their confinement. The lodge is parked well away from Churchill, out on the tidal flats where the bears mill about and teach their cubs how to be ornery. The attraction is that instead of riding in the buggies, the bears come to you so that you can bask in their nearness while you sip your morning coffee or clip your toenails before bed. Extreme isolation, punishing weather, and wild animals known primarily for their malicious temperaments: it's like *The Shining* meets *Jaws*, but with a really touchy septic system thrown in for extra horror value.

The teens had already been together for the better part of a week, and they were beginning to exhibit the giddy intergender familiarity that makes parents cringe. Underwear hung in conspicuously exposed locations, kids lolled on each other's bunks with practiced indifference, and the air was thick with pubescent pheromones. No wonder bears were so attracted to this place.

Buchanan had sent the kids inland by helicopter so they could walk on the spongy tundra and peer inside an abandoned polar bear birthing den. I felt distinctly out of my element as I wandered through the sleeping cars, but the kids put me at ease by failing to acknowledge my existence in any way. The Grim Reaper could walk down the hall wearing sequined stretch pants and I doubt that any of the students would remove a single iPod earbud in his honor.

But when Buchanan came through the door with a clap of his hands and a holler, the buggy fell silent.

"Did everybody have a good time?" he asked.

"Yes!" They all screamed in unison

"Are you inspired?"

"Yes!"

"Are we gonna save the polar bears?"

"Yes!"

"Are we gonna change the world?"

"Yes! Yes! Yes!"

"All right then! Let's go do it!" The buggy erupted into a jumble of cheers, squeals, and applause. "But first let's have lunch," Buchanan said, his voice lost in a din of irrepressible teen joy.

In the dining car, the kids set upon a lunch buffet with murderous intensity. The polar bears could learn a thing or two from this predatory frenzy. Whoever had planned the menu had done so with a keen understanding that any parents were thousands of miles away. You could have your pick among hot dogs, hamburgers, pizza, and fried chicken fingers, with cases of Mountain Dew to wash it all down. For dessert there were cookies, tarts, pans of brownies, and trays of cupcakes. And for good measure, every windowsill held a bowl full of jellybeans, gummi bears, and other sugary gut-bombs that belong to the class of youthful delicacies that are completely indigestible to anyone over the age of twenty-five.

The dining car itself was like all the others, except that instead of bunks bolted to the walls it had tables bolted to the floor. The décor was reminiscent of a Cracker Barrel restaurant, with snowshoes and cast-iron skillets on the walls to lend frontier credibility. The difference being that when you look out the window of a Cracker Barrel you usually see a parking lot and a Sbarro's Pizzeria. Here, all I could see was rocks petering out into the water, and the ass end of a polar bear poking out from behind a bush.

Buchanan sat at a rear table, wearing a baseball cap and a slightly crazed expression. He has an almost feral, badgerish look, and if you were to replace his high-end outdoor gear with buckskin pants and a raccoon cap, Buchanan wouldn't look out of place in a trapper's cabin or a boomtown saloon circa 1849. He has widely spaced teeth, a blunt nose, and eyes that are nearly always bloodshot and puffy, a result of too little sleep, too much sun, and perhaps a fondness for good booze. He covers a weak chin with a salty, scraggly beard that isn't so much long as extensive, crawling farther down his neck than most men would find comfortable. Like some teenagers, Buchanan always looks as though he has just been woken from a deep sleep, an effect he heightens by continually removing his ball cap and scratching his balding head in a bewildered manner. His most distinguishing characteristic, however, is his laugh, a high-pitched, wheezy gasp that arrives without warning and makes you worry that he's about to choke on his own tongue.

"I'm fifty emails behind," he told me as I slid in next to him with a bowl of soup and two apples that looked very much the worse for wear.

"Anything important?" I asked.

"They're all important. CNN, BBC, *Entertainment Tonight*. I just can't keep up." He shook his head ruefully, but it was obvious that being overwhelmed was nourishing to his soul.

The kids appeared to be having a wonderful time, but I didn't have a clue what they were doing here, or why Buchanan had spent so much time and money to make their trip possible. And so I asked him.

"We're empowered to teach these kids how to make a difference," he said. "It's an enormous responsibility. Saving the polar bear is in their hands."

I nodded my head sagely. I had no idea what he was talking about. "That sounds great, but *specifically* what are you doing to . . ."

Buchanan cut me off, wagging his finger vigorously to show that he knew exactly what I was going to ask. "We're giving them the facts and the tools so that they can lead with their heads, but at the same time never be afraid to express the passion that they feel in their hearts."

I hadn't survived a loosey-goosey Bay Area childhood just so somebody could tell me that the solution to global warming was as simple as expressing the love we all feel but are too repressed to share. If I'd wanted a group hug, I would have stayed home.

"They seem like great kids," I said, trying not to scream or tear my hair out. After all, PBI had paid for my helicopter ride out to the Tundra Buggy Lodge, and it's never a good idea to grab your meal ticket by the shoulders and shake him until he stops talking like a part-time yoga instructor. "On a day-to-day basis when these kids get home . . . what are you expecting them to *do*?" I asked.

"I'm expecting them to lead. I need leadership and I need leaders. They come in here as bunny-hugging enthusiastic kids, scared to death of speaking in front of a group. And they leave understanding that kids can make a difference. The politicians aren't doing what they need to be doing. The churches aren't doing it. The schools aren't doing it. And so PBI is doing it."

"Doing what?" I asked.

"Building the Greatest Conservation Generation that the . . ."

". . . world has ever seen. Got it," I said, scribbling in my notebook. "The Greatest Conservation Generation the world has ever seen."

"We're just trying to spread the word," he continued. "Is everybody going to listen? Is everybody going to change their behavior? Some will. Some won't. So what. Who's next?" Buchanan gave me a grin; he was proud of that last line. I was having no trouble seeing Buchanan's roots as a corporate marketing genius. "Where did you say you worked before you retired?" I asked, switching tacks.

"I was the head of marketing for a major beverage corporation."

"Which one?"

"A major beverage corporation. Let's just leave it at that." I'd asked him this question before, and had gotten the same answer, verbatim, every time. Maybe he thought it made him seem mysterious. I just thought it made him frustrating.

"Thanks for lunch," I said, standing up and clearing his dish along with mine.

"Anytime. Anytime at all. You're a friend of PBI now, so what's ours is yours. All you have to do is ask." He grinned up at me beatifically and spread his arms wide in welcome. "Go get yourself a cookie. Don't be shy."

CHAPTER 16

The Greatest
Conservation Generation

[Protecting the polar bear] is going to make Americans
do what they've never done before, which is say,
"What am I willing to pay for that species, in the Arctic,
in the far north, that I'll never see, and if I did it would
probably try to eat me?"

—KENNETH GREEN, RESIDENT SCHOLAR AND
CLIMATE CHANGE SKEPTIC, AMERICAN ENTERPRISE INSTITUTE

A S THE LOCAL REPRESENTATIVES of the Greatest Conservation Generation inhaled their processed lunches, I invited myself to sit down with four of them. They chattered about the helicopter flight they'd taken and all of the acrobatics that the pilot had performed for them. Apparently, someone had had to make use of an airsickness bag.

"Do you guys have a minute to talk?" I asked.

"Just a minute," one of the girls said, sighing. "And then we have to blog."

A girl named Annabel, a high school junior with an attitude so severe and serious that she seemed haunted, explained what she planned to write. "The den was collapsing," she said. "The permafrost is melting and if it keeps going like this, the moms won't have any place to deliver their cubs. We came here to the tundra and we actually saw that. We have pictures. Global warming is happening." She bit a half-moon out of her sandwich and nodded her head gravely as she chewed. "We have to do something soon. It's all up to us or the bears are going to die."

"That's pretty heavy," I said.

I looked outside the dining car window. A bear wandered lazily from one side of the buggy to the other and back again, sniffing at the bare dirt and chewing on some grass. He lifted his head to look directly at us only once, when a particularly loud chorus of squeals rose from one of the tables. After the commotion died, he scratched out a little spot in the ground and went to sleep.

"He's been here for a couple of days," Annabel said. "He feels safe with us." Ah yes, the pure simple friendship between man and beast. Step off the Tundra Buggy and it's group hugs all around, cue the theme from It's a Small World and then . . . some big-ass bear punches you in the throat and eats your kidneys.

One of the other girls shrugged. "He got really excited when we were grilling hot dogs and hamburgers the other night. Maybe we can do that again tonight. That would be so cool." I watched as the bear got up, turned from head to tail, and then lay down in the same spot, facing the opposite direction. It was like watching a house cat: we were each mildly interested in the other, but there was no affection beyond the fact that it's nice to be in the same general vicinity as another mammal with a beating heart.

But the girls felt differently. "He needs us," said one of them.

"We can't let him down. We just can't," Annabel said with a pleading tone to her voice. She looked at me without blinking. "A lot of my friends don't buy into global warming. They're supportive, I guess, but they don't understand why I'm here. And what I've learned at Leadership Camp is that you can't get into debates with people who don't care. You can't waste your time on people who won't ever try to change. Some will, some won't. So what. Who's next? That's what I always say."

Annabel was freaking me out. In fact, all of these kids were. They had the trappings of teen silliness—the digital lives and the self-conscious attire—but at their core every single one of them was as serious as a heart attack. Weren't kids this age supposed to be self-absorbed gossip girls who spent their free time sending text messages about the latest advances in halter tops? The counselors kept them in lectures and discussion groups until 11:00 at night; the kids looked drawn out and tired, but I never heard a word of complaint. Why weren't the boys trying harder to score, I wondered? Why weren't the girls busying themselves with catty infighting and intricate clique-building rituals? Why wasn't anyone, even one single kid, sitting in the back of the classroom making snide comments and trying to undermine the authority of the adults in charge? Hell, even the bowls of candy on the windowsills and the cases of Mountain Dew in the fridge were going almost entirely untouched. Were these actual teenagers or bioengineered conservation-bots from Buchanan's secret laboratory?

"Do you really think that you kids can have an effect on something so big?" I asked.

"I don't have a choice," Annabel said. "My whole life has changed because of this week. Kids don't want to listen to adults preach at them, but *we* can make a difference. *We* can influence our peers."

The kids quickly lost interest in me and drifted back into a conversation about their "forward action plans," by which I think they just meant their plans. They were going to give lectures at middle schools, set up recycling programs at their parents' workplaces. They were going to save the polar bear one compact fluorescent light bulb at a time.

AS THE DISHES WERE BEING DRIED, a mother bear and her cub nosed up to the dining car. The cub wasn't tiny, not one of those little downy furballs that make such good postcards. In Hudson Bay, polar bear moms keep their cubs alongside them for upward of two years; farther north, where conditions are harsher, they may stay together for an additional year. This sort of long-term bond is exceptionally rare among animals;

in most cases you want your offspring to do well, but you also want to get rid of them so that you can get busy producing another litter. But the polar environment is harsh and mercurial, and there's so much to learn that keeping cubs close is the only way to survive. If a mother dies or is killed, the odds of a new cub surviving are zero. Maybe that's another reason that people identify with polar bears so closely.

At the moment, this particular bear was teaching her cub what garbage smells like. And the little guy loved it. Although the lodge carts out all of its sewage, the dishwater is a different matter. A squat metal tube runs from the belly of the dining car down into the earth, and all of the rinse water just dribbles out a few feet below the rocks. The bears can't get anything there, but the remnant odors of our chicken mini-potpies must have been maddening. The mother bear pawed at the ground; it had been months since she'd been able to eat, and the bay was nowhere close to freezing. The cub stood alongside, looking hopeful. An entire roomful of teenagers abandoned their cleanup chores and pressed themselves to the windows. Seeing bears scavenge for untreated gray water was a whole new thrill, and not to be missed.

"Aww, how cute," the kids cried in unison as they snapped off a few thousand digital photographs.

"I love you, little guy," said Annabel, her face pressed to the glass like an inmate at the end of visiting hour.

Eventually, the cub wandered off to play with a piece of black plastic garbage bag that came skipping across the tundra. He grabbed it in his teeth and thrashed wildly, practicing for the day when he'd snap a seal's neck in the same way. The kids all cooed and hugged each other.

"This is going to set us back," Buchanan said grimly. "Seeing bears always throws us off the schedule."

In the narrow lounge car, the kids flopped down on two rows of chairs, facing each other, their backs to the windows. A dozen laptops flipped open in unison; I'd never seen so many MacBooks in one place. They had Facebook pages to update, Twitters to tweet, photos to Flickr. Heads bent and faces alight with screen glow, the defenders of the bears documented their action plans. The revolution would not be unblogged.

ON THIS PARTICULAR WEEK, a medium-market network weatherman was riding along on the buggies—How ya doin', Toledo!—and sending home several dispatches a day. I watched him interview Buchanan on the back deck, with a sleeping bear as the backdrop.

"I can make him lift his head for your shot," Buchanan said before the camera started to roll.

"That would be great," said the weatherman. "I'd really appreciate that."

"Watch this." Buchanan grabbed a cellophane tortilla chip bag and wrinkled it vigorously. The bear didn't flinch. Buchanan looked disheartened, his trick with the Doritos bag having failed to bring him into Doolittle-style communication with the beast. But the weatherman forged ahead with his report from the front lines of the climate change disaster. Later, he told me that he'd probably have to use some snowy stock footage, supplied by PBI. "It just looks all wrong to have a polar bear without any snow," he said. "I know the whole story is supposed to be about the melting, but it's still weird to have a bear lying in the dirt like that."

Knee-deep in networking, the kids had spent the past several days cramming and rehearsing for a series of teleconferences beamed straight out of the lounge car. Their goal was to reach out to the carbon-spewing urban world, to chat up a succession of middle schools, community groups, zoo organizations, and hometown media outlets. "It's the power of friends helping friends," Buchanan said, his eyes boring into me with messianic fervor. "The politicians aren't doing it, the churches aren't doing it. . . ." He had approximately ten great lines, and I had learned every one of them by heart.

The kids sat in the lounge car, readying themselves for the first video-conference. They rolled their shoulders and did vocal calisthenics, arranging their faces into camera-ready masks of calm and competence. When the big screen at the front of the room sizzled to life, they would all be perfectly ready, looking just like the perky professional spokes-advocates that they all looked forward to becoming.

"You guys have *got* this," Buchanan said, switching into cheerleader mode. "You know all the facts and we've given you the skills to do this right. If you get lost or off track, just remember to stick to the science.

This isn't a right issue or a left issue. It's a human being issue. It takes twenty years to build credibility and twenty seconds to lose it. Everybody ready? Go!"

As they waited for the linkup, the kids vibrated with anticipation as if they were backstage at the Apollo. One of the counselors motioned frantically for silence; the screen blinked, the audio crackled and . . . into focus came a classroom full of glassy-eyed junior high school kids, staring at the Leadership kids over a few thousand miles of Internet cable. The twin triumphs of global interconnectivity and teen enthusiasm were upon us in all their fearsome glory.

And then . . . silence.

The kids from the distant classroom fidgeted at their desks, their adolescent awkwardness painfully apparent even through the herky-jerky pixilation of the video hookup. One kid picked his nose; another reached under the table for some Twizzlers. Across the daunting expanses of murderous wilderness, boredom reigned supreme. The kids in the room with me were as engaged and excited as any human beings I'd ever seen, but back home in the classroom, on the receiving end of some heavy peer-to-peer knowledge, every tick of body language said, "Dear God, please don't let this be on the test."

Finally, with all the enthusiasm of a POW reading out a forced confession, one of the students reluctantly asked a question. "What is the bear population in that area and how has it changed in recent years?"

Buchanan exhaled visibly; the game was on. "I can handle that," said a lanky kid, straightening up in his chair. "The population in western Hudson Bay is about 935 animals, and that's down from 1,194 animals just a few years ago." He continued on with a litany of dire numbers, recounting the findings of the Heavy Hitters with such crisp efficiency that it seemed he might have somehow gotten the kind of face time with Steven Amstrup that I wanted so badly for myself.

"Can you see evidence of global warming from where you are?" somebody asked.

"Oh, definitely," Annabel chimed in; the question was tailor-made for her brand of overwhelming seriousness. Her brown eyes fixed on the video camera and she sat very still, with her hands in her lap as if she were in a witness box. "The bay should be frozen by now, but as you can see behind me, it hasn't even started yet. If it keeps up like this, the bears will starve." I shot a glance toward Buchanan, who grinned and flashed a big thumbs-up.

There was only one problem: what Annabel was saying wasn't true.

In fact, it wasn't even close. This was still early October, and the bay wouldn't freeze for a solid month or longer. In fact, freeze-up had reliably been a mid-November event for decades. Although it might drift a week or ten days to one side or the other, freeze-up was not the biggest part of the problem; it was the spring thaw that was changing so dramatically.

More important, how could these kids possibly think that they were seeing global warming unfurl right in front of them? These were smart, hardworking students, completely capable of grasping the fact that climate change only makes sense when viewed as a long-term trend. And yet here they were, promoting the sort of snapshot conclusions that turn complex scientific issues into muddled messes whenever they reach the public arena. This was exactly what Rocky had warned me about, the sound bite-ification of science, the risk of letting emotion overwhelm good data. Annabel pointing to a warm day in Churchill was as irrelevant as a conservative columnist pointing to a freak June snowfall as evidence that global warming is a hoax. She was just a well-intentioned kid, and you could hardly blame her for getting a few facts crossed, but still: this wasn't helping.

"What can we do to stop global warming and save the polar bears?" was the next question, and the Leadership kids jumped on it. This was their money shot, the reason for everything. They piled on with suggestions: Unplug your toasters! Take shorter showers! Ride your bike to school one day a week!

"If everybody unplugged their cell phone chargers when they're not using them, we could reduce the amount of carbon released into the atmosphere by 10 percent," said one girl. *Ten percent?* Buchanan's jaw dropped a little at that one, and even some of the other kids looked alarmed. But in the end they all pushed through. It was just a slip of the tongue and their hearts were in the right places.

I couldn't really blame Annabel or the others. In their eagerness to be eyewitnesses to one of the greatest calamities ever, these kids were stumbling all over each other just to get ahead of themselves. These were heady times, their generation's Vietnam War. On a broad scale, they all knew that they were right. The children may lead you . . . but details and statistics shall be the business of grown-ups. As the conference ended, the mood in the buggy was triumphant. Working together, we can make a difference! If we all work hard, and if we all want it bad enough, the polar bears will be just fine!

For all their dedication and smarts, I couldn't buck the feeling that these kids were deluding themselves on an epic scale. Sure it's fun to scream and cry and feel like you're part of a groundswell, but to use an analogy from my own glorious teen years, it's not exactly like the We Are the World video eliminated hunger in Africa. I mean, what American students haven't already heard that they should recycle their soda cans? And if another kid—even one speaking by futuristic astral video projection from a land far, far away—tells you to ride your bike to school, are you really going to be guilted into a world-inverting overhaul of your entire carbon footprint? With every megacorporation on the planet already pledging to "go green" and every unnecessary plastic object arriving prestamped with a tiny recycling triangle, is more consciousness-raising really what we need?

Every time I heard Annabel and her friends declare victory because they'd started an environmental club at their high school, I wanted to scream. With India industrializing, the Chinese quadrupling their meat consumption, and the Brazilians hacking away ceaselessly at their forestlands, I felt like this Save the Bear campaign fell somewhere between sentimentalism and sophistry. Every one of these kids had flown thousands of miles to get here, and each would be going home to Miami or Louisville or San Diego with a brand-new, PBI-provided, expedition-weight parka that would probably never again see the outside of a basement closet. No matter what these kids eventually did with their mandates for change, would they even be able to offset the resource costs of coming to Churchill in the first place? I liked these kids, and I liked

Robert Buchanan, but the whole enterprise was so small bore. If video-conferencing was the future of conservation, then polar bears were as good as dead.

THE MALE BEAR WAS UP from his hiding spot in the willows and moping around outside the window again. Tomorrow a group of paying customers would arrive, and these idealistic kids would be sitting in various airports, plotting strategies for reversing the past two hundred years of American industrialization and materialism. For the last time of the trip, and maybe of their lives, they gathered around the windows to watch bears.

"That one is looking out for us," Annabel said, sidling up beside me. "I thought you should know that."

"How do you mean?"

"Well, yesterday this other male came up out of nowhere and our guy backed him down. He knows that we're here to protect him and so he's watching out for us, too." I liked her conviction and even her magical thinking; the certainty of youth is the most wonderful drug ever. "Nature didn't leave those bears lacking in anything," she said. "They're beautiful and profound. They're the most profound, best example of the Arctic, and we're messing it all up. Do you want to hear my elevator speech?"

"Your what?" I asked

"My elevator speech. It's what I'll say if I'm in an elevator with some-one and they ask me what I was doing up in the Arctic."

"Sure. Let's hear it."

"I went to the tundra to learn how to save the world and to empower other people to do the same after seeing these beautiful bears in their natural habitat. I will lead the people of the world into an environmen-tally healthy future. . . . What do you think?"

"It's good," I said. The mean kids back home would destroy her if they heard her say that, I thought. "Are you really going to say that?"

Annabel regarded me as if I'd asked why the sky was purple. "Of course that's what I'm going to say," she answered. "I know they call it an elevator pitch or whatever, but that's not what it is to me. It's how I really feel. I'm not the same person that I was before I came up here."

LATE THAT NIGHT, as the dining car chairs sat upended on the tables, and the only view out the darkened windows was a smudgy reflection of oneself, the kids gathered in the lounge. They tried out their elevator pitches and made solemn pledges to stay in daily communication for the rest of their lives.

I found Buchanan sitting on his bunk, the farthest one in the farthest car. His ball cap was off and the long thin hairs that ringed his bald spot stood straight on end in the dry staticky air. He pecked away at a laptop balanced on his knees, looking up like a hunted animal when I appeared beside him.

"I'm eighty emails behind," he said, his air of perpetual exhaustion seeming especially pronounced. "And that's just from today." Whoever invented retirement never considered people like Robert Buchanan. One week of tee times and early bird suppers and he'd die of irrelevance.

I sat down on the bunk opposite and watched him work by the blue glow of the screen.

"If you wanna ask something, just go ahead and ask," he said. "No secrets here."

I didn't really want to ask the question that had been on my mind, if only because I was already pretty sure of the answer. I took a deep breath and asked anyway. "Are you giving these kids false hope?" I asked. "Even if they convince everyone in America to shut off their porch lights and unplug their toasters, is that really going to make any difference? Aren't the polar bears basically dead no matter what we do?"

Buchanan set his laptop aside and looked over his glasses at me. "Who am I to say what will work and what won't?" he said, after a long pause. "My job is just to put the facts out there and let the people decide for themselves."

But Buchanan knew the facts better than I did. He knew that if the Heavy Hitters were to be believed, nothing short of a wholesale reinvention of modern society was going to reverse the decline of the bears. Unplug your toasters . . . my ass. What the polar bears needed was for the United States to sink into the ocean and for the Third World to stop being so uppity and successful and go back to being a whole lot more Third World-y.

I'd watched him give one interview after another and cheerlead tirelessly about the power of small, personal changes that could save the bears. Marketers market; it's in their DNA. But at some circular point in time, the fact that a product sells is all the proof you need that it's worth selling in the first place. Pipe dream or not, the American public was clamoring for every last bit of hope that Buchanan had for sale.

"No offense," I said, "but do you ever feel dishonest telling people that they can save the polar bears?"

We looked at each other in the darkness. We'd had versions of this conversation, but this was the first time I'd been so direct. The wind rocked the buggy like a ship at sea, whistling through tiny pinholes and firing laser beams of frigid air.

"Look," he said. "We both know you're right, but that doesn't mean we should stop. Recycling is just separating your garbage. We're hemorrhaging right now, and all of this stuff is Band-Aids. Are we going to stop this slide? In a hundred years are we still going to be able to go out in these buggies and see bears like this? That's what you keep asking, right?" I nodded at him; he stared back at me as if unsure whether he wanted to keep going.

"Are we going to save the polar bears? No. Probably not. Not in a really significant way." He closed his laptop and put his hands on his knees.

I didn't know what to think anymore. I'd spent the past few days trying to get Buchanan to admit that everything was hopeless, and now that he'd done it, I felt like a perfect piece of shit. When I was at Nestor Two, Rocky had planted the idea in me that polar bears might actually be OK, and now that I was at the Tundra Buggy Lodge, Buchanan—the bear's greatest champion—was telling me that they might not, even despite his own best efforts. What a mess.

"Come on," Buchanan said, taking off his glasses and rubbing his drooping eyes. "Let's go do something." I followed him into the lounge car, where the kids were tapping away diligently on their blogs.

"Wrap it up," he said. "We're going outside."

Out on the back deck, the starlight lit up the night. That same male bear, the one that had been with the kids all week, lay sleeping a few body lengths away.

"Hello, handsome," Buchanan said, and then turned to the kids "You see that? That guy is your guardian angel. He's the one who's going to make sure you follow through on everything you've promised this week. It costs about $15,000 to bring each one of you here. Now I'm not trying to put a guilt trip on you, but I need some leadership. It's all up to you not to let 6 billion people down, and I need to know that you can do this."

The kids looked beleaguered. Not only had they been made guardians of the entire population of the earth, but they were also standing in the wind and cold and most of them were in T-shirts and socks. Buchanan plowed ahead. "As you continue on this journey," he said, "you're going to start feeling emotions as you start touching your soul. Don't ever be afraid of that. But I want you to close your eyes and imagine if that bear disappeared. Imagine if they all disappeared. Imagine if you were the last generation ever to see polar bears in the wild." The kids were all sobbing, while also bouncing up and down spasmodically to stay warm.

"Wouldn't that be an incredible loss? It is my generation that has caused this, and your generation is the only one that can fix it." Buchanan was drifting, getting carried away with the power of his own inspiring oratory. "If you give up, if you don't use these skills you've learned, then the polar bear isn't going to be out there anymore." The kids clung to each other. "Actually," he said softly, speaking just to me or maybe only to himself, "those bears probably won't be out there anymore no matter what you do." He looked my way and winked.

CHAPTER 17

Scare Them and They Will Come

Ah, bullshit! It's the hunting! In Quebec they've got
totally unregulated bear hunting. The Eskimos are
selling them for $100 a foot. The Hudson fucking Bay
fucking Company has four hundred polar bear skins in
a warehouse, and they can't even sell one of them.

—BRIAN LADOON, CHURCHILL
DOG BREEDER AND POLAR BEAR EXPERT

B Y MID-OCTOBER, bear season was fully under way. Tourists washed over Churchill like breakers on the shore. They trundled in and out of buses, packing into the gift shops along Kelsey Boulevard with fistfuls of dollars aching to be spent. They filled their shopping bags with tundra-berry jam, oversized polar bear T-shirts, earrings in the shape of ptarmigans and inukshuks, and the assorted fudges and taffies that all tourist towns are required to sell. On their buggy-free "town days," they made the stations of the cross, dutifully visiting the Eskimo Museum and the Anglican Church, getting their passports stamped at the post office, and attending the ranger talk at the Parks Canada building. They'd make a few laps around town, wander the aisles at the hardware store to figure out if it had anything more to offer than the usual assortment of tenpenny nails and electrical tape. If they were feeling flush, they would treat themselves to a helicopter ride; if their portfolios had tightened a bit of late, they'd opt instead for the "dog sled experience," riding around on giant wheeled sleighs made necessary by the absence of good snow. Almost without exception, they were ecstatic over their trip. Churchill had been exactly what they had hoped it would be. I only heard one significant gripe, by a man from Tallahassee who grumbled that pictures of polar bears on dirt instead of snow were worthless and that "unless it dumps really damn soon here, I'll consider this trip to be a failure."

And though they were happy to have seen so many bears, the common thread running through the conversations I overheard was always the same. "They looked so skinny to me," people would say. "I could tell from the way they were pacing around and licking the ground that they're not feeling right, that they're scared." As people traded bear stories, the subtext of every conversation was the question, How close to dead do you think they really are? No matter that all of the locals thought that the bears looked healthier than they had in years. It had been a good, long, cold winter, and the bears were as fat as they could hope to be during this lean time of the year.

One afternoon I sat at the kitchen table in the PBI house, watching the swirl of activity surrounding Robert Buchanan. At one point a publicist for a major environmental organization sat down next to me. "It's just so sad," she said, pushing her lips into a long pout. "They all look so skinny that it's hard to look at them." A few minutes after she got up, her chair was filled by a senior biologist with the Manitoba Conservation Department. "The bears look good," he mused. "I haven't seen them this fat in years." Apparently, he hadn't gotten the message from the PR wing.

Experts aside, most of the tourists had written the narrative of their trip long before they ever set foot in town. You don't take a trip to Auschwitz because you're a fan of the Polish countryside, and you don't necessarily go to Churchill because you want to see healthy, happy bears. Where were all the tourists thirty years ago, when global warming was just a glimmer in Al Gore's eye and the polar bear had yet to become anyone's poster child for anything? Nowadays, amid the cluck-clucking over energy policy, there is also no mistaking the shimmy of excitement that runs through the tourists' collective gonads. It is not entirely unpleasant, as it turns out, to be a witness at the beginning of the end of the world. Terrible that it has to happen, but so lucky that we all got here in time to see it for ourselves!

There is only one problem with the narrative: none of the locals want anything to do with it. Every time I brought up the subject of global warming with one of my new neighbors, they would either change the subject or begin cursing my idiocy.

One night I sat down with Kevin Burke, the ranger I had gotten to know when we were both out at the field station with Rocky. His wife was out of town, so a home-cooked meal was out of the question. We muddled through as best we could with a bottle of something brown and fiery and a pile of Snickers Bars.

"So what do you think about global warming, then?" I asked. "Is it all about to come crashing down?"

Kevin thought a minute and then said, "You know, I've worked with a lot of scientists over the years and I have a lot of respect for all the work that goes into getting those PhDs, but honestly, Zac, I just don't see it. I had this Dutch film crew here and they wanted to interview me sitting on a snowmobile. 'Course it's all about global warming, global warming, global warming. They set it all up and they know exactly what they want before they even start."

Kevin scratched his head and yawned. As far as I could tell he was one of the hardest-working men in Churchill, and he looked tired. "So I just try to be as honest as I can," he continued. "I don't want to come across as being an idiot. They ask you what changes have you seen. And you know what? I haven't seen much change. I really haven't. Except for maybe the falls seem to be a little bit later. I hear it from some local people, too. They say, 'We don't get the winters we used to.' Ah, whatever. You don't remember three fucking years ago, how harsh the weather was. All I know is that the bears still seem to leave pretty much on time, mid-November. I always see some stragglers, some of them who stay behind for whatever reason. I don't know why the bears do what they do, and I'm not sure the scientists do either."

Kevin broke a piece off his Snickers. "God, I love these things." He drained his cup and leaned back in his chair. Tomorrow was going to be another in an endless series of long days, and it was well past the time when we both should have been asleep. But Kevin had one more thing to make clear. "I'm not saying that everything is fine and that there's no such thing as climate change. Not at all. What I'm saying is that all of these scientists and do-gooders and TV people . . . when they talk about making changes and 'saving the polar bears'"—he made little air quotes with his fingers—"it might be as much about themselves as about the bears. As long as people are around, you're not going to stop them from taking planes, taking trains, taking ships, driving in cars, driving trucks, and you might as well throw in space shuttles as well. It will never end. It will never stop. You can't stop that."

ALONG WITH THE TOURISTS, the media machine was also revving into high gear, as if for Fashion Week or a visit from the pope. But bears don't take direction well and the weather isn't exactly Hollywood clear, so there are inevitable conflicts between the producers and the locals who sign on to wrangle them. In the past, film crews have not always behaved with the best interests of the bears in mind. They hover too low in helicopters; they bait the bears or goad them into doing something more pictur-esque than groin-scratching; they bribe their buggy drivers into going places they shouldn't.

Often, the problem is that the Beautiful People and the producers who service them don't know how to behave above the 58th parallel. The scene isn't exactly what the media elite is accustomed to: there are no spas in Churchill, no organic sushi bars, no place to see or be seen by the people who matter. With no cell phone service, you can't even send a text message—a thought more horrible to some than global sea rise. One year, a famous TV weatherman came to Churchill with nothing but a light windbreaker, apparently mistaking an Arctic winter for an afternoon of golf in the Hamptons. On strict instructions that it was only a loan, somebody handed the weatherman a rugged, fur-and-feather down coat. Despite more than a few reminders, the weatherman took the coat home with him and had the gall to show up in Manhattan—on camera—wearing the thing. The coat's owner made a phone call and was informed by the weatherman's assistant that he had immediately donated the coat to charity upon his return from Churchill, but he'd liked it so much that he'd bought one of the exact same model and color for his very own.

For the most part, the locals regarded the fall frenzy with benign good humor; this was the year's meal ticket, after all. All around me, a shift in attitude was taking place. People were girding themselves for long hours and inane questions, pushy foreigners with outlandish demands. At the same time as they were opening up their town, they were closing down parts of themselves, planning temporary retreats into closely guarded circles of intimates. People have always gone north because they wanted to get away from something. But when you live in Churchill, the polar bears always bring the wide world right back to your doorstep.

AS WE SETTLED INTO OUR LIVES in Churchill, Percy and Mac and I took to dropping in at Gypsy's Bakery in the afternoon. We'd stuck with our no-furniture plan, so sitting at a real table on real chairs was a luxury, as were the brownies and mugs of hot cocoa that were placed in front of us.

Early in our stay, we ate dinner at Gypsy's most nights—dinosaur-shaped chicken nuggets for the kids, Chicken Caesar for the grown-ups, or maybe a plate of Caribou Stroganoff to split. But in the heart of the season, Gypsy's was off limits at breakfast and midday, and then again between 5:00 and 8:00 at night. The place was filled by multiple seatings of tour groups, all of whom had made reservations weeks in advance.

Even the long communal table up front, usually reserved for locals straggling in one at a time, was reset with candles, menus, and tightly rolled napkins.

Long experience with Canadian cuisine has taught me to be wary of any restaurant that the guidebooks suggest is the best in town. There's nothing terribly wrong with prime cuts of Northern game—caribou and reindeer taste just fine, although bear meat of any kind leaves something to be desired. But it's also nice to make the acquaintance of a fresh vege-table every once in a while, and that's just not possible in the extreme latitudes. Man cannot live on frozen peas and pearl onions alone.

The Canadian culinary repertoire relies heavily on ingredients that could be considered complete meals when served by themselves. Re-quired staples include Corn Flakes, cream of mushroom soup, vanilla pudding, teriyaki Slim Jims, and the like. The semi-official national snack is poutine, which does double duty as the number one national health crisis. Poutine, for anyone who has not had the opportunity to sample it, is French fries smothered with cheese curds smothered with gravy. For maximum cardiac benefit, it is usually served as the center of a three-part tasting menu, bookended by jelly doughnuts and filterless cigarettes.

But Gypsy's takes the unusual step (for a Canadian restaurant) of serving food that is actually delicious. The owners, a Portuguese family named Da Silva, do not recoil at the thought of a salad, and they do not adhere to the philosophy that the human body can only digest items that have been battered and deep-fried.

If the way to a man's heart is through his stomach, then the way into Churchill runs right through the front counter at Gypsy's Bakery. I've never been much of a pastry fan myself, but the bear claws and apple fritters here proved irresistible. I developed a mild addiction to Nanaimo bars, a uniquely Canadian treat involving layers of chocolate, coconut, and nuts held together by creamy yellow custard. It sounds disgusting, but trust me.

A line of tourists stood just inside the door of the café, their bellies rubbing up against a glass case full of pastries and wheels of cheese. They looked enormous in their down coats, which had been issued to them by their trip leader the moment they stepped off the plane. Two of them, one in red and the other in the green of a competing tour outfit, struck up a conversation as they waited for their goodies.

"We had a fantastic day out there," said the first.

"I was out yesterday," said the other. "The guide said he's never seen so many bears in a single day.

"How many did you see?"

"Gosh, I would never *count*. I just feel fortunate to see any at all."

"We saw thirty-eight," said the man in red, his chest puffing out slightly.

"Now that you say so, I think my wife said we saw forty." The two men looked at each other grimly, locked in a battle to the death over who had had the more wonderful Churchill experience thus far.

"We also saw three different sets of cubs," said the red-jacketed man, his cheeks and nose turning the color of his coat. "Really tiny ones. *Super* cute."

His opponent shrugged. "*We* saw two enormous males fighting, really going at it, not that play fighting. Also an Arctic fox."

"Yeah, but were you up at three this morning for the northern lights? Best show I've ever seen . . ."

Mercifully, the woman behind the counter took their orders before they could come to blows over who was the more talented sightseer. They took their food and retreated to opposite corners of the room, where they scrolled through the images on their digital cameras in order to calm themselves. By tomorrow, I felt certain, they would each claim to have seen over a hundred bears. If the scientific community used tourists instead of researchers to do the census, the polar bear population problem would have been solved years ago.

"How's it going, Fred?" I asked, as my little entourage made its way past the front counter, shedding a thick trail of hats, mitts, and scarves. Fred Da Silva is the oldest son and the public face of the Gypsy's empire, a constant-motion machine of hospitality and good cheer. In addition to being the maître d' of the restaurant, Fred is the unofficial fixer for the entire town. All gossip flows through him, and should you ever need anything of any kind, Fred always knows a guy who knows a guy. He wears vaguely fashionable clothes (for Churchill) and gels his hair into a spiky little 'do that wouldn't look out of place in New York or LA. Fred spends the entirety of bear season inside his restaurant, hovering several inches off the ground and making everyone, tourist and local alike, feel like Gypsy's exists solely for their benefit.

"It's busy," he said. He flashed his hands at me over and over to indicate how many days remained until the end of tourist season.

"But who's counting, right?" I joked.

"*I* am," he replied, stone-faced. "And I'm really, really good at counting."

"Sorry to hear that."

He broke into a broad grin. "Just kidding. I wouldn't trade this time for anything." He rubbed his thumb and forefingers together, the universal symbol for money. Ten thousand tourists can eat an astonishing number of sausage rolls and chocolate éclairs. "You guys wanna go in the back and see the bakery?" he said, getting down on one knee and handing out doughnut holes. Mac looked temporarily flummoxed; his mouth was already stuffed with the lollipop that Fred had slipped him about three seconds earlier. This is one of the most important lessons of childhood: when sugar is involved, you can always find a way to open your mouth a little bit wider.

Mac looked at me with a moment's hesitation. He'd never been behind a counter before, and I was forever chastising him for his tendency to casually destroy anything within arm's reach.

"We've got a great big knife machine to cut the bread back there," Fred said. "And the mixers, too. If you're not careful, they could take your arm off."

This was too appealing to resist, and Mac practically collapsed into Fred's arms. Fred lifted him by the ankles like a chicken on the way to slaughter and carried him into the kitchen. The waitress shook her head, then grabbed a mop to clean up the drops of cherry-red lollipop drool that my upside-down son left behind. Mac's squeals of delight filled the room. Another satisfied customer. I think Fred sees it as his responsibility to send his customers out into the world feeling dopey and content, their lips and fingertips glistening with saturated fat, fortified for the cold and prepared to be the best possible nutritional feast for a hungry polar bear.

WALKING AROUND OUTSIDE in Churchill took a little getting used to. A number of people told me that if I was ever about to have an encounter with a polar bear, I would be forewarned by a distinctive tingling along the length of my spine. But I had been feeling that tingle since the minute I landed, and it reappeared every single time I tied my boots and stepped outside. Either my every move was being followed, or my bear detector was seriously on the fritz.

The problem was that I didn't know exactly how scared I ought to be. The edge of town—and our house was right on that edge—was forested with signs suggesting that you'd be an idiot to go one step farther. I knew that *I* could obey the signs, but it seemed unlikely that a bear would be so respectful of posted warnings. On the other hand, one of our neighbors had what appeared to be several dozen young children who played out in the street unsupervised at all hours of the day.

"Do you ever worry about running into polar bears on the street?" I asked one of the local park rangers.

"Never," he replied, in a heavy Quebecois accent. "Polar bears like to eat seals and I am not a seal. Besides, if he really wants to get me, then he'll get me, whether I worry about him or not." This was probably a sound philosophy for life, but not exactly the reassurance I had been hoping for when it came to the responsibilities of parenting.

"Do you ever worry about polar bears?" I asked a young mother I ran into at the playground.

"Constantly," she said. "These little kids look just like seals in their snowsuits. I wouldn't walk anywhere in the winter, especially after dark."

"Do you ever worry about polar bears?" I asked an old Native man who could be found standing on his porch smoking at any hour and under any weather conditions.

He laughed and waved his hand in the air dismissively. "I don't worry about them at all." Now this was what I wanted to hear, a little Cree wisdom about the mutual respect between species. "I don't need to worry," he said, "because I've got a great big gun." I followed his gaze to the ancient shotgun resting against the door frame. The thought of using it to blow a bear's brains out delighted him, and he went from chuckling to making little *pow-pow* sounds like a kid with a new set of plastic army men.

One morning, Shona informed me she had spoken with a neighbor who had wanted to know whether we'd seen the polar bear in our yard the previous night. Mac's eyes widened at the news. Apparently, the bear had nosed his way through the front yard near 7:00, which would make it approximately ten minutes after we'd all walked home from dinner at a restaurant. "I couldn't tell if he was pulling my leg or not," Shona said. Because there wasn't any snow on the ground yet, we couldn't very well look for paw prints. "Maybe that's just something they tell new people to freak them out."

"Nope," Mac said with authority. "I knew he was there. I saw him. I mean, I heard him." I'd been promising Mac a bear sighting ever since we'd made the decision to come to Churchill, and he was ready for me to make good on my pledge. Percy, on the other hand, couldn't be bothered to look up from her crayons even if a dozen polar bears marched through our kitchen in formation.

Whether the neighbor was having fun with us was beside the point. The important thing was that there *could* have been a polar bear in our yard, that there probably had been one there at some point in the past, and that there doubtless would be one again in the future. One sure thing was that *we* had been in our yard last night, and that our chances of running across a hungry polar bear were substantially higher than they had been back home in Oakland.

DESPITE THE MANIFEST DANGERS, I decided that we, as a family, needed to quit being such a bunch of sniveling weenies. It's not every day that you get to be in Churchill, and we couldn't waste our trip bunkered inside our apartment like it was some kind of Arctic Alamo. Besides, didn't all of the people who stayed inside the Alamo die, anyway?

We'd make a foray to Ladoon's Castle, which lay just beyond the Polar Bear Alert signs, on the hillside that separated us from Hudson Bay. This Ladoon was Brian Ladoon again, the slightly shifty-seeming dog breeder and polar bear wrangler I'd met with Marc Cool and the miners. And his castle was a stunning—if uncompleted—testament both to his creativity and to what some people in town thought of as his mild insanity. His plan, as I understood it, was to build a castle on the hill for eventual use as a hotel and tourist mecca. It would be two stories tall, with thick walls and bay windows affording spectacular views of the water. And it would be built using nothing but local materials, which in this particular location meant nothing beyond irregularly shaped chunks of rock.

Ladoon hired a Scottish stonemason to teach him the semi-lost art of Celtic Random Rubble Piling, and then did the rest of the work himself, hand-carrying every last bit of rock. The stones around the base were joined together with perfect precision, each one placed in a spot that made the best possible use of its natural contours. Say what you will about Brian's mental status (and people certainly do), but his artistry and skill are undeniable. The place was as sturdy and impressive as a medieval fortress, and it was clear that Brian had poured thousands of hours into coaxing his castle up from the earth.

Yet he never even completed the first story, much less the entire hotel. No fan of authority, Brian hadn't bothered to get any permits or permission from the local government before he started to build. In fact, the land wasn't even his; he just figured that since nobody was using it, he might as well put it to good use. What's odd isn't that he did all that building without permission—renegade squatting is de rigueur in these parts—but that the various city bigwigs let him work for as long as they did. It's not like Churchill is an ungovernable metropolis, and the castle isn't exactly hidden away in the shadows. I would venture to guess that most people in town must have seen Brian at work on most days. And yet somehow they let him build many hundreds of linear feet of rock walls before it dawned on them that maybe he ought to be stopped. Brian might be on the razor-edge of propriety, but what can you say about a town council that would prefer a ruined castle and its pissed-off builder to the greatest man-made tourist attraction in the Arctic? Instead, what they got was a sprawling construction footprint, piles of abandoned stones, and hundreds of sun-bleached milk crates, which Brian had used to carry rocks from one end of his folly to the other. A few million more hours of labor—and possibly a valid building permit—and Ladoon might really have had something to be proud of.

"Hold my hand tight so you don't get eaten," I said to Percy, who somehow looked both stricken with fear and also utterly bored by the entire enterprise. With her gap teeth and long blonde hair held in place by haphazard barrette work, she looked up at me uncomprehendingly through tasteful, understated pink Barbie eyeglasses. She couldn't understand why somebody would want to go explore a bear-infested castle when you could be ensconced in a nest of sleeping bags with an Amelia Bedelia book and a box of Cheddar Goldfish.

Mac, on the other hand, has always resented the fact that he is forced to sleep on sheets and pillows rather than pine needles and animal hides. "Could we really get eaten?" he asked eagerly.

"Oh, absolutely," I said, not wanting to disappoint. "Do you know where your kidneys are? Bears like that part the best." I patted him in the appropriate spot, and he weighed the potential excitement of a bear attack against the value of an organ he'd only just learned he possessed.

We picked our way over the rocks as slate-gray clouds spat out flecks of stinging snow. It hadn't seemed all that cold to begin with, but at 10°F, the air cut through my clothing like a knife. I'd been trying to go as long as I could without wearing my heavy North Face parka; I thought it made me look like a bumbling tourist and I was willing to endure any misery in order to keep people from thinking that I looked like the sort of person that I actually was.

"Fucking wind," Shona said, wrapping a third scarf around her face. When you are born in the Yukon you have enough credibility—not to mention intelligence—to dress however the hell you want without worrying about what somebody else might think. We should all be so self-possessed.

Brian's castle was impressive by any measure, and it would have made a fabulous place to watch bears from. Somebody told me that Brian had once suggested that the town build a metal rack from which they could hang seal carcasses. Tourists would be able to have a cup of coffee and a stack of pancakes while watching polar bears destroy the frozen meat. The drawbacks of such a plan are almost too numerous to mention, but let it never be said that Brian Ladoon has an insufficient understanding of what tourists want. It must have been hard for him to abandon his dream of the best bear-watching hotel on earth. Sometimes late at night I would look out the window toward the castle and see the glow of running lights and the outline of a truck idling at the castle base.

I climbed on top of the highest wall, dragging Mac after me. He clung to my leg for balance and we looked out at the sea in one direction, then back toward our house in the other. I couldn't see any bears, but in a place like this, height doesn't convey any particular advantage. Polar bears look like snow, obviously, but they can also look like rocks or hide in bushes that would be barely big enough to camouflage a full-grown man. Bears could be anywhere.

"Is your spine tingling?" I asked Mac.

"What's my spine?"

"It's the bone in your back."

"My spine's OK," he said. "But my nose is cold."

I stepped down off the wall and scooped up little Zeke, who was eating pebbles. His coat was misbuttoned, his hat was askew, and his scarf was tied in a fashion that was more noose-like than warmth-giving. A two-year-old California boy has difficulty understanding the direct relationship between how he dresses and how comfortable he will be. I'm quite sure that he would have happily frozen to death rather than submit willingly to having a down coat put on him. He always fought valiantly as we headed out the door, but I outweighed him by a solid 150 pounds, so I usually won.

Holding Percy's hand tightly, Shona looked as nervous as I felt. "Should we really be up here?" she asked, nodding at the Polar Bear Alert signs.

"We'll probably be fine," I said. "I saw some kids playing around here yesterday." It occurred to me that all of the bear warnings were as much about the Churchill brand as about any actual danger. The unofficial town motto could be Scare Them and They Will Come.

"We'd feel pretty stupid if we got eaten by a bear, though," Shona said. True enough. As if to agree with his mother, Zeke squirmed and whimpered, bait-like in my arms. In the end we decided that Mac and I would stay and explore, just for a few minutes, and Shona and the others would go back. In my quick and stupid calculus of risk, I figured that I could grab Mac and run with him, but that Shona and the others would have more trouble. Besides, this was a four-year-old boy we were talking about, with a long-standing interest in construction projects, rocks, and ruination in general. Showing him a crumbling castle might be worth a minor mauling.

After Shona and the other two kids left, Mac rambled without fear while I peered around corners and tried to keep him close. It was easy to imagine a sleeping bear nestled down in a roofless bedroom or prowling around possessively like an impotent emperor surveying the trappings of a nobility that had long since eroded.

"We should go, Mac," I said. "It's not really safe here."

He considered my statement for a minute. Even back home I was constantly telling him that he was on the verge of killing himself, and he'd long since decided to be selective in regard to the advice he was willing to take. "It's not really a person place anymore," he responded at last, giving a respectful nod to my paranoia. "It's kind of like he built a castle and gave it to the polars. And polars don't need roofs."

I wished I could share Mac's calm, but I was glad to be going. I lifted him over the last wall and watched as he trundled off, zigzagging out of his way in order to smash the ice on top of every puddle. "Heeeere polars," he sang as he ran. "Come on out big bad beary-bears. . . . You can have my little broooother."

CHAPTER 18

Never Look a
Polar Bear in the Eye

Get indoors and stay there.
Children should be driven to and from all locations.
Running is not a good solution. It may invite pursuit.
A bear rearing on its hind legs is not always aggressive.
As a last resort, play dead. . . . It takes courage to lie
still, but resistance would be useless.

—FROM "POLAR BEARS IN TOWN: WHAT TO DO?"
A PUBLIC SERVICE POSTER ON LIVING IN POLAR BEAR COUNTRY

MAC FROZE AS THE POLAR BEAR LUNGED for his throat. Small and compact, the bear was moving so quickly that Mac didn't even have time to throw up his hands in self-defense. With a low, guttural moan of aggression, the bear was upon him. Mac fell to the ground, squirming to break free and kicking at the air. Again and again the bear attacked, its paws swiping at my son's fragile ribcage.

From ten feet away, I watched the horrible scene unfold. Then I cracked another pistachio nut and licked the salt from my fingers. Mac giggled uncontrollably.

"Do you know why that polar bear attacked you?" asked Max Burke, another four-year-old boy who had become Mac's partner in crime approximately three seconds after they had first been introduced. He held aloft the three-inch plastic bear figurine that had been pressed, vampire-like, to Mac's jugular just a few seconds earlier.

"Why did he?" Mac asked.

"Because you looked him in the eye. Never look a polar bear in the eye." Max Burke was the son of Kevin Burke, the park ranger who had worked with Rocky out at Nestor Two. Kevin was also the senior driver for one of the buggy companies, and during tourist season he pinballed around town, leading helicopter tours, escorting bear-crazed dignitaries on sightseeing trips, and helping film crews get in position for the perfect shot. Although it goes without saying that all boys possess an encyclo-pedic familiarity with vicious wild animals, there wasn't a four-year-old on earth who came by his knowledge more honestly than Max Burke. He wagged his finger at Mac and proceeded with the lesson plan. "If there's one thing you need to know, it's that you should never, ever look a polar bear in the eye."

"What do I do, then?" asked Mac, his eyes wide as he soaked up valu-able knowledge.

Max Burke nodded gravely at his new pupil. "You put your head down and you walk away slowly and then you get in a car and then you drive away down the road going the speed limit."

"Oh, OK," said Mac, squirreling the information away into the por-tion of the immature male brain reserved for large carnivores, space travel, and catapults. "We don't have a car but my dad said he's going to get me a quad."

"That's cool. My dad drives a snowmobile. And he has a gun."

"That's cool, too."

AFTER A FEW WEEKS IN CHURCHILL we had learned the basic self-defense tips for survival in bear country. No sudden movements, don't run away, don't act like you're challenging him. Pay attention to the tingling in your spine. We'd learned that when bears were around, private property rules no longer applied; people left their houses and cars unlocked, and if you were feeling threatened it was perfectly good form to open some stranger's door and duck inside.

What we had not done, however, was show the kids an actual polar bear. Although I had seen plenty of bears on my various day trips out to the tundra, Mac was becoming increasingly dubious. What category of monster did they belong to, he wondered? Were polar bears real but nonexistent, like dinosaurs? Or were they unreal *and* nonexistent, more like dragons and the tooth fairy? I kept promising that he'd get his bear, but he would have to be patient, which was not his strong suit. "Did you see any polars today?" he would ask whenever I came back to the house after a day out. And I always felt bad if I had.

One day, he greeted me at the front door, stripped to the waist in the tropical heat of our apartment. "We saw one today!" he crowed. "I mean, I saw it. Mom didn't. I saw a face behind a rock. And it wasn't a dog face because it was bigger and whiter and had a different nose than a dog face. It went behind a rock and lay down and we couldn't see it, but I'm going to count it anyway. It was a bear, right?"

"Sure it was," I said. "Good for you." I couldn't blame the kid for ginning up an imaginary bear encounter after I'd been unable to engineer a real one. A lot of adults would do the same thing if a trip to Churchill left them empty-handed.

Truth be told, I was getting a little antsy to see a bear inside the city limits myself. I mean, I thought this town was supposed to be overrun with bears. Weren't they supposed to be as commonplace as pigeons?

There had been a bear attack a few days before my arrival, when a worker was painting the exterior of a research facility outside of town. I'd been there a few times, and in my experience the place had never failed to smell of bacon, which seems like a fairly strong risk factor to me. A mother bear with cubs in tow had crested the rise at the edge of the building and been surprised by the man she found there. She took a swipe at his face, cutting him badly. Another hit sliced open his shoulder. Things might have been worse had the cub not made a noise. When the mother bear turned to see what was wrong with her baby, the man staggered inside. The wounds were serious but survivable; the psychological trauma was far worse. I tried to talk to the victim, but it was clear that he was uninterested in being used as material for anybody's bear-attack stories. Maybe in a few years he could spin a good pub tale out of the incident, but for the moment he just wanted to be left alone.

But within the city limits, this whole terror-dome aspect of Churchill had been proving rather lame. Not only had I failed to see even one halfway decent mauling, but I hadn't even been able to show my eager warrior/caveman son so much as a single tuft of tail disappearing behind a rock. Where was the danger? Where was the adventure that I'd promised everyone before we set out on this trip? Mac liked Churchill's Complex well enough; the indoor playground had a giant wooden polar bear with a slide that dropped out of its mouth, but it was no substitute for the real thing. And where, oh where, was this goddamned embattled frontier that I was supposed to be reporting from? The tourists all scuttled about casting worried glances over their shoulders like nervous suburbanites who'd taken a wrong turn into a bad neighborhood. But the locals seemed unconcerned.

Churchill seemed like a conventionally quirky Northern town, where you were more likely to be accosted by an overly friendly drunk than by a mean-ass bear. Could it really be true that the riskiest part of my trip had been the bus ride to the Oakland airport? These townsfolk had it all figured out. Danger sells. Nobody would pay to go bungee jumping off a four-foot bridge, or to swim with goldfish in the wild. And nobody would come to the Polar Bear Capital of the World if they knew that the bears were as docile as puppy dogs and as rare (in town) as snowstorms on a sunny day.

As it happened, the first time I saw a bear in town, Mac was nowhere around. He'd gone over to Max Burke's house to join him in his favorite indoor activity, which was watching old Johnny Cash concert videos on DVD. At the Burkes, there was a beautifully preserved polar bear skin hanging from a banister above the television. Mac could often be found standing underneath it, staring up wistfully. "Bang bang," I heard him say under his breath one time. "I looked him in the eyes but then I shot him and now he's a rug."

While Shona and the big kids were eating Kraft Mac & Cheese and doing a "Man in Black" sing-along, little Zeke and I were getting ready for a trip to the grocery store. After a prolonged battle, I wrangled his squirming body into winter clothes and down the front stairs. There's something faintly ridiculous about pushing a collapsible stroller on ice-crusted roads in a sleet storm, but the grocery store was far away, and I didn't want to have to carry the little guy if he pulled one of those non-violent sit-down strikes that two-year-olds are famous for.

By early November, the snow had finally arrived with a vengeance, blanketing the town with successive waves of white. Front loaders worked all day, building twenty-foot-tall mounds that quickly iced over and froze solid. The local kids made sleds out of pieces of plastic and hurtled down the gravel-studded slopes and out into the middle of the street. Bloody noses were the must-have fashion accessories of the fall season. The snow fell daily, and almost every night as well; lethal icicles hung off our house, some five feet long and thick as my leg. Going outside meant full-fledged battle against the wind, and on walks into town, my scraggly little starter beard acquired the kind of spiky hoarfrost that means you've really been out there working like an Arctic superstud. Or at least pushing a stroller with a balky back wheel.

Without school, friends, jobs, or responsibilities of any kind, going to Churchill's only grocery store, called the Northern, had become a focus of our lives. At home we are your typically insufferable Bay Area food snobs, plying our children with low-sodium sprouted barley wheat toast and cruelty-free probiotic yogurts. But in Churchill, where if you try to "eat local" you will be limiting yourself to a diet of caribou, caribou, and more caribou, all bets were off. Although at first they may have thought we were up to some sort of bait-and-switch, the kids adjusted remarkably quickly to eating frozen pizzas every second night, with Chex Mix and Fudgee-O's to keep up their strength during the day. The best we could do was count Ragu tomato sauce with garlic as two servings of vegetables.

You can buy candy bars at the Northern, but you can buy bed sheets, lawn furniture, self-serve nachos, and a flat-screen television there as well.

Just past the video rental counter, there's a full-sized ATV—excuse me, *quad*—parked next to the blue jeans. In a nod to the times, there's even a small health food display to help wayward environmentalists feel at home. Outside of tourist season, I imagine the cigarette counter gets considerably more attention than the organic case.

"Hey, banana boy!" yelled the checker, a middle-aged Native woman. She giggled as Zeke beelined for the fruit bin near the front of the store. I had tried, on many occasions, to explain to him that fruit needs to be weighed and paid for before it is consumed, but he had proven willfully ignorant of the finer points of microeconomics. Usually, we just arrived at the checkout counter with a handful of skins and a guilty shrug.

Today was no different; Zeke inhaled three Costa Rican bananas while I pondered what sort of meal I could make from tortillas, mozzarella cheese, and canned salmon, all of which were on special that day. Prices in Churchill are staggering. A gallon of regular milk runs close to $10, a head of wilted Romaine lettuce is $4.50, and buying meat requires that you assiduously ignore the numbers on the receipt even as you sign the bottom of it.

Everything has to come to Churchill by air or by rail, and because the Northern has no competitors, the population is a captive audience. Over the previous summer, two successive food shipments had been disrupted and the store shelves went bare, forcing people to get creative with powdered milk, pickle slices, and whatever else remained for purchase. Although the much-maligned railroad was blamed for the shortages, more than one conspiracy-minded local suggested that it was all a scheme to punish people for complaining about prices.

We made our way home, a banana-full Zeke babbling happily as I pushed him along roads as slick as skating rinks. Had I been a little more graceful, it could have been like something out of a Gene Kelly movie. As it was, I just fell on my butt a lot. Once we reached the house, Zeke foundered in the snowbank outside the front door while I wrestled with the folding stroller. "Dog!" he yelled. "Dog, dog, dog!" The poor puppy across the street had become increasingly unhappy as the temperature dropped; he spent most of his time looking miserable and testing the limits of his chain. "Big dog," Zeke babbled on. "Bark woof." I looked toward the spot where Zeke was pointing with two outstretched hands. "It *my* dog," he said, toddling into the street.

What I saw on the low rise across the street from our house was not Zeke's dog. In fact, it wasn't a dog at all. Instead, a polar bear sauntered from right to left, sniffing its way along the hillside toward Ladoon's Castle. From where we stood, it looked to be a small bear, not particularly skinny or desperate, but a polar bear nonetheless. Its fur was dirty and bedraggled, and it moved with a heavy, plodding purposelessness.

The neighbor's dog slept soundly on top of its chain; so much for my early warning system. The bear was a good two hundred yards away and showing complete disinterest in us. I felt oddly unthreatened, though not nearly as blasé as Zeke, who was bobbling across the street and directly toward the animal. Still, it seemed prudent to get some walls between the bear and us as quickly as possible. I grabbed Zeke and tossed him inside, abandoning our stroller with its tempting cache of fragrant groceries, which were now reduced to chum for any wild animals that cared to claim them. *Damn,* I thought as I double-locked the door behind us. *I paid $19 for that stew meat.*

Zeke piled a stack of books by the window and climbed up on them. We stood over the heat grate, dry air blasting into our faces as we watched the bear pick its way through the rocks. It lifted its nose and sniffed the wind, then changed course and headed directly for us.

"Here dog!" Zeke yelled.

"It's not a dog," I said.

"Doggy doggy dog dog."

"It's not a dog."

"Monkey?" he said, his forehead wrinkling with concern.

I had to admit that I was inordinately excited by the prospect of seeing a polar bear rip apart $100 worth of fresh groceries. It wouldn't be as good as a mauling, clearly, but to have a front-row seat at a feeding frenzy would still be pretty good.

But such a demonstration of carnivory was not to be. It hadn't even occurred to me to dial the number for Polar Bear Alert, but apparently I wasn't the only one with an eye on the situation. Somebody else must have called 675-BEAR, because before the bear made any significant progress toward our dinner, a Manitoba Conservation truck rolled by. Soon the sound of cracker shells peppered the midmorning quiet, just three little pops, widely spaced. With a resigned and weary swing of his head, the bear turned away from us and reverted to his original course, northward along the edge of the bay. The bear knew the drill; he had probably been harried like this a dozen times already, and he didn't want a fight. Soon he was gone from view, blending into the snow and the rocks and the distance.

"Bye-bye dog," Zeke waved, shooting me a nervous look. "Bye-bye *monkey*," he corrected himself.

All things considered, it wasn't what I had been expecting from a bear encounter. No blood, no panic, no life flashing before my eyes. Instead it had been just a minor annoyance, like when you cross the street to avoid a thuggish character coming toward you. The worst part of the whole experience was Mac's heartbreak upon hearing that his little brother had seen a bear and he hadn't. "That's so not fair," Mac said, his typical stoicism turning to a pout at this most egregious of injustices. "He probably didn't even know what it was."

"He knew," I lied. "He thought it was very special. And I'll try really hard to show you a bear."

"Promise?"

"Promise."

"Good," he said. "Because showing me a polar bear is the whole reason you came to Churchill."

How I planned to make good on my promise was not quite so clear. I considered taking Mac and Percy on a Tundra Buggy ride, but at $400 per person per day, it was out of the question. I didn't know whether my kids, at their age, even had the capacity to develop lasting memories, and

I certainly wasn't about to drop that kind of cash unless I could be assured of their lifelong adoration.

In the end I did what all good middle-aged dads do when the chips are down and a vacation is on the line. I rented a minivan. We'd stick to the back roads, explore abandoned military buildings, and rumble along the rocks down by the coast in hopes of surprising a bear in its natural habitat. We stuffed the kids into their coats and piled them into the van. The novelty of getting to ride without car seats was at least as exciting as the chasing of bears, and Mac and Percy kept pointing out that they could move from seat to seat inside the van *while we were moving*.

"If the van crashed while we aren't wearing seatbelts, would we be thrown out of the window and into the snow on our heads?" Mac asked.

"Probably," I said.

"That's cool."

Until a few years ago, the easiest place on earth to see bears was at the Churchill town dump. In all their wisdom, the town bureaucrats had opted for an open-pit dump, overflowing into the tundra with food scraps, dirty diapers, and other delectables. Imagine your own local dump, but replace the pigeons with polar bears, and you'll have some idea of what the place looked like. Scientists liked the place, too; they'd catch bears at the dump and spray paint foot-tall identification numbers right onto their backs. Photographs from that period—and there are thousands of these—show grubby, tagged bears standing atop mountains of garbage. Sometimes, spontaneous garbage fires would erupt and bears would singe themselves or emerge from the pile blackened with soot. It's almost impossible to imagine a scene less worthy of a *National Geographic* cover shoot.

Even worse, at the dump, bears acquired a taste for garbage and a familiarity with people. How were the bears to know that eating trash at the dump was all good fun, but that doing the same thing on Kelsey Boulevard would earn them a flurry of shotgun pellets in the face? So in 2004, the town moved the dump indoors, to an abandoned military building known as L5. But, hot on the trail of chicken bones and Cheetos wrappers, the bears broke in time and again. An arms race ensued, with the Public Works Department constructing ever-hardier armaments to fortify the building. The bears just got craftier. One time, a bear snuck through the gate and got locked *inside*, unbeknownst to sanitation workers, who brought the ecstatic animal tons of fresh garbage to pick through every day.

But L5 had the disadvantage of being finite. By 2008, garbage was spilling out of the sides. When Linda Gormezano and Quinoa did their scat work near the dump, they found undigested string, Styrofoam, aluminum foil—and all manner of other junk that looked none the worse for its journey through a digestive tract. On an earlier dump visit, I surprised a bear who was rooting around in a smashed refrigerator lying on the ground outside the building. He seemed baffled by how something that smelled so delicious could be so devoid of anything good to eat.

Today, unfortunately, the dump was bear free. If only we could have been here in the halcyon days of free garbage and semi-domesticated scavenger bears. We sat in the idling van for a few minutes, hoping for something delightful to appear. Mac tried valiantly to hide his growing disappointment.

"It's OK, Macky," Percy said. "Do you want to have a page of my coloring book?"

"No. I wanna see a polar."

Percy handed him a page anyway, one that she was willing to part with because it was already completely filled out. "Do you see what a good job I did staying between the lines?" she asked.

Mac noted her achievement, but he remained disappointed. Zeke fiddled with a stuffed polar bear on his lap and babbled away cheerily. "Monkey, monkey, monkey."

"It's not a monkey," Mac snapped, in a rare show of ill humor, then pressed his forehead against the rear window as I fired up the van and drove back to our apartment.

CHAPTER 19

Dial 675-BEAR

One bear attack will ruin your whole day.

—TOM SMITH, BEAR EXPERT,
BRIGHAM YOUNG UNIVERSITY

YOU KNOW WHAT'S DIFFERENT about this town than about Oakland?" Mac asked me.

"What's that?"

"Here people let their kids go outside and play, and at home you have to have a grown-up with you even if you just go on the front porch." He was right: despite the apparent danger, kids of all ages spent hours rolling around in the streets, smashing toy cars into piles of dirt and swinging on the rusty play set in our back alley.

"How come kids get to go outside here without grown-ups?" Mac repeated.

"I'm not really sure," I said. "Maybe because there aren't as many bad guys here as there are at home."

"Why aren't there?"

"Because it costs too much to get here," I said. "And because bad guys don't like the cold."

Mac chewed on that. He'd considered becoming a bad guy as a career and seemed to think that he would be undeterred by weather. "So can *we* play outside without a grown-up today?" He had the look of someone who knows his request is about to be refused but still can't stop himself from asking. Which, if you think about it, is pretty much the definition of childhood.

"Sure," I said, surprising both of us. "But stay right there where I can see you through the window, and you have to promise to come in the second I say so, no excuses." What the locals had been telling me all along was correct: it's important to have a healthy fear of polar bears, but you can't let it dictate your life. Besides, sending my kids out to play in the snow made me feel more like I belonged in Churchill and less like one of the terrified masses from out of town.

"We'll come right inside if we see any polars," Mac said, pouncing on my moment of weakness. "And I promise never to look them in the eyes."

ALTHOUGH THE STREETS of Churchill currently reflect something less than the gun-fightin' frontier that the marketing geniuses would have you imagine, such a peaceful kingdom was not always the norm. Over the years, the number of bears in town has waxed and waned, more in response to human activity than to anything climatological. In the 1950s, during the heyday of the military presence, polar bears were shot on sight by soldiers looking to relieve the tedium of their Northern posting. But twenty years later, the decline of the military coincided with the global imposition of bear-hunting restrictions, as well as a burgeoning eco-consciousness that made blasting away at every bear in sight uncouth. With the cease-fire, polar bear numbers exploded all over the Arctic.

Between 1966 and 1969, there were three serious maulings in Churchill and one fatal attack. In the 1970s, so-called defense kills, in which bears were shot by townsfolk who felt themselves to be in imminent danger, were logged at a rate of about a dozen a year. On average, the Manitoba Conservation Department killed an additional six bears a year, and everybody was on edge. Bears feasted at the dump and roamed the edges of town, prying into outbuildings, dog sheds, and cabins, and generally causing trouble.

It was against this backdrop of ever-increasing defense kills that the government of Manitoba got serious about protecting Churchill. The result was the Polar Bear Alert program, and three decades later it's the reason I could—reluctantly, and with great misgivings—allow my kids their unsupervised playtime in the front yard.

The basic idea behind the Alert program is simple. You give people a telephone number to call when they see a bear, you beg them not to kill the bear before you get there, and then you have the problem dealt with by professional wildlife officers who are better trained and presumably somewhat more sober than the guy cowering in his house with a shotgun.

"When you call that number, do the guys come like it's an emergency or do they just drive there?" Mac asked one day as we looked at one of the Alert program's ubiquitous street signs. Mac had wanted to go down to the water, but the signs had the unfortunate effect of foreclosing most of the town's best real estate. Apparently, you're taking your life into your own hands if you want to gaze over the ocean at sunset or kick a rock along the railroad tracks down by the river.

"They come like it's an emergency," I said.

"But do they *always* bring guns with them?"

"Yes, they do," I said. "Lots and lots of guns." Upon hearing this, Mac nearly passed out from the excitement. The only thing that could possibly be cooler than polar bears is polar bears being chased by men with guns in trucks. I'd only just confirmed for Mac what he already suspected: Churchill was the most wonderful place on earth.

THE FOLKS AT THE MANITOBA Conservation Department had grudgingly agreed to let me ride along with them and see the Polar Bear Alert program in action. Like everything else involving polar bears, getting permission to sit in the front seat of a pickup truck for a few hours involved months of planning, multiple layers of bureaucracy, and no small amount of obsequious pleading. I had long since given up my pride and grown accustomed to all the genuflecting. If you want to be a tough guy and get right up next to some bears, then you have to be prepared to beg like a little girl.

The Alert office, like many things in Churchill, was housed in a flimsy trailer. This particular trailer was on the edge of town, sandwiched between the Lazy Bear Lodge and the helicopter company. It was a featureless November day, and as I walked to the offices I noticed that not another soul was out on the streets. Snow gusted along the ground in nasty wisps, and mounds of furry white ice rose up out of the gloom. It felt as if the entire population had taken one look out the window and then decided to spend the day sleeping in. If I were making a horror film, I would say it was the perfect kind of day for a bear attack. I tried to put such thoughts out of my mind. Certainly, it would be too cheap and easily ironic for me to get eaten on my way to visit the bear patrol.

The secretary let me inside, and I spent fifteen minutes pretending to be enthralled by a pamphlet on local fishing ordinances. The ranger I was supposed to meet was nowhere to be found, which probably meant that I had just missed a dramatic bear-fighting escapade by two minutes. Either that, or else he was simply late, the way everybody in Churchill is late for everything. There must be some sort of space-time wormhole that envelops the areas nearest to the North Pole because in my experience, people from the Arctic seem constitutionally terrified of punctuality. When nighttime lasts for three months, you can be forgiven for smashing your wristwatch with a hammer.

Just as I had thoroughly exhausted the literary potential of the Manitoba catch-and-release regulations, Shaun Bobier—the head ranger for the district—nudged through the door, stamping snow from his boots.

"Sorry it's such a lousy day," he said.

"No problem," I said. "It's not your fault, is it?"

He smiled nervously, and fumbled with some papers. With his bald head and slightly doughy midsection, he looked less like a bear slayer and more like a certified public accountant. I'd been expecting somebody hairy and immense, a backwoods vigilante type, but Bobier seemed deferential and almost dainty, right down to the Frenchified silent "r" in his last name. Then again, guns have a way of making anyone look bigger. Apparently, he wasn't planning on winning a footrace with the bears or besting them through hand-to-hand combat.

"Are you here for the ride-along?" he asked, not quite meeting my eyes.

"Yes."

"Sorry I'm late. We had to chase a bear off the runway at the airport."

"No problem," I said. "That's your job. I was just catching up on some reading."

He looked at me for a moment without speaking, his nose and cheeks pinking up in the overheated trailer. After a long pause, he wrinkled his brow and said, "You don't speak Japanese do you?"

"Excuse me?"

"Do you speak any Japanese? Or Korean? Was it Korean?" He looked toward the secretary's desk for corroboration.

"Sorry, I don't speak either one," I said.

"That's too bad, we could really use you if you did. We've got this film crew coming in right after you and I can't tell what the heck they're saying." He seemed genuinely disappointed, and I wished that I could help him.

"You don't need to take any pictures, right?" Bobier asked.

"Right."

"So what exactly is it that you'd like to see?"

"Nothing special," I said. "I'd kinda just like to punch a bear in the teeth and maybe shoot off a bunch of your guns. If that's okay."

Bobier looked momentarily stricken, before coming to the conclusion that I couldn't possibly be serious. "You actually have no idea how close you are," he said, letting out a long breath. "People ask me for the craziest things. Why don't you get in the truck and we'll ride around for a bit."

We headed toward the airport, parking at last in front of yet another decommissioned military building that the town had repurposed. Churchill is how the entire world would look if every architect was employed by the US Army. The windowless, corrugated metal dome in front of us looked like a giant piece of culvert pipe split lengthwise and plopped unceremoniously onto the ground. A few Polar Bear Alert signs were tacked up around the grounds, along with some stern warnings to Keep Out!

"So this is the polar bear jail?" I said. I'd heard a lot about it. Nobody was allowed inside, and the Conservation Department officers kept their comings and goings as quiet as you can in a small town.

"You mean the Polar Bear Holding Facility? Yeah, that's it."

The polar bear jail—and really, it can't possibly be known by any other name, bureaucratic doublespeak be damned—is the centerpiece of the Alert program and one of the key components of the Churchill mystique. You'd have to be almost dead inside not to be transfixed by the image of dozens of bears in tiny cells, dreaming of seal blubber and counting the days until their release. It's the final step in anthropomorphizing the hairy beasts: not only can they stand on two legs and care for their young like we do, but when they're bad, they even go to jail. What will Churchillians think of next—dressing them up in bonnets and having them join tourists for lunch at Gypsy's?

Much to my disappointment, I learned that the jail was designed neither for punishment nor rehabilitation. Bears weren't given sentences based on the severity of their crimes against humanity. Instead, problem bears get trapped, occasionally drugged, and then deposited unceremoniously into individual cells. Once inside, the bears are given snow to drink and no food whatsoever, because polar bears don't eat at this time of year, and you wouldn't want incarceration to be a treat. When the ice eventually comes onto the bay, the bears are driven down to the shore and released into the wild, not to be seen again until the following fall. It's more of a purgatory than a prison, a temporary interruption of their ursine criminality. I guess the theory is that no bear is truly bad at heart, but they just get caught in the wrong place at the wrong time.

I rolled down my window to get a better view. Everything was quiet—no rattling of cages or cries for justice from the imprisoned.

"Can I go inside?" I asked.

"No."

"Can I just look in the door?"

"No."

"Can we get a little closer at least?"

"No."

"Why not?"

"Because you can't."

"Can you describe it for me at least?"

"A little," Bobier said, though it was clear he didn't even want to do that. This prison was further off-limits than Guantánamo. Inside the building was a series of cells, Bobier told me, each measuring about fifteen feet to a side. Problem bears are held one to a cell, with moms sharing space with their cubs. In total there are twenty-eight holding pods, with an aisle running down the middle. Bears are usually held for only a few weeks at a time. And because the animals aren't eating anything during their incarceration, cleaning the cells isn't a big problem for the conservation officers.

"How many bears are in there right now?" I asked.

"I dunno, maybe eighteen," Shaun said. How could you not know how many bears you had in jail? They must not have been worried about an escape attempt. All was quiet and still; it was hard to believe that so many polar bears were peacefully coexisting in one giant, unheated room just a hundred feet away.

SHAUN BOBIER WAS FEELING DONE with me. He drummed his fingers on his lap, and at one point he even put his head down on the steering wheel. For him, bear season means lots of 3:00 AM phone calls and early mornings spent driving around in search of ghosts. Here he was, answering my stupid questions while the rest of the town was taking a snow day. There was also the small matter of the upcoming Japanese invasion to deal with. "Sushi," he said. "Sony, Toyota, Toshiba. You think I'm fluent enough to handle them?" he asked me.

"I doubt it," I said. "But if you get them footage of your guys shooting a bear in the ass, they probably won't care at all what you say."

We drove around the deserted streets, peering behind outbuildings and bouncing over the rocks down by the shore. Much to the tittering delight of the tourists, a bear had walked down Kelsey at dinnertime a few nights earlier, but now it was nowhere to be seen. Some bear or other had been systematically going from restaurant to restaurant over the previous week, scavenging in the dumpsters and making a nuisance of himself. We pulled up behind the Northern Nights Lodge, where a metal garbage cage bore the telltale signs of a solid pounding. The bear had broken the latch and eaten the scraps of the previous day's meal. "The willows are so thick around this end of town that it's hard for us to see what's going on," Shaun said. "Even when you fly over with a helicopter, you can't always see the bears." The town would be bulldozing the vegetation soon in order to make the job easier.

Apparently, there were bears everywhere. But of course, now that I was sitting in a truck full of shotguns, the town was as quiet as a graveyard. Where was my adventure? Where was my man-meets-beast moment? I'd come up here to feel their hot, fishy breath sneaking up behind me, and all I got to do was drive around in a truck like a thrill-seeking idiot.

"Sorry about this," Shaun said, suffering from the uniquely Canadian disease of Politeness Overload.

"It's not your fault."

"Closing the dump was the biggest thing," he said, explaining the recent dearth of bears in town. "Our numbers just dropped off a cliff after that."

"That's good," I said.

"Yeah," he said halfheartedly, "but we're all loaded up and ready to go."

As a firefighter, I knew how it felt to eagerly await the next disaster. "You hope you don't have to go out and do it, but it's still fun when you have to, right?" I said.

"Nope, it's pretty much just fun to do it," Shaun said.

TECHNICALLY SPEAKING, the Polar Bear Alert guys don't actually shoot bears, they just shoot *near* them. Churchill's streets are choked with environmentalists and wildlife biologists, so it wouldn't do to have bears with gunshot wounds staggering around. Instead, the rangers use noise-making cracker shells and the occasional rubber bullet. They chase the bears out of town and down to the water. Over the previous few weeks, I'd grown accustomed to the occasional *pop pop pop* of cracker shells in the distance. If I was pushing a stroller when the gunfire erupted, I would take a quick peek over my shoulder and then quicken my pace, like a lineman pushing a blocking sled through the snow. If I was on my own, I would turn around, against all good judgment, and walk toward the shots, hoping to see something interesting. But I almost never got there in time; usually all I could make out was the smoking tailpipe of the Conservation truck and the half-imagined shape of a polar bear retreating into the snow. Before long, I didn't even notice the sound of the shotguns anymore. But Mac did; he would grow still and his eyes would narrow, ever alert to the delightful possibility that he might be called upon for close-quarters combat with a beast forty times his size.

If a bear is smart, he'll keep walking northward once chased out of town by the rangers. If he's young or feisty or particularly ornery, he may have to be trapped and serve out the rest of the fall in jail. Bobier and his guys set out bear traps—nothing more than a length of culvert pipe with a closed end and a piece of rotting seal meat hanging in the back. The bear trips a trigger, the front gate comes down, and the whole thing can be hitched to the back of a truck and taken to jail. No muss, no fuss.

"So you don't kill them very often?" I asked Bobier.

"Try not to sound so disappointed," he said. "That's a good thing, remember?"

Although there's nothing like a good marauding bear to spice up the tourist trade, the Alert folks have become awfully good at what they do. In the ten-year period that ended with the 2007 bear season, the rangers had dealt with 2,219 calls to the bear hotline, and not a single call ended with a fatality to the bear. In fact, the department hadn't had to destroy a bear since 1983.

Bobier and his gang had been so successful that it seemed the only way to have a little adventure around here was to be a borderline moron. As we passed the dump, Shaun pointed out an unremarkable patch of earth. "We had a guy from New York who came up on the train once and pitched a tent out there for a month. We told him that you just don't *do* that, you don't camp around here." But technically there wasn't anything illegal about it, so they let him be. "You can't arrest someone for being stupid," Shaun said, shaking his bald head. "But there's times when I'd sure as heck like to." It's a long-standing frontier sort of thing; times may change and new rules come and go, but as long as there is a shred of wilderness out there it will always be every North American's God-given right to go out into that wilderness and get himself killed in the most ridiculous way imaginable.

We drove a few more laps around town, checking out Ladoon's Castle, the port, the dump, and a few other common points of ursine entry. As we circled, I couldn't help but think about the pointlessness of it all. Here you had a perfectly nice little spit of land that polar bears had happily occupied for thousands of years. Sure, they're bloodthirsty killers and all, but it's not like they tried to expand their territory in search of man-flesh. Then, all of a sudden people showed up, built a town, and—surprise!—the whole damn place was overrun with polar bears. So the people shot the bears until they were almost extinct, at which point they realized that they actually *liked* polar bears and would be sad if they all died. Then people stopped shooting polar bears, but instead of showing gratitude, the damn bears went right back to menacing the very folks who'd just committed to protect them. In their infinite wisdom, the town residents created a bear patrol, because they liked bears, but they just didn't like having them that close. The bear patrol worked great except for the fact that they had an open-pit dump, and too many little children running around just taunting the bears with their squirmy deliciousness. The bears, once the prime local nuisance, then became the town's main source of income. And in one final, towering insult to logic, when the bear population started to crash because of mankind's thirst for fuel, the tourist industry redoubled its efforts to put as many people onto planes as possible so that they could see the dying bears before their own leisure activities destroyed every last one of them. If the town's polar bear plan had an honest marketing slogan, it might be "I Love You, You're Scary, Come Closer, Go Away." It would have been a whole lot simpler if they'd just declined to put a town here in the first place. It's not like the 6 billion people in the non-Arctic parts of the world couldn't absorb 934 Churchillians.

"Come on," Bobier said, eyeing the flickering neon sign of the Seaport Restaurant. There'd been much talk of coffee and home fries all morning, and it was time to make those dreams a reality. He parked the truck outside and grabbed his radio, almost as an afterthought. "There's no bears out here," he said. "This town is dead."

CHAPTER 20

Nice Day
for a Drive

*All these people run these businesses from somewhere
out of town. They're from the fucking United States and
Japan. I can't even afford to spell out the word "Japan"
in those wooden block letters that they make for kids.*

—BRIAN LADOON, CHURCHILL DOG BREEDER
AND POLAR BEAR EXPERT

I F CHURCHILL RESEMBLES a polar bear theme park, then the
Tundra Buggy is the gondola ride that connects the distant corners
of the magical kingdom. A trip to Churchill without a ride on one
of the buggies would be like going to Yellowstone and skipping Old
Faithful. Two companies—Great White Bear and Frontiers North—have
cornered the buggy market, and between them they take nearly 10,000
people out for a ride every year.

When you want to see a grizzly bear, you can get yourself a sturdy
pair of boots and a plane ticket to Montana, and the rest will be easy. If
a crocodile is your beast of choice, a rented canoe and a few hours in the
Everglades is what it takes to get your itch scratched by a row of razor-
sharp teeth. But if you want to see a lot of polar bears, your tough-guy
capabilities are irrelevant; the main requirement is that you be willing
to be treated like a third-grader for the duration of your journey.

Polar bears have three things going for them: they're dangerous, they live in a really unpleasant place, and they enjoy the full protection of any number of national and international treaties and regulations. So even though you might get lucky and see a bear in town, if your goal is to see as many bears in as little time as possible, you're going to have to head out into "Buggyland," the flat, rocky wilderness outside of town. But you can't just strap on some snowshoes and go out there yourself. Access is strictly limited by the Manitoba provincial government, so there's no choice but to pick one of the two companies and let it rummage around in your wallet.

Because I'd long since decided that this entire polar bear experience was about me and me alone, I of course opted for the longer, more exhaustively expensive tour package. It would involve two full days on the buggy, a dogsled ride, a helicopter tour, innumerable lectures, tundra walks, and a guided tour of Churchill, during which we'd probably all be expected to pick buddies and hold hands while crossing the street. I'd always avoided group travel of this sort, because being herded around with a bunch of self-righteous, middle-aged yuppies was my idea of hell. Never mind that I fit that description pretty well myself; there's nothing hypocritical about loathing one's own peers.

But unfortunately, if you want to see a polar bear, then you *will* ride on a yellow school bus; you *will* sit through science lectures and raise your hand to be called on; you *will* be encouraged to mingle at mealtimes; and you *will* drink innumerable cups of powdered hot cocoa topped with stale mini-marshmallows. Call it what you like: the "Polar Bear Adventure of a Lifetime" or "Lords of the Arctic Learning Experience" or "Bear Safari Photo Extravaganza." What you're really buying is a package vacation complete with food, lodging, out-and-back airfare, professional guide services, and probably some sort of promotional T-shirt/coffee mug/earmuff freebie gift to take home with you. The infantilization and the claustrophobia are gratis.

And so, luggage at my feet and Arctic parka across my lap, I sat in the lobby of the Tundra Hotel, waiting for the shuttle van that would

begin my immersion program in group travel and polar bearology. The
motel's owner had just arrived for the day with her dogs in tow and a
shotgun slung over her back. Apparently, she never went anywhere without it, which was good protection and also great PR for the assembled
guests, who had gathered in the main room for coffee and toast. They
might not rave about the quality of the mattresses, but they'd certainly
tell everyone they knew about the desk clerk who was packing heat.

An elderly man in oil-stained pants and a non-ironic trucker's cap
stepped in front of me and clicked his coffee cup against mine with such
vigor that you would have thought we were toasting the end of a major
war. He had a weather-beaten face, a drinker's nose, and eyeglasses that
were so scratched that he had to bob like a Parkinson's patient to keep
his eyes on me. He and the three women with him—whom he declined
to introduce—lived on a farm in Saskatchewan and had spent thirty
hours on the train in seats that defied all their efforts to make them re-
cline. Churchill seemed like an odd vacation choice for a man who already spent his life eking out a living on the rocky Canadian prairie. I
don't think anybody would have blamed him had he opted to go to Or-
lando instead.

"That's true," he said, when I mentioned that he might think about
trying someplace sunnier. "But I've always been real into the nature." I
liked the way he said that, as if "the nature" was a discrete attraction for
which you might gain entrance with a string of carnival tickets. And with
the Tundra Buggies, that's about how it was.

"Besides," he continued. "I've always wanted to see the bears, and
the way things are going I might not get another chance. How many did
we see yesterday, honey?" He looked back over his shoulder at the
women. Two of them started to speak at once; obviously, there was
some confusion as to who was his rightful honey. After a brief stare-
down, the older woman persevered.

"We saw twenty-nine yesterday," she said. "Well, twenty-nine confirmed, at least. We saw thirty-eight total, but I can't say if we saw the
same ones on the way out as on the way back in."

"Aw, heck," the man said, scowling. "I thought we might see one or two, but there's so many I don't even know why she bothers to keep track. You know what, though," he said, surveying the small lobby, "this is a great little town, even if it wasn't for the bears. You ever been this far up north before?"

I told him that my wife was from the Yukon, and his eyes narrowed a little.

"Is she white or Native?" he asked.

"White," I said, and he relaxed visibly.

"I thought this whole town was going to be Native, but it turns out it's really nice. They actually don't have hardly anything run by Natives at all. The restaurants and the stores are white owned. Even the guy sweeping the ice rink was white," he said with approval. Attempting to be agreeable, I smiled and nodded as if to say that I, too, had long suffered under the oppressive yoke of a First Nations Zamboni driver. These particular folks wouldn't be coming along on my trip, but with growing dread I realized that there were many hours of awkward chatter like this in my near future. There are a lot things that I don't do well, but chief among them is hiding the irritation I feel at the extravagant inanity of strangers. Polar bears or no polar bears, it was going to be a long week.

Before he could deepen what he assumed to be our bond of shared racism, the farmer was interrupted when a truck with the logo of the Churchill Northern Studies Center pulled up outside. This was the outfit that I would be touring with, and the driver hustled through the front door of the motel, clipboard in hand and pen between her teeth. She eyeballed me and I introduced myself.

"Unger. Check," she said by way of greeting, shaking my hand after she ticked my name off a piece of paper. She was a remarkable-looking person, not so much heavyset as completely round, an optical illusion owing to pronounced shortness overlaid on a stevedore's stocky physique. Never before had I been physically intimated by a woman who stood at eye level with my bottommost rib.

Ridiculously underdressed for the weather in a light windbreaker and thin toque, she had an all-business air about her, something one rarely encounters in Churchill. "I'm Leann. I'm a scientist," she said. "But sometimes I drive, too."

"Nice to meet you," I said. "Oh please . . . don't, I can get that myself." As I was getting myself scarfed, hatted, and mittened, she shouldered my duffel bag and loaded it into the truck. I'm not exactly infirm, but the dynamic was clear: she was the guide and I was the client. The fact that I was there meant that I must have money to burn, which, almost by definition, made me next to useless at all practical tasks.

As she backed the vehicle away from the building, I asked a long, digressive question about the quality of life in the North, a real stem-winder designed to elicit maximum philosophical rumblings. She looked over at me and smiled humorlessly.

"We're here," she said, pulling into the parking lot at Gypsy's, which was almost directly across the street from where she'd picked me up. "This is where you get off."

"I'm sorry," I said. "You didn't have to come pick me up. If I'd known where we were going I would have just walked."

"We're in charge of your safety now. We want to make sure that everybody gets where they're going alive." She pulled up next to an idling school bus, placing the passenger door of her truck directly in line with the bottom step so that I didn't even have to touch ground as I transferred between vehicles. I felt like a high-value dignitary under Secret Service protection. The farmer from the motel lobby strolled past as I boarded; he must have followed us out the door while Leann was loading my bags. "Good to see you again," he said. "Nice day for a drive."

"Nice day indeed," I replied, stepping carefully from one armored vehicle to the next. "Be careful out there. Bears everywhere." I figured it was better not to fight what was happening to me. Despite the fact that I'd walked this way on my own dozens of times without serious incident, for the next week I'd give up all pretense of independence and slip into the warm, fetid waters of group travel.

I WAS THE LAST PASSENGER TO ARRIVE, and the bus driver revved the engine as soon as I was seated. I was a good twenty years younger than the rest of the adventurers, and I took my seat in front of a large woman who was hacking up bits of lung into a tissue that she folded into ever smaller squares. Bags of luggage were piled in the aisles, and the men did their best to squeeze into the child-sized spaces provided. Most of the voices around me were European, and one bald, vulpine Brit knelt on a seat in watchful anticipation. He was bristling with camera gear, long lenses slung across his chest like guerrilla bandoliers. Satchels of photographic whatnot teetered on the seat next to him. As we rolled through town, his trigger finger clicked epileptically, the camera emitting staccato fake shutter-snaps. It was hard to imagine what it was that he was capturing—a coffee shop, some abandoned military buildings, the rusted minivan-cum-taxi puttering along in front of us.

"You getting any good ones?" I asked.

"Nah. Complete rubbish," he said, clicking away without pause. It was just exuberance probably, the excitement of being up north, of finally being close to the holy grail of the polar bear.

He let his camera dangle on its strap momentarily and then said soberly, to no one in particular. "I'm worried that we haven't got enough gin."

A chorus of giggles erupted from the middle-aged women sitting around him. "We'd better have," one shouted. "Or else how will we have the courage to face all of those bears?"

"There's one now—a big one!" screeched the bald guy, and everyone hurled themselves to his side of the bus, cupping their hands around their eyes.

"Gotcha," he said, and everyone groaned. Is it possible that every single tourist to Churchill has played this same trick? The mere possibility of a bear is apparently too much to endure in silence, transforming well-heeled travelers into giddy pranksters. Like I said, it was going to be a long week.

The bus wheeled out of town, and people rubbed at the frosty windows with their forearms and tittered with excitement at the views. My new companions were literally bouncing off the walls, switching seats and poking each other in the ribs, acting for all the world like third-graders who'd been spared a day of social studies in favor of a field trip to the best zoo on earth. From England and South Africa and Japan, after months of planning and endless hours in stuffy airplane cabins, these people had finally arrived. At long last they were *here*. The primal rush of being this close to bears was overwhelming, thrilling them with the knowledge that there were deadly animals around every bend and that despite all of our protections—our steel cages and shotguns, our big brains and opposable thumbs—in the true natural order of the world, we're still no better than human jerky, just two-legged snacks for the all-powerful bears.

Conversation ebbed as we rumbled out of town, the rhythmic *thwack-thwack* of the school bus tires lulling me into a stupor that was occasionally broken by the agonal respirations of the pneumonia patient alongside me. Everyone sat transfixed by the view of Hudson Bay. The gray sky funneled downward toward the grayer water, the two meeting in a hazy line like a charcoal sketch, some indeterminate number of miles offshore. It felt like we were on the edge of a vast and cruel-hearted ocean, the kind that routinely swallows luckless mariners.

We rolled past a forest of communications towers, each one anchored to the ground with multiple guy wires, thick ropes of cable to keep the towers earthbound in the relentless winds. Occasional scrap heaps dotted the shoreline, twisted nests of metal and rusted steel drums at the ends of stubby spur roads. Helicopters shimmered in the sky, some banking in tight circles for sightseeing tours, some heading out of town in straight lines, on errands either scientific or commercial. The area resembled a war zone, but one in which the battle has long since been lost.

"Bears!"

Somebody with better eyes than mine spotted a pair of bears, and the bus driver let us coast to a stop in middle of the highway. Everyone crowded to one side as we fought with the tiny latches to lower the windows. Separating the bears from the landscape was tricky, but we pointed them out to each other with limited success: "See? Over there? By that big rock that looks like a fist? It's a gray rock, just to the left of those three other gray rocks. About ten o'clock or so, just where that spit of ice goes into the water. Can't you see? It's right where I'm pointing."

Eventually, we all saw the bears for ourselves, or at least claimed to; there's nothing worse than being the only one on the bus who can't see what everyone else does. There were three bears in all, maybe four, creamy yellow in color and utterly indifferent to the uproar they were creating. One of the bears sniffed at the ground and another paced away from the group. Seeing bears this far away, and engaged in such uninspiring behavior, should have been as thrilling as seeing a squirrel in Central Park, yet everybody was utterly absorbed. We grudgingly ceded window space to one another and jostled for better position whenever anyone shifted weight or stepped away to fiddle with camera gear. When two bears reared up on their hind legs and started battering each other playfully, a swell of Cockney squealing rose inside the bus. Squirrels *never* do that.

"I can't believe I'm really seeing this," said a woman who'd suddenly materialized alongside me on the bench seat. She had fashionable clothing and a casual, expensive-looking pageboy haircut. Everything about her said good taste and money, though I was sure she wouldn't hesitate to describe herself as being unpretentious and down-to-earth. "I . . . just can't believe they're really here," she continued, in a light English accent. Her hands were clasped in front of her face, then her shoulders began to shake. A horrible premonition came over me and I willed myself to stare out the window. But when she whipped out a little lace hankie, my worst fears were confirmed. The woman was actually sobbing.

"Are you all right?" I asked. Normally I'm not one to get involved in the business of strangers. But when an elderly British woman is quite literally crying on your shoulder, it seems rude to pretend she doesn't exist.

"I'm wonderful, darling," she said. "And terrible. I've wanted to see a polar bear for just ages. And now I'm here, and they're all about to die. And the thought that I'm partly to blame for it all . . . it makes me feel sick."

I gave her a perfunctory little pat on the shoulder, hoping that small gesture might be enough to keep her from eventually needing a hug. "It's not your fault," I said. "I'm sure there are much worse people than you."

"I'm doing my best," she acknowledged, wiping away a tear that threatened to roll off her nose and onto my pant leg. "But it's not like I can, well, go live in a mud house and eat yard trimmings all day."

"I don't think anyone wants you to do that." How had this lady managed to get so old and still feel so guilty? It's one thing to have back-to-the-land flirtations as a teenager, but did people in their fifties still struggle with whether or not to live in a yurt?

"I should, though," she said. "I should do it all. For *their* sake. For their sweet little cubs. If this keeps up, they're going to starve, you know."

"I know," I said. We turned back toward the window, which had frosted over from all the sobbing. She handed me the tear-stained hankie, and I cleared a porthole. What would she say if I told her about Rocky, about the idea that reports of the polar bear's demise had been greatly exaggerated? A message like that should fill her with delight, but probably all she'd be able to do was mistrust the messenger. She had her story and she was not about to be dissuaded.

"Fight! Fight!" somebody screamed, as if we were watching the bully and the fat kid square off during recess. Sadly, it was a halfhearted battle, with just a few jabs and one lackluster roundhouse from the bigger bear. When they finished, they remained standing, regarding each other coolly.

We settled into our seats and relived the minutes-old experience by looking at digital stills from the man with the longest lens, my bald British friend. The photos were every bit as exciting as the real thing, possibly more so, and we gave the tepid brawl a blow-by-blow dissection worthy of *SportsCenter*.

AFTER A WHILE, we pulled up next to a long two-story building with metal walls, the former military rocket range that had now been repurposed as a science support facility and tourist hostel. A few scattered windows were covered by thick bars, like an Arctic Alcatraz Island. Part dump, part ghost town, part active enterprise, the facility's dereliction was reminiscent of the port, as well as of Churchill's downtown, for that matter. Stacks of pallets teetered precariously along one side of the building; yellow fuel drums sat in snowbanks, quietly rusting; a telephone pole with no wires reached up toward the flat sky, like a weak imitation of a tree in the middle of a deforested plain.

Somewhere in the middle of the bus ride, the Arctic winter had arrived in earnest, with whipsaw winds and the thermometer dipping well below zero. We herded inside and pressed ourselves into a long hallway, shoulder to shoulder in our bulky jackets. Leann reappeared and gave us a rundown about the Churchill Northern Studies Center, an orientation that had less to do with the bathrooms, the quiet hours, and the laundry facilities and more to do with how to keep ourselves from being killed.

"Don't go outside," she said. "If you'd like to have a cigarette, now is your chance to quit." People laughed, which may have been the reaction she was aiming for, though not, seemingly, one that pleased her. She wanted us to understand the severity of the situation. Bears can hide behind parked cars, she explained, lurk next to doorways, waiting patiently for somebody to exit. "It is not safe to go outside," she repeated. "If you do happen to be outside for some reason"—she rolled her eyes, as if going outside were too ludicrous to mention—"be ready to get inside the building quickly. And then keep moving so that the people behind you can get inside, too."

The exasperation in her voice suggested that she'd seen the rules violated too often, and with too much rank stupidity to have much faith in this new batch of half-wit tourists. The week before, in fact, an oddball German traveler who imagined herself to be a soulful Bear Whisperer had opened a side door and stepped outside directly between a polar bear mother and her cubs. A staffer looked out the window just in time, and the woman was physically dragged inside and then sent packing in the time it took to warm up the motor of the nearest vehicle. "We get one of those every year," Leann said. "Every one of them thinks that they've got some kind of special connection, like 'Oh no, he wouldn't possibly eat me.'" I wondered if it might be better if somebody *did* get mauled; never underestimate the value of a bloody glove on a plaque next to the front door.

CHAPTER 21

Don't Touch the Bears
and Don't Feed the Bears

*If we would declare officially that bears are friendly,
it would be deadly for the industry. So it's a secret
we'll keep. Or we will lose our industry.*

—RAYMOND GIRARDIN,
RANGER WITH PARKS CANADA

AFTER MILLING ABOUT IN A HERD for a few minutes, we assembled in the kitchen for an introduction to our guide, who was standing off to the side, waiting to be adored, as all good trip leaders hope to be. Given his occupation, it feels almost too easy to describe Rupert Pilkington as bearlike. And yet, were his passion anything but bears, were it anything from salamanders to semiconductors, no other description would fit him nearly as well. He is tall, gentle, and a bit soft, though it's the kind of extra weight around the midsection that is less the result of sloth and more like a deliberate storing-up for winter. He has a closely cropped beard and is given to wearing earth-toned woolen sweaters, raggedy at the edges and with the occasional moth hole. When he's outside in the snow, he wears a fur cap with the flaps pinned up jauntily alongside his head. Despite years of exposure to direct sun and harsh polar winds, his face is unwrinkled, rosy-cheeked, and playful.

Even his voice, a fluidly generic British accent with a trace of Scottish brogue, could easily work as the voice-over for a friendly cartoon animal.

"Would anybody care to join me for a brief walk about the grounds?" he asked. As we were standing three abreast in the tiny entranceway, the idea of physical motion of any kind sounded delightful. We issued a low moo of approval. "Let's get ourselves kitted up then, quite warmly, please, and meet back here shortly." Rupert smiled benignly and said things like "jolly good" and "splendid," as wave upon wave of tourists funneled past like pilgrims come to touch the hem of a holy man's garment. Having spoken less than twenty words, he already had our entire group eating from the palm of his hand.

"Ah, DELIGHTFUL," Rupert intoned as we reassembled wearing heavier clothing. "We won't stay out long, just enough to get a feeling for this desolate, yet supremely beautiful landscape." He spoke as though narrating a *Nova* special on the Arctic, his script full of carefully chosen adjectives and artfully placed dependent clauses. "Safety is paramount today, and every day, when we depart the safety of our structures and venture out afoot. Our best defense is remaining together as a group. We appear quite large and unpredictable in that way, and it is unlikely a bear would attack us when we are en masse. Try not to stray from the group; individually you are in great peril." He made a grand gesture of checking the chamber of his rifle before ushering us outside. *Nobody really talks like this*, I said to myself. *But my God—he must get laid a ton and pull down some enormous tips.*

"Follow on closely," Rupert said, and we shuffled after him, amoeba-like in our desire to adhere as closely as possible to the man with all the answers (and the gun). One tourist in particular attached himself to Rupert's hip and fired off questions designed more to demonstrate his own knowledge than to elicit any new information. I had met this guy—Steve from Jersey—earlier when he dropped his gear on the bed above mine and without so much as a hello, launched into a reminiscence about the rampant top-bunk sex he remembered from his college days. He had the hunched spine, enormous round glasses, and icy pallor indicative of someone who spends a lot of time online pretending to be a warlock. Everybody on the course had instantly pegged Steve as the guy you didn't want to get stuck sitting next to at lunch. His gaze was just a little too avid, his attempts at conversation and flirtation too aggressive by half. He struck me as the sort of lonely middle-aged guy who eats a lot of canned food and goes to arena rock concerts by himself.

"It's not nearly as cold as I thought it would be," said Steve. "I've been places that were a lot colder than this."

"It's certainly not as cold as it was when I first came here," Rupert replied. "It's remarkable to see such dramatic changes even within my relatively short tenure."

"This global warming stuff is the real deal then, huh? I heard that even if we all stopped driving today, it would be too late to turn it back. So we've pretty much screwed ourselves then, huh?"

"That is certainly a plausible scenario," Rupert answered, edging away from Steve.

"You know, these polar bears kinda remind me of gorillas, you know?"

"And why would that be?"

"Well, you know," Steve said. "I've seen gorillas in the wild, too. In Africa. Also lions, lotsa lions."

"So would you say, then, that the point of connection these divergent animals share is that they have all been viewed by you, Steve?" Rupert's voice was without sarcasm.

Steve, of course, missed the point entirely. "Have you ever been to Glacier National Park?" he yammered on. "Well, I have and there's lots of bears there too and . . ." The wind kicked up and I cinched my hood into a cone around my face.

THE CENTERPIECE OF THE CHURCHILL Northern Studies Center is the building that used to launch rockets, a squat, bombproof-looking affair with a firing tube pointing skyward at a haphazard angle. They launched all the big rockets back in the day, the Black Brants and the Nikes and the Ajaxes—more than 3,500 in all. They even launched a satellite or two. Locals report that the Americans used to scuttle about the tundra, collecting the top-secret remnants of the tests.

But now, except for the main hallway where we slept, the rest of the once cutting-edge facility was stunning only in its dereliction. The military didn't just leave this place, but abandoned it. Ancient jeeps sat frozen into the snow, hoods raised as if someone were planning to come back momentarily with a fresh set of spark plugs. In the old days, engineers walked between buildings through a series of tunnels. But now the passageways had collapsed, adding to the endless heaps of rubble that are still, fifty years on, too much trouble to deal with. Apparently, this spot makes as good a dump as anyplace else.

"Tundra, saltwater sea, and boreal forest—we stand at the intersection of three distinct biomes," Rupert said.

"We stand at the intersection of Lame Avenue and Freezing Street if you ask me," Steve muttered into his parka.

"In reality, it's quite lovely here," Rupert said, pointedly gazing out over Steve's head toward the distant sunset. His hand rested on the shotgun strap at his shoulder, and he looked like a modern-day heir of Davy Crockett. "I feel very fortunate to have spent as much time here as I have. Anyplace that's good enough for a polar bear is a place that I deeply wish to be."

BUT THE POINT OF AN ARCTIC Learning Vacation isn't to walk around in a circle in the snow. Despite the fact that we were all outdoorsy hiking-club types, the point was to spend as much time in enclosed spaces as possible. To hell with physical exertion; the meat of this trip was sitting on one's ass in a Tundra Buggy.

Jumping from foot to foot to keep warm, our merry band of eco-tourists crossed the threshold of the buggy and milled about in the next phase of our slaughterhouse experience. I only say this because after herding us onto the school bus, we had literally been driven to a raised wooden cattle chute where our delicate hooves were never forced to touch the ground, and a series of gates directed us precisely where to go.

I fully expected that Steve from Jersey would require a touch or two from the electric prod before this day was through.

People jostled for seats next to the window, and there was anxious discussion about which side of the buggy would be facing the bay, and which way was the bay, anyhow? With no mountains on the horizon and the wan sun emitting a flat, directionless glow, it was impossible to get a sense of bearing. In the Arctic, people always say that the expanses are so open and wide that they can see the curvature of the earth. But to me it feels like the opposite, like you could be forgiven for believing the world is flat in a place like this. Without trees, structures, or topography, the earth stretches forward with a bleak sameness, equally punishing in every direction. The only flux is the tide, which sneaks in and out with imperceptible effort, transforming the flat gray waters into mile upon mile of ankle-breaking stone.

"All of the seats provide ample viewing," Rupert reassured us. "And we will have the opportunity to switch seats over the course of the day."

"I just don't wanna get stuck on the aisle, you know what I'm saying," said Steve from Jersey, frowning and looking aggrieved. "It would really suck to not be able to see anything." He sounded like a kid who just *knew* he was going to get a worse piece of birthday cake than everyone else. We assessed one another and sorted ourselves out using the careful social calculus I hadn't employed since lunch period in junior high school.

Rupert took his place at the rear, cleared his throat, and waited for us to settle down like good schoolchildren. "We're all aboard so I'd like to welcome you to the Tundra Buggy . . ."

"It's not a Tundra Buggy," interrupted a young man who had just come inside and slammed the door shut behind him. "The other company"—he rolled his eyes—"trademarked the name 'Tundra Buggy,' so you can call this whatever you like as long as you don't call it a Tundra Buggy. We call 'em Polar Rovers."

"All right then, Rover it is," said Rupert, with a small, gracious bow. "We'll see many bears no matter the name." Pointing to the newcomer, he said, "I'd like to introduce you to our driver for the day. He is called . . ."

"Kyle," said Kyle.

"Kyle," confirmed Rupert. "He has some things to tell us about the vehicle, so let's give him our full attention."

Kyle was in his early twenties, endearingly scruffy with a month's worth of whiskers that could generously be called a beard. Like most of the people I'd met up here, he seemed badly underdressed, in little more than a cotton sweatshirt. Kyle's one concession to the weather was a large pair of handmade sealskin mitts. He welcomed us to Churchill and to his bus and launched into a safety shtick that he'd obviously delivered a few thousand times in his short life.

"Don't touch the bears and don't feed the bears," he began. "There is no food allowed on the back deck and nobody is allowed on the ground for any reason. Don't touch the bears and don't feed the bears. The windows open like this," Kyle pounded on the frame just so, squeezed the metal push tabs in the correct sequence and the window dropped fluidly. The rest of us attempted to follow suit, but with our big gloves and complete mechanical ineptitude, most of us failed and then pretended we never wanted the window open to begin with.

"It's going to be hard to push a sandwich out if I can't get the window open," said Steve from Jersey in a stage whisper.

"Don't touch the bears and don't feed the bears," said Kyle, sending out a surprisingly powerful death stare given his young age.

"Aw, I know. I was just kidding," said Steve.

"Don't touch the bears and don't feed the bears."

Steve slunk low in his seat and Kyle continued. "Feel free to move around the vehicle and go out onto the back deck whenever you like. Just be careful not to drop anything. I've seen thousand-dollar cameras go over the side and get turned into chew toys. Nobody's very happy when I can't get them back." Two dozen pairs of hands dropped simultaneously into camera bags, caressing precious Nikons. As we considered the health of our gadgetry, Kyle passed out the obligatory stack of small-font waiver forms. I assumed we'd be taking responsibility for being mauled, nibbled, mishandled, decapitated, dismembered, disemboweled,

or otherwise dispatched in any foreseeable way mechanical, climatological, or at the hands of all animals prehistoric, modern, or yet to have
evolved. I ignored it entirely and signed with a flourish.

POLAR BEARS ARE SLEEK and efficient and well adapted to their environment. Tundra Buggies—sorry, Polar Rovers—are the opposite. Not
one single thing about them is graceful or suggestive of ease. They lumber. They whine. They growl with effort as they hammer their way
through the pitted landscape and half-frozen ponds across which the
bears glide so effortlessly. And, with passengers packed inside like
matchsticks while being surrounded by approximately a half million
square miles of open space, the buggies are a further exercise in the
semivoluntary incarceration that I had come to recognize as one of
Churchill's hallmarks.

   We crept forward at five miles an hour. I could have walked faster,
except for the problem of being eaten alive. Kyle told me that over the
course of a typical day's thirty-mile journey, our bus would burn twelve
gallons of fuel. Riding in one of these things requires that you award
yourself a little vacation from your pledge of carbon neutrality. The bulky
heater at the rear of the bus chugged away nonstop, never quite getting
the bus to the point where I wanted to remove my coat. Rupert and Kyle,
of course, acted like they were inside a sauna.

   Despite shock absorbers as big around as small tree trunks, every
spine-fusing bump served as a reminder that in the grand scheme of
things, we were most definitely not meant to be where we were. We
swayed from side to side as the buggy climbed dirty berms of ice, and
then we braced ourselves for impact as the vehicle descended into axle-
busting potholes that had filled with water and frozen solid. The motor
growled an incessant, low-grade rumble, and the windows fogged over
constantly. Occasionally, Kyle cleared a peephole, but often he seemed
to be relying on instinct, keeping the wheel mostly straight and his foot
steady on the gas. It was as if he were flying on instruments, except that
there were no instruments, not even a speedometer.

Everything about the buggy suggests labor, a bankrupting investment of fuel and metal and effort to get us into inhospitable territory. This was underlined when we saw our first bear, a midsized female lying in the snow, fast asleep and without a care in the world.

"She should walk around or something," said Steve. "She's probably cold."

"I assure you that she's not," said Rupert.

"She looks cold."

"She's not cold."

"She looks cold. I'm just saying."

Rupert raised his chin and stared over Steve's head.

BEFORE LONG, DOZENS OF BEARS popped up on every side of us. Although the lady with walking pneumonia had taken on a corpse-like, bluish hue, she proved to be a remarkably good spotter. In between death rattles, she shouted out directions for where we all should be looking. Kyle brought the buggy to a stop, and after my eyes adjusted to the light and the whiteness, I noticed that the landscape around me was in constant motion. Bits of rock transformed into black snouts and dirty tails; mounds of snow revealed themselves to be bear cubs gamboling about as their mothers walked purposefully toward nowhere.

The tourists withdrew cameras from their bags and snapped outsized lenses on top, like hit men assembling their arsenals. A bear that Rupert identified as a female stood a hundred feet off. Our presence disturbed her not a bit, and she made a long slow arc, walking in a semicircle around us. We followed her around the bus, first crowding around Kyle's driver's seat, then pressing against the windows on one side of the vehicle, and finally pushing to get outside onto the observation deck. Occasionally, the bear stopped and regarded us, but mostly she kept her own counsel.

"How big is that one?" asked Steve.

"Possibly seven hundred pounds or more," said Rupert. "Though it's quite difficult to tell at this distance. I can tell you that she is certainly quite reduced from her winter weight."

"It's a pretty lame life they got here," Steve said. "I wouldn't mind seeing a fight."

Rupert raised a reproachful eyebrow. Steve backpedaled. "You know, I don't want to see 'em get hurt or nothing, but a good fight would be really cool, you gotta admit." For once, I had to agree with Steve. Actual bear watching was a poor substitute for watching a show about bears on television. Out here, there was nobody to edit out the slow parts. And at this time of year, a bear's whole goal in life is to be as slow as possible.

"They're just waiting in the longest lunch line of all time," Kyle piped up from the driver's seat. A lot of his job involved keeping up the illusion that watching a sleeping lump of fur was the thrill of a lifetime.

"Longest lunch line of all time," Steve said, mining for a laugh that wasn't coming. "Man, I heard that." We were about forty-five minutes removed from a breakfast of bacon, eggs, potatoes, oatmeal, fruit, and pastries, and the idea of more food was nauseating.

And then, all of a sudden, something startled the bear and her torpid demeanor changed in a flicker. She lifted her head and held it perfectly still, testing the wind for whatever might be coming, be it threat or opportunity. And when she decided to go, she was gone in an instant, covering a hundred yards in seconds. Powerful muscles shimmered beneath the fur at her shoulders and she navigated the broken ground as if it were flat earth. She wasn't elegant, not like a gazelle bounding into the bush; her haunches jiggled and her gait was stocky and uneven. But she plowed over the land like a bulldozer, kicking up puffs of loose snow and thrashing the scrubby willows in her path. I'd been watching her move for well over a minute when I realized that the buggy was silent; we'd all forgotten to breathe.

THE FREEZE-UP POINT would be upon us soon. The waves of Hudson Bay broke malevolently against the shore, half a dozen shades of gray overlapping in constant motion. Small plates of ice surfed on the tide and were beaten into foam against the rocky shoreline. The shallows were transforming into a gelid slurry, not quite ice and not quite water. Waves that began as swift, gentle forces far out to sea morphed into languid breakers as they hit the transition zone, exhausted by the effort of carrying the jumble of ice up onto shore.

Over the rest of the day, seeing polar bears went from being an exceptional experience to being merely commonplace. Dozens of bears of every size, all milling about aimlessly. The male bears tested each other, wrestling and fighting not in anger, but in an attempt to measure themselves and establish a pecking order. The bears were tired and hungry, so the feinting and posturing was halfhearted at best. It wasn't time to mate and there was no food anywhere, thus the stakes were exceptionally low. Mostly, they just wanted to be left alone.

"It's getting a little slow, wouldn't you say?" I said to Eileen, my British seatmate who, thank God, had long since stopped crying. It was getting on into afternoon, and I was finding that my tolerance for bear watching had expired several hours ago.

"Oh, heavens no," she said. "I could watch them for days." I probably should have been able to guess that from the way she had left her bag lunch nearly untouched, preferring instead to spend her time with palms and forehead pressed against the glass in a posture of extreme supplication.

"You don't ever feel like they all kind of look the same? You know, seen one, seen them all?"

She pulled her face away from the window to give me an angry schoolmarm look. She pursed her lips and said, "Different people look quite a bit alike, but that doesn't stop me from talking to you, now does it?"

Before I could make a further ass of myself, Rupert came to the rescue. He'd spent the day wandering around the bus like a maître d', making sure that all of his patrons were happy. He would kneel alongside someone's seat to answer a question or offer a comprehensive minilecture. His knowledge of bears was encyclopedic, but he treated every subject on earth with the same careful scholarship, giving the impression that he spent his nonexpedition days tucked away in the stacks of the Oxford Library. Cold war history, Greek word origins, and the subtle differences among brands of Irish whiskey—these subjects and a thousand more were respectfully analyzed by Rupert and then presented to us, his eager acolytes, as if they were Scripture. The syrupy slowness of his delivery only enhanced his authority, and when Rupert spoke, even if it was only to recommend that you choose the strawberry Danish over the apple at breakfast, you got the feeling that all would be right with the world if you did exactly what he said. All the senior citizens in our group would gladly have stripped down to their socks and stuck their heads into an ice puddle if Rupert suggested that it was next on the list of the day's activities.

"It's lovely to be able to watch them like this, isn't it?" he said.

"Oh, *yes*, it's divine," said Eileen, answering the question before I had the chance to say anything that made me look like a bear-hating cretin. "They're such regal animals, so much poise. It's like having an audience with the queen, or the pope, or wait . . . no, no, that's not it at all. It's more like being in the presence of the Dalai Lama!"

"Yes, well said," Rupert responded, placing a hand on Eileen's shoulder. "They are utterly without artifice, totally at peace with their place in the world. And they have no idea what is about to befall them." Eileen looked as if she were about to cry again. We watched as the bear gave a great yawn and then stood up, wiggling his haunches from side to side.

"Is he doing what I think he's doing?" asked Eileen all of a sudden, two fingers covering her mouth in the universal symbol for having been scandalized.

Rupert knelt down on a vacant seat to get a better look. "Oh my, yes," he said with genuine excitement, as a gray-green stream splattered onto the snow at the bear's feet. "This bear is indeed having a bowel movement." Like all of the bears around here, this one had probably not eaten a substantial meal in months. "They feed on kelp during these lean periods," Rupert explained, excitement rising in his voice, "but it's generally more for the minerals and the taste of salt than for any actual nutrition. It is *quite* rare to see a bear having a bowel movement at this time of year. You're quite fortunate to have seen this." The bear turned around twice and then lay down in the liquid puddle of his own shit. We are fortunate, indeed, I thought.

"How big is that one, do ya think?" hollered Steve from the back of the bus.

"He is precisely as big as he appears to be," Rupert responded without turning around. "Neither bigger nor smaller than that."

CHAPTER 22

Looking
for Narnia

C AN I, UM, BUM A SMOKE?"

After another enormous dinner—meals seemed to arrive every thirty minutes in this place—I was standing outside the Northern Studies Center's front door, giving myself a brief respite from the stale air inside. Another tourist stepped through the door, looking alarmed to see me, and asked for a cigarette. I briefly considered telling him that I'd just smoked my last one. Instead I came clean.

"Actually, I'm faking it," I said.

He looked immensely relieved. "Oh, thank God. So am I." Smoking, we had been told, was the only permissible reason to go outside unattended. The general feeling was that if you were a smoker, you probably deserved to be eaten alive. But I'd begun to feel like a fatted veal calf inside the Center, and so my faux smoking habit was approaching two packs a day. With a few notable exceptions, these were active, healthy people who probably spent hundreds of hours per year jogging or doing Pilates. And yet they seemed more or less content to stay inside the claustrophobic dormitory for days on end, with none of the nightmares I kept having about a poor man's version of *The Shining*.

It also seemed as though I was the only one having trouble thinking of this entire experience as a vacation. For this amount of money I could be lying on a beach in the Caribbean or watching Parisians walk past my table at some charming Left Bank café. Instead, I was wearing four layers of thermal underpants, I'd been admonished not to shower too often because of water rationing, and I was sleeping in a bunkroom with five world-class snoring champions. A room in which the windows were jammed shut and barred over, so that by midnight the locker-room aroma made sleep impossible.

My new nonsmoking buddy and I stood in the snow, dancing around in circles and watching our breath disappear into the cloudy darkness. For once, the wind was still, and when the front door to the Center opened, a blast of hot air shot out onto my back. The cook came out, wearing nothing but a light apron over a T-shirt.

"It's a hair bit nipple out tonight, eh boys?" he said in an inscrutable Canadian accent.

"Excuse me?"

"It's cold, I said, it's cold," he explained.

"You could put a jacket on," I offered.

"Ah, it's not *that* cold."

The cook, an actual smoker, had joined me outside on numerous occasions. He was good company, unfailingly jolly, and he never mentioned the fact that I wasn't sucking on Marlboros the way I should be in order to merit these trips outdoors. Tonight, he was taking a break in the infinitesimally small window between putting dinner on the table and prepping for tomorrow's breakfast. The cook took a deep drag on his cigarette and then looked at me. "American?" he asked. It was the first time we'd spoken about anything other than the weather. I nodded.

"Check this out, then." He handed me his cigarette pack, which featured a picture of a black, rotting lung underneath the brand name. "Pretty cool, eh?" he asked.

"Very cool," I said.

"That's one thing we've got that you don't." He smiled with satisfaction, tapped the pack, and slid it into his pocket. Being married to a Canadian, I'm used to this sort of cross-border one-upmanship, and I'm usually willing to let them have the little things. Strong FDA warnings do not a superpower make.

The cook, the other escapee, and I leaned against the wall and stared at the sky. The clouds were breaking apart in places, opening up huge swaths of stars in an ever-shifting pattern. It was the kind of night that should be perfect for northern lights. But there was nothing. Nothing but an immensity of stars, crackling more intensely than any I had ever seen. I know that "north" isn't the same thing as "up," but it still felt as if coming this far toward the Arctic had also brought me closer to the heavens. Maybe it was that this place, in its desolation and disregard for human comfort, felt a lot like outer space.

I climbed on the roof of a truck for a look around. Lights from communications towers twinkled at odd intervals, and a dull glow emanated from the direction of Churchill proper. The cold hurt my lungs with each breath, and I'd forgotten my hat and gloves. But it felt delightful to have a break from the canned heat and fluorescent lights of the station.

"No Aurora show tonight, eh?" the cook said, stubbing his cigarette out on the sole of his shoe, then crushing it between his fingers and letting the bits of paper and tobacco evaporate into the breeze. He and the other guy finished their smoke break and headed inside. "Don't stay out here by yourself too long," the cook said. Before he let the door close, he stood on the threshold, raised his hands like claws and bared his teeth at me. "Aaargh!"

"Yeah," said the nonsmoker. "If you get eaten I won't have anyone to not bum a smoke off of."

After they left, I thought about the German tourist I'd been told about, the one who went outside with the specific goal of encountering a bear. "She was looking for Narnia," was how Rupert described it to me. "Who knows what sort of packaging went into her head over her lifetime?" he said. "She was thinking about cartoons and stuffed animals." If she had managed to get outside without being rescued, the bear would have taken a swipe at her, and in the natural order of things, he would have had every right to do so. But the world stopped following the natural order a long time ago. If she'd gotten so much as a scratch on her arm, that bear would have been dead, called an incorrigible or a problem bear, hunted down and killed for doing what was in its nature. "She forgot that a bear is a bear," Rupert told me, with a small harrumph that made it seem he thought the world might have been better off if she'd gotten what was coming to her.

Danger aside, it was hard to shake the feeling that this was a glorified petting zoo. Sure, we were the ones inside the cages, but if the bears did anything threatening, it was they who would die, not us. And although the bears had room to roam, human beings were still building cages for them. "Don't come around here," we essentially said to them, when they nosed their way near towns. "Go out there, where the ice is." But that's a cruel trick, too, because the ice isn't there anymore, at least not like it used to be. We tell the bears to come close because we love them, to get the hell away from us because they frighten us, and to make their way in a world that we're rapidly stealing from them.

Unlike the German tourist with the death wish, I hadn't forgotten what a bear was, and I had no interest in meeting up with one. But the sterility of all things Churchill was overwhelming. In town, there were pictures of bears everywhere, but no real adventure. And out here, on the buggies, there were bears everywhere, but no real connection to them. We could have just as easily been on a people mover at the state fair, with the role of the polar bears being played by animatronic dummies. I wanted to feel the hot breath on my face. I wanted to know what a polar bear smelled like. I wanted to see what Steven Amstrup and the rest of the Heavy Hitters saw when they flew over the tundra, feel what they felt when they knelt down next to a tranquilized animal. I wanted to care about what happened to polar bears because I *knew* them, and that was never going to happen from inside a school bus.

Outside in the eternal night, every shadow was on the move, and phantom footsteps and nonexistent snuffling noises echoed from every direction. I scanned the darkened ground for lurking shapes, took one final glance skyward through the fog of my exhalations, and headed inside.

SOMETIME NEAR MIDNIGHT I gathered pillow and blanket and left the ca-
cophony of my dorm room. Steve from Jersey made soft whimpering
noises in his sleep, and the bunk next to mine was occupied by an enormous Australian man who spent the hours bouncing on the squeaky
bunk as though it were a trampoline.

I avoided the committed alcoholics drinking wine in the dining
room, stole past the employee's quarters, and climbed the ladder into
the observation deck on the roof of the building. We'd been specifically
admonished not to be up here at night, but at some point you have to
remember that you're a grown man and that even if you get caught, the
chances of being sent home to mother are small.

The observation deck was the derelict Northern Studies Center's
best feature. It was about eight feet in diameter and nine feet high at the
center, with a wide Plexiglas dome enclosing the entire space. I laid
down my bedroll, turned on the defroster and watched as the world
around me sharpened into focus. Although moonlight enlivened one
corner of the sky, the heavy cloud cover made it feel as if the universe
abruptly ended a hundred feet above my head. The lights of Churchill
twinkled warmly in the distance. And over the bay, a jagged streak of
open sky hugged the horizon, accentuating the suffocating darkness
that reigned elsewhere.

One of the staff emerged from the front door directly below me. He
swept the parking lot methodically with his flashlight before letting the
door swing shut behind him. As he walked he checked for bears behind
each vehicle, turning completely around and shining his beam into the
middle distance. The Manitoba flag flapped stiffly in the wind, then fell
slack, straightened again and fell slack. The man did his business, something mechanical by a row of old snow-moving equipment, and then
hurried back inside. He stood in the doorway a moment longer, casting
one more searching look into the gloom. No bears here. Not now, at
least. Not visible.

Over the course of the night, however, as sleep failed to find its way
to me, I saw dozens of bears. Solitary bears and mothers with cubs; big

males walking with the arrogance of great size; subadults in the new-found bloom of their independence. I saw bears with their noses to the ground, haunches swaying as they trekked along some invisible highway that led beneath my perch. Some bears appeared to have weathered the summer well, but others were desperately skinny, ribs protruding underneath empty bags of fur. I saw some bears skulking at the edge of the light given off by the dorm-hall windows, and some brazen ones licking the snow right at the edge of the Center's front wall. All night long, as I tossed on my uncomfortable pad, the ground below the dome became my own private parade ground, as bears of every size and description presented themselves for my inspection.

Or not.

Because every time a bear caught my attention, it disappeared before my tired eyes could focus. I rubbed frost from the window with a corner of my blanket, and the bear I thought I saw was always disappearing around a corner of the building; a single hind leg would flash and be gone. White plastic sheeting atop a gravel pile shifted amorphously in the wind, acquiring paws, a stubby tail, a great lolling head. Had I really seen even so much as a single bear? Somehow, even with dozens of bear sightings under my belt, the idea of a bear remained as powerful as a bear itself.

In the morning darkness, I snuck downstairs and deposited my bedroll before anyone noticed my out-of-bounds camping. The smell of hash browns filled the air, and the cook scrambled eggs in time to the music, singing along to an old sea shanty about a tragic wreck off the Newfoundland coast. Nobody noticed as I headed outside for my first noncigarette of the day. A single set of tracks meandered across the parking lot, doubling back and forth, tamping out a resting spot in the snow.

An hour later, when we all emerged together from the front door, a stiff wind and a fresh dusting of snow had rubbed out any trace of what I might have seen the night before. At some point, probably sooner rather than later, the idea of a polar bear may be the only thing that exists for any of us.

CHAPTER 23

The
Bear Whisperer

I came, I saved, I protected, and I studied.

—TIMOTHY TREADWELL, BEAR ENTHUSIAST AND SELF-APPOINTED DEFENDER OF
WILDLIFE, BEFORE HE AND HIS GIRLFRIEND WERE KILLED BY A GRIZZLY BEAR

T HE SECOND DAY OF BUGGYING started off grimly. The temperature had dropped from just above freezing to deeply below. The moment the bears had been waiting for had come, and now the bay was a solid slab of ice. Tourism was over and the seal hunt was on.

It was alarming how precipitous the change was, how quickly one world can transform itself into something utterly different. With the exception of a forest fire, I couldn't imagine a landscape altering itself so fundamentally in such a short space of time. It's a stark lesson for anyone who would say that a few degrees one way or the other can't make much difference. A few days earlier, the endless ocean was a slurried mess, and we watched bears laboring through the shallows, half swimming, half crawling as they broke through the thin crust time and again. Now they were in their element. Meaning that they were gone. For a very long time, we rode in silence without seeing anything at all.

Kyle glassed the horizon. The mood was tense; if we didn't see bears—a *lot* of bears—then all of these people would have spent several months' salary on what amounted to a midwinter, Midwestern trailer-park vacation. Nobody wanted to admit, exactly, that they were just here for the bears. But I also didn't hear anybody saying that they'd be just as happy if all they got to do was listen to Rupert's lectures and visit the Eskimo Museum.

Moreover, we'd been missing the seminal Churchill experience, the moment in which a bear comes up to the side of the buggy, stands on its hind legs and paws at the windows. All the tour agencies feature pictures like this in their literature; every television and film crew that heads to Churchill needs this shot, the slavering jaws beyond the glass, the whiff of musk for the narrator to breathlessly describe.

"Come to Daddy," Kyle cooed. We looked out the windows. We waited. We drove. A line of buggies appeared on the horizon, idling as though at a drive-through. We'd gotten a late start; Rupert had held court at breakfast, discoursing grandly about the white cliffs of Dover or Pre-Raphaelite painters or the Norwegian public school system or something. As usual, the guests were rapt, but it also meant that we were the last buggy in line, and the people up front were seeing something cooler than we were.

Bears nuzzled around the tires of the buggies up ahead, looking up warily at the visitors crowding above. The people in the front bus must have been as ecstatic as we were envious. How quickly things change— earlier we'd counted ourselves lucky just for having come this close to the Arctic Circle. Now getting to see a bear from a few bus-lengths away felt like a monumental letdown.

"How big do you think *that* one is?" asked Steve. "That one way up by the front bus, I mean."

"He's quite large, no doubt a senior male. He could quite easily be in the neighborhood of 1,200 pounds," Rupert said.

I borrowed a pair of binoculars and trained them on the lead bus. People crammed themselves through open windows, getting as much of their bodies outside as their own morbid obesity would allow. Several people pounded on the side to get the bear's attention; he regarded the now he cleared his throat and addressed us like a philosophy professor expressing grave concerns about the state of the human condition.

"Do you think that this is a good idea?" He lowered his voice an octave for the occasion, becoming James Earl Jones to convey his seriousness. "Does anybody really think that we ought to be out here like this? Are we hurting the bears by viewing them in this manner?"

The assembled crowd looked at Rupert dumbstruck. How could somebody whose entire livelihood depended on keeping things exactly as they were suggest that there was a problem with the status quo?

"Are we helping the bears by coming out here, or are we harming them? Can we pretend that this"—he made an expansive gesture to emphasize the otherworldly proportions of the bus—"really has no effect on the bears and on their habitat? I must say, I am not so sure. I am not . . . so sure."

This was not a subject that made the people on the bus happy in any way. Rupert was, after all, indicting them for buying the very product that he was selling. You could almost smell the gears burning inside people's brains, wondering why they had to be here in the back of the buggy line while all the cool kids up front got to pound on the side of the bus and holler at polar bears. It was all well and good to ask us to feel bad about the polar bears, but now we had to feel bad about ourselves, too? People don't go on vacation to be told that they're acting like jackasses.

Eileen, my feisty little seatmate from England, raised her hand cautiously and suggested that perhaps what we were doing *was* a tad too easy. "Maybe we should be required to make more of an extraordinary effort," she said. "All I did was cough up a few thousand quid. It's almost like I'd rather go out in the cold with a trapper instead of in a great big lumbering palace. I'd almost be happier seeing them at a distance." The rest of us murmured our halfhearted agreement, though I doubt anyone shared her desire to see fewer bears, farther away, while enduring greater personal discomfort.

The fact that a trip like this was full of ethical pitfalls was not exactly a news flash. It was, however, more than anyone wished to say aloud.

spectacle with the same dispassion with which bears confront
things. I could almost hear the people whooping and hollering, s;
"Here beary beary, here beary," and making the universal clucking
that we believe attracts all animals and human babies. The windows
ten feet off of the ground, easily reachable should the bear decide t(
up. And in addition to the obvious idiocy of offering one's arm to a s
ing carnivore, there's something hopelessly tacky about waving (
hands and making kissy noises to a polar bear as if it were a mischie
puppy. The bear poked his snout upward and a dozen heads retre
in unison; the squealing must have been deafening.

"I don't get it," Kyle said. "Nobody ever walks up to an airplane
sticks their head in the propeller just to see what it feels like."

"You ever see anybody get hurt?" Steve asked eagerly. Tourists
carnage.

Kyle rolled his head in a yes/no non-answer. "People always sa'
can see into his soul. He would never hurt *me*.' But *news flash everybc*
You can't see into his soul, and he will definitely hurt you."

"They seem so placid," Rupert intoned in his grave, *Masterpi*
Theatre voice, "but we can never join them." Rupert envisioned him:
as something far grander than a guide, a sort of freelance Ambassac
to Beardom, the Undersecretary for Ursine Affairs. Although he has
official government responsibilities and no PhD, in his dream world he
sail to Russia to investigate post-Soviet hunting regulations and then d
camp to the Canadian Rockies to help a resort town get a handle on i
problem bear population. In between, he'd advise Congress on issues (
genetic bottlenecking in the grizzly community, and then petition th
UN on the plight of Asiatic black bears, which are held in squalid cap
tivity in order to have their bile milked for its aphrodisiac qualities. T(
no great surprise, the call for a man of his qualifications is slim, and s(
guiding has remained his mainstay.

Nonetheless, Rupert doggedly attempted to raise the discourse above
simple tourism. The obnoxious behavior of the lead buggy gave him an
opening. All week he'd been tiptoeing around a sensitive subject, and

Coming here was meant to be an *escape* from the constant harangues and harbingers of doom that followed them around their daily lives. This trip to the Arctic was their reward, the treat they gave themselves in return for their socially aware shopping habits. *I get it, I get it,* they seemed to be thinking. *I'm part of the problem and I'm part of the solution. But right now can we just forget all that and go see some bears?*

"Human beings are just so treacherous," Rupert pressed on, repeating a line I'd heard him say a dozen times. Poor guy. Here he was trying to be the World's Greatest Bear Rescuer and instead he ended up playing hall monitor for a bunch of entitled rich kids. How many times had he beaten himself up just for doing his job?

As always, Steve from Jersey saved the day. "Is that the same bear we saw the other day?" he asked, pointing to a midsized female snoozing near the front of the bus.

"You mean the white one? With all the fur and the four paws?" said Kyle. "Oh, definitely."

A mother bear herded her two cubs over a snowbank. With the possible exception of big males fighting, playful cubs are the ultimate "get" of the Tundra Buggy experience. Earlier, we had seen a cub sliding goofily down a small hillock, and the bus erupted in giggles and sighs. The perfect postcard moment.

The mama bear noticed a large male noticing her, and she regarded him with a taut alertness that was rare to see. Bitter cold and months of starvation aside, the lack of genuine threats must make for a stress-free lifestyle. You'll never see a polar bear demonstrating the low-grade twitchy panic that characterizes the behavior of most animals in temperate climates.

As the male bear closed the gap, the female prodded her cubs along, casually but carefully. Even when food is plentiful, big males are not above taking a swipe at a cub, and moms usually keep their brood far away from unpredictable brutes. The cubs were ignorant of the danger, and they got distracted and fell behind the way children do. Everyone on board immediately recognized the situation for what it was: a made-for-TV chase scene!

Suddenly, the male broke into a deliberate run, covering half the gap in five seconds flat. Somebody was about to be eaten whole—how delightful! The female bear came alive and forced the cubs into flight. They ran, scrabbling and stumbling over the broken ground, a pell-mell race to survive.

The big male looked up, saw the panicky morsels in flight, and . . . stopped. He turned around and lay down on the ground. Eating a couple of cubs would have been wonderful, but having to actually work for it? The bear thought not. Better just to wait a week and kill some dumb seal rather than chasing down a scrawny little bear.

The tour group let out its collective breath. The cubs were safe. And I, for one, was mildly disappointed, a feeling that I'm sure was not unique to me. True cannibalism. Of *infants* no less. Now that would have been something to write home about. Instead, the mother gathered up her cubs and set off from the male at an oblique angle.

"Their solitary lives are kind of sad, in a way," Rupert said wistfully, before catching, then castigating himself. "No! That's not it at all. They're *solitary*, not lonely. They're singular animals. It's just what they do." Even for the most committed naturalist, it's nearly impossible to resist the urge to anthropomorphize.

"WE'RE RUNNING OUT OF DAYLIGHT," Kyle said. "Probably ought to head for home." It was 1:30 PM, but Kyle was right. The sky was shifting to the grainy colors of dusk, and cold pushed through cracks in the windows, leaking through the metal floor and chilling me from the feet upward. I made my way to the front of the bus, where an immense thermos dispensed lukewarm water for coffee and hot cocoa. Over the past few days, I'd eaten my weight in mini-marshmallows; today, a bottle of Kahlua was quietly making the rounds and I added a splash of coffee to my booze.

People shook off their postlunch torpor with the news that we had only a few hours of buggying left in our lives. (This isn't the kind of trip that people repeat; Paris is eternal and Hawaii never gets old, but once you've seen a polar bear, you've pretty much seen a polar bear.) There was a rush to get the last best shot, the perfect capper for the inevitable slide shows that I'd already heard people selecting background music for.

The fact that I was without a camera made me not only an oddity, but also a second-class citizen. When a "good" bear came into view, people crowded around the nearest windows; when that window happened to be mine, people were annoyed by the fact that I was holding a notepad instead of a Nikon. Why should I be hogging prime real estate, when at the end of the day I was going to have nothing tangible to show for it?

When photography went digital, the cost savings removed any restraint that the budding nature photographer of a previous era might have felt. The snapping of photos is a newly evolved vital sign, measuring excitement as reliably as blood pressure or pulse rate. You can gauge the intensity of a wilderness encounter in megapixels per minute. It's physiological and involuntary; when you're on vacation, taking pictures simply means that you're alive.

"No camera?" I was asked time and again. There was always a hint of resentment in the question, as if they thought I was adopting a holier-than-thou stance. But Google Images currently offers upwards of 100 million pictures of polar bears, and I can't do any better than the postcards on sale in every store. "Could I get in there?" people would ask, pressing against me with shrugs and apologetic half-smiles as if to say, "It's not me, it's the camera; there's nothing I can do."

There was one final piece to the perfect bear tour that we still needed to photograph (and, incidentally, to experience), and Kyle maneuvered to get us in position. What we needed was to be attacked, and now we had our chance. A giant male, easily the biggest we'd seen, circled the bus proprietarily.

The group of tourists moved like a wave from the right side to the back deck to the left side. Kyle opened his window and leaned out ever so slightly. This bear wasn't undernourished: his big belly swayed, his neck heaved with rolls of fat. Kyle kept up a steady patter—"Hey buddy, how ya doin'? Whatcha lookin' for? You hungry? You hungry? Hey buddy . . ."—and the energy level in the bus rose from late-afternoon naptime to near fever pitch.

"Quiet now," Rupert admonished feebly. "We mustn't disturb him, we mustn't get overexcited."

"Hey buddy, hey buddy, hey . . ." The bear vaulted onto his hind legs, slapping heavy paws against the side of the bus. His head swayed and his expressionless eyes bored in at us. At last he approached the open window, almost entering the bus before Kyle slapped the window shut with a bang. Kyle made a *tsk-tsk* scolding noise and the crowd went wild. Everyone high-fived each other and cheered and began to write the narrative in their heads of *the time that Kyle almost got eaten!* Kyle beamed. Rupert looked stricken.

I was finding it hard to get into the spirit, though. The encounter wasn't nearly as thrilling as I had always imagined it would be. What had happened to me? When I first came here, all I wanted was what everybody wanted. But along the way something had changed.

Part of it was the doubt that Rocky had introduced. Despite everything you heard on the news, there was a scientifically plausible argument to be made that all was not lost. Sure, Rocky was in the minority, but he wasn't a crackpot. And the gaps he'd shown in the armor of the Heavy Hitters were very real. I wondered how many of these people on the bus knew that polar bears were doing vastly better today than they had been doing thirty years ago. And how many of them understood that under the most dire of predictions, the polar bear population would only return to its 1950s level? That would be sad, to be sure, but the Arctic would go on being the Arctic, the world would go on being the world, and the remaining polar bears would hunt and eat and mate and live and die as best they could, just like now, just like they did 100,000 years ago.

But for most people, doubt had been banished, the most unwelcome guest of all. Uncertainty existed, but it simply wasn't discussed in tasteful circles. The World Wildlife Fund had done its job. Robert Buchanan and

Polar Bears International had done their job. There are a million problems to choose from, a million sad stories demanding our attention every day, but only a few of them break through the static. Polar bears had broken through, embraced by the nonprofit watchdogs and the corporate social responsibility image-tenders and the celebrity endorsers and the media talking heads who like to end the hour with something a little bit sad and a whole lot cute.

On the ride home, Kyle chattered away happily. He'd done exactly what a good guide is supposed to, delivering the ultimate polar bear goods. The bears might well be dying, and that made him sad. But there was nothing he could do about it, and besides, the notion of scarcity sent bookings through the roof. He was unafflicted by doubt, a good guide and a good guy, plying his trade as responsibly as he knew how. He was in that sweet spot between adolescence and adulthood, when the world lays itself open in front of handsome young men with solid skills and limitless confidence. It might have been a bad time to be a polar bear, but it was a great time to be Kyle.

Sitting in the back row, Rupert looked tired and defeated. We both had our misgivings about this industry of bear tourism, it seemed. Looking at it from the point of view of the people on the bus, I found the whole thing shallow and overhyped, adrenaline tourism masquerading as environmental activism. But Rupert looked at it the other way, from the perspective of the bears. With all that he knew and all that he believed, how could he justify this? Late at night, I wondered if he had nightmares of polar bears with hats and tiny bicycles, riding around the tundra. And Rupert, astride a buggy, their reluctant ringmaster.

The buggy rolled through a covey of willow ptarmigan, their feathers shimmering brilliant white in the sunset. The birds fluttered off in every direction as we barreled through, and this time there was no discussion of our impact, no hand-wringing about the effects of our disturbance. Theoretically, Rupert would probably have wanted us to appreciate the ptarmigan as much as the polar bear, two rare creatures uniquely suited to life in a harsh environment. The difference, of course, is that only one of them can rip your fucking head off. And that's a very appealing characteristic to have when you're a wild animal. No amount of lecturing or education could keep each one of us from slipping into our own private wilderness idyll, a place where the bears are simultaneously fierce and friendly, where each of us has special communicative powers, where we alone among all the people on earth can see inside the animal brain and experience a kinship bond with something wild and untamable.

Just before we reached the end of the road, we saw a set of bears standing on a frozen lake. A ray from the vanished sun shot straight up into the air like a spotlight, and with the bears in the foreground it made a perfect tableau for the last picture of the day. Rupert joined us as we piled onto the back deck, his magnanimous smile and good nature restored. That night he'd stay up late, drinking scotch and regaling us with stories like the world's best pub companion. The storm that roiled him earlier in the day would be swept aside in the bonhomie of a warm room on a cold night. But I couldn't help but think that over time, these tours he leads will diminish him. He's dedicated his life to preserving the dignity of bears. But the only way he can live that life fully is by bringing us up here to make sport of them.

CHAPTER 24

Bunny Huggers

*Though such tremendous animals they are very shy of
coming near a man; but when closely pursued in the
water they frequently attack the boat, seize the oars,
and wrest them from the arms of the strongest man,
seeming desirous to get on board; but the people on
those occasions are always provided with firearms and
hatchets, to prevent such an unwelcome visit. The flesh
of this animal . . . is far from being unpleasant eating.*

—FROM THE JOURNALS OF SAMUEL HEARNE, 1769–1772

WHEN WORD GOT OUT that I was obsessed with polar bears, friends began to email me a set of pictures that had been circling the Web. In the traditional viral path, the photos came from everywhere, over and over and over again. From relatives, from co-workers, from my college roommate's wife's uncle from Bombay. If you've been anywhere near the Internet, you've probably seen the pictures, too; they've been featured on every nature show and browser home page and animal lover's blog.

The first picture shows a polar bear approaching two huskies. The dogs hunker low to the ground; a bear heads right toward them. Blowing snow whips around their feet, giving the scene a smoky, Middle Earth feel. The accompanying text usually tells the story of a photographer (or sometimes a hunter) who emerged from his tent when he heard the dogs barking. "He was sure he was going to see the end of his Husky sled dogs. But the polar bear didn't seem to be hungry. Just lonely . . ."

The subsequent photos are the key to the popularity of the series. In one picture, the bear reaches out a paw, and instead of taking a swipe, it looks like he's going to pat the husky on the head. In the next shot, the dog jumps up and the two animals embrace. Finally, the bear lies down on its back and the dog dances around him playfully. What the viewer expects to end in bloodshed instead results in a joyous moment of interspecies affection.

Every version has the story a little different, but the gist is always the same, a saccharine parable about love and coexistence, the peaceable hand of Mother Nature. (Any piece of writing that includes the phrase "tummy rub" doesn't deserve to see the light of day, as far as I'm concerned.) The website of an outfit called the National Institute for Play notes that "the bear's eyes are soft"—though they look like typical black dots to me—and the husky's "mouth is open without showing fangs." The website details "something magical happen[ing]" as the animals "begin an incredible ballet" in their state of "mutual bliss." The story always ends the same, with the bear "returning every night" for a week or two while the amazed hunter looks on in slack-jawed appreciation of the harmonic spirituality of the animal kingdom.

IF ONLY IT WERE ALL TRUE. The pictures are real; that isn't the problem. And the bear *did* refrain from killing the dog. But beyond that, things get very complicated very quickly. The pictures are redemptive and pretty, but if you knew the circumstances that led up to the moment when the shutter snapped, you might have a different idea. Or you might not. How a person reacts to the facts behind the bear-on-dog love story is like a Rorschach for the entire issue of bears and people and who belongs where in the Arctic.

First of all, there was never any hunter, and never any surprise. Bears in Churchill act like that all the time. But only in one specific place: the land where Brian Ladoon raises his sled dogs. Ladoon's place was where I'd gone when I was driving around with the gold miners who wanted so badly to see a bear. What I remembered best about that ride was how wary everyone seemed. "Don't piss Brian off" was the dominant theme. "Don't piss him off or he might . . ." Might what? Nobody seemed to know for sure what Brian might do if rubbed the wrong way. "Complicated" was the most generous word you might use to describe Brian. And the story of how those photographs came to light up the Web was one tricky piece of business.

Brian agreed to meet me for lunch at Gypsy's, and I sat outside on a splintery bench, waiting for him to arrive. Ten minutes passed, then twenty. Half an hour. At last, his truck approached. He slowed down, took one look at me, then gunned it down the road, his tires kicking up a hail of pebbles. I went inside and ordered alone.

Ten minutes later, he appeared in the doorway and nodded at me.

"I will have two egg rolls," he told the waitress. "Warmed, but not too heavily fried."

Brian was wearing what I came to recognize as his uniform. It started with a black leather band encircling his forehead, keeping his long, stringy hair out of his face. He wore dark sunglasses, often indoors, and he constantly scanned the room as if trying to determine whether each new diner was friend or foe. The wide lapels of a white dress shirt were folded over the top of a ribbed sweater with shoulder patches suggestive of epaulettes. The overall effect was somewhat martial, like a jumpy rebel soldier. He completed his look with the accessory of unrelenting foul language, which he deployed unself-consciously around anybody within earshot.

"Did you grow up in Churchill?" I asked, looking for something non-confrontational to start the conversation with.

"I am from here," he said, bristling. "Churchill is my home." He acted like I had said something offensive, and maybe I had. Brian rarely laughs, and when he does it's without mirth. His mouth makes the right shape and the appropriate noises come out, but it's a binary thing, a clear delineation of now-I'm-laughing/now-I'm-not. When his sunglasses are off, his eyes never stop squinting at you.

Brian's parents came to town in the 1950s to do construction. Apart from some travels as a young man and a few stints as a merchant seaman, Brian has spent his whole life in Churchill. A lot of people say that they like the leisurely pace of small-town life, but Brian is a man in a hurry. He asked me to tear a page out of my notebook so he could illustrate why he doesn't take vacations.

"People don't realize how short life is, and how little time there is to fuck around. Say you live to be a hundred years old," he said, writing down the number 36,500 in a slow, careful script to indicate the numbers of days available in an extraordinary life. "Then you have to subtract out thirty-three years for getting old and for being young." He did the relevant math. "Now you have to subtract out twelve years for getting educated."

"Wouldn't those years be included in the years you already took out for being young?" I asked.

"No!" he said, stabbing his pencil at the paper. "No!"

"Why can't youth be counted toward your usable life?"

"Because you don't have no decision-making power. And if somebody else is making your choices for you, you don't have no real quality of life." Brian subtracted out days for illness, for mechanical failure, for bad weather. At the bottom of the crumpled paper, he beheld his final number of worthwhile days and let out a low whistle, as if the smallness of the sum were a surprise, even though he'd probably calculated it dozens of times before. "Think about all the things you have to do and how little time there is. Eating and sleeping and sex . . . Jesus, sex! If you have sex every three days"—he held the napkin sideways and squinted at it—"well, that's not too very much sex."

The waitress appeared and set the egg rolls in front of him. He looked up and said, "I require a . . ."

She cut him off midsentence, producing a steak knife before he could finish demanding it. Apparently, she'd been through this with him before. As we spoke, Brian cut each egg roll into quarters, and then cut each quarter in half. Eating seemed like a chore, and he dipped each piece into the sauce deliberately, as if the entire enterprise was distasteful. "I eat very little," he said as he dissected his meal. "Half as much as most people. A little meat, a vegetable, possibly some soup. I always try to leave half on my plate." Sure enough, Brian was one of the few people in town for whom I didn't have to conjure a synonym for the word "heavyset."

IF BRIAN ONLY RAISED SLED DOGS it would be easy to dismiss him as another typically eccentric Northern character. But Brian raises sled dogs in polar bear country, and in proud defiance of the conventional wisdom about how people and polar bears should interact. (Ladoon refers to his dogs as Eskimo dogs, not huskies; apparently, there's some controversy about the lineage that's well beyond my ability to understand.)

From early fall until a little while after freeze-up in late November, Brian's dog yard serves as home base for up to a dozen polar bears. And not just any polar bears. These are the big males, the ones with deep scars on their snouts, rips and gouges in their flesh from years of battle. They've got paws the size of dinner plates and the utter indifference to humans that comes from having survived a hundred encounters with cracker shells and rubber bullets. Every fall, the big males congregate at Ladoon's place, nestling in the willows not fifty feet away from where the dogs yap at the ends of their chains. The dogs bark, the bears sleep. Later, the bears pace while the dogs sleep. Brian is in and out of his truck all day long, throwing globs of frozen meat to his dogs without any fear of the bears that lurk nearby. It's hardly nature red in tooth and claw. Where's the mayhem? Where's the killing? And how in God's name do you end up with cutesy pictures of gigantic, battle-scarred male bears playing kissy-face with a dog? If anything, it seems that Brian should be regarded as more Dr. Doolittle than town troublemaker.

But there's a catch. Many people allege that Brian Ladoon feeds the bears. He'll curse you up and down if you ask him, and deny it until he's blue in the face, but even among his supporters, there's no real disagreement about what's going on. Brian has a lot of dogs to feed, and a lot of dogs eat a lot of meat. Brian used to feed his dogs with beluga whales that he caught in the Churchill River; for a while he even hunted polar bears to use as dog food until the government shut him down. Nowadays, Brian spends $1,000 a week on frozen necks and guts and unidentifiable chicken bits scooped up from the floor of a slaughterhouse down south and shipped to Churchill by the trainload. He dishes it out twice daily, slogging through the deadly winds and the knee-deep snow.

In the midst of all of that hauling and feeding and fighting the elements, if some of the meat should end up beyond the reach of the dogs, how is Brian really to know? And if some hungry bear manages to eat that meat, that isn't Brian's fault. It's not like he's going to shoot a bear over a pound of frozen beaks. He'll tell you that he's just trying to make a living, and that sacrificing a few dollars' worth of feed to the polar bears is the price of doing business.

His critics allege that he's doing much more than losing a little dog food here and there. They say that he's actively feeding bears as much meat as they want to eat. They say that when no one's looking, he throws great shanks of meat onto the tundra for hungry bears to feast on. How else would he get the bears docile enough to romp with the dogs? And more important, how else would he guarantee that there would be bears on his little patch of land, the land behind the gate, the gate where he sits and charges admission to people who want to be absolutely assured of seeing a polar bear every single time?

"I don't have time for Brian Ladoon, nor do I give a shit," said PBI's Robert Buchanan, sounding very much like a man who gives a shit about Brian Ladoon. "I'm trying to save an entire species here, so Brian Ladoon is low down on my priority list. It's a fantasy he paints that animals live together, that you see mothers and cubs and dogs in love and you all go do a big group hug. He attracts the bunny huggers and that's fine, but I don't have time for it." It was interesting to hear Buchanan, head of the most prominent polar bear conservation group on earth, dismiss a small-time hunter and dog breeder as a "bunny hugger."

The scientists and resource management people I spoke with were just as pointed in their criticism. "As my nonreligious friends say, there's some awful shit going on out at Brian's place," was how Tom Smith phrased it. Smith, a bear behavior expert at Brigham Young University, has devoted a big chunk of his career to figuring out how to keep people and bears from killing each other. Time and again, when the relationship gets too close, somebody ends up dying. Whereas Ladoon might not have any cohabitation problems, Smith said, he was teaching bears that people are harmless, that the sound of dogs means free food nearby. Reports had been coming in from settlements to the north of Churchill about big male bears—possibly the same ones that were seen at Brian's—coming into towns, killing dogs, and having to be shot in self-defense. Polar bears are smart, but they're not *that* smart; you can't fault a Ladoon-trained bear for acting one way near Brian and then expecting the same treatment everywhere else. "There's not a bear biologist in the world who thinks that Brian Ladoon is doing a good thing," Tom Smith said. "Quite frankly if there's ever an incident in town where someone is dragged out of a car or killed, if I was Brian I'd be pretty worried about my liability in the whole thing."

CHAPTER 25

They Know
They Are Safe Here

It seems that every time mankind is given a lot of
energy, we go out and wreck something with it.

—DAVID BROWER, FIRST EXECUTIVE DIRECTOR
OF THE SIERRA CLUB

DESPITE MY PROMISES, Mac still hadn't seen a bear. Our time in Churchill was running short. I'd dragged my entire family to the end of the earth, and although they'd had a nice enough time at the indoor playground, that wasn't exactly what they'd come here for. High-minded environmental ethics aside, I had a four-year-old boy experiencing a serious need for some face time with a polar bear. So I rented another van and we headed out for some wildlife viewing at Brian's place.

When we arrived, Brian was nowhere in sight. The barrier chain was up, and a rangy yellow dog snarled at us, hackles up as it paced back and forth in the middle of the roadway. Mac was crestfallen.

"I'm sorry, buddy," I said. "We can't get in. I don't know where Brian is." It was now or never for Mac, and it was starting to look more and more like never.

Mac tried to hide his disappointment. He climbed into the front seat and leaned over the dashboard. "I'm pretty sure I see one over there."

He pointed to a clump of snow and chattered on amiably about how good polar bears are at keeping themselves hidden, and how he was just glad that he had such good eyes and was able to see them anyway. He shares his mother's boundless optimism and utterly aggravating ability to make the best of a bad situation. Fortunately, Percy—a committed realist after my own heart—couldn't have cared less whether we saw polar bears or not. Oblivious to our failing quest, she sat in the back seat singing tunelessly and eating peanut butter crackers. We sat in the car and waited. The guard dog growled.

The chain across the road is one of the PR problems that Brian is so good at creating for himself. Specifically, everyone I talked to told me that the land on the other side of the barrier isn't his. They say he doesn't own it, doesn't lease it, doesn't even have squatting rights. What he does have is that fat metal chain. And so far that's been enough to keep a disorganized and slightly cowed local government from shutting down his operation. Once, when I asked him how he interpreted the law, and what made him think that he had the right to set up shop on public land, he dismissed me with a wave of his hand and reminded me of his calculations regarding the brevity of life. "I understand that people might not like what I do, but I don't have time for all that. I've got no phone, no TV, and no fucking idea how to use a computer. I do what I want and I don't waste time and it works for me. Some people might not like how I treat 'em, might get their feelings hurt, but while they're up in heaven making fluffy fucking cream cheese biscuits on a cloud somewhere, I'm shooting right past 'em like a missile."

Just as we were preparing to abandon the mission, Brian arrived in his pickup truck, two powerful dogs bounding in front of him like heralds. "Put away your camera," I hissed at Shona. Cameras changed Brian's attitude for the worse, and I wanted him in a good mood for Mac's sake.

Brian's assistant, a young man named Caleb, sat beside him in the truck, and the front seat was littered with tools, ammunition, and miscellaneous supplies. A shotgun was propped against the dashboard. I tried to roll down my window to talk with him, but it had iced over. Brian looked on warily as the fool from the South banged on the glass and struggled ineptly. Finally, I got out and stood next to his truck, slipping on the ice as we spoke.

"Hi there," I said. "The kids were hoping they could see the dogs, would that be OK?" Brian's official stance is that the tourists are there to see the dogs, not the bears.

"You're that doctor, eh?" he said through a crack in his window.

"No, a writer. Any bears down there today?"

"Always. We've seen two at least. Big males."

Brian wasn't moving to unchain the gate or invite us down the road. "You been busy lately?" I asked, hoping to move the conversation in the direction of his tourism operation.

Brian sneered. "I get 1 percent of 1 percent of all of the tourists who come to Churchill. It's nothing." I knew from our earlier conversations that Brian's relationship to math was tenuous, but wouldn't 1 percent of 1 percent of Churchill's 10,000 annual tourists work out to 1 single tourist per year? I decided to let it slide.

"Go on down," he said at last. Mac vibrated in his seat, pounding his fists against his thighs in excitement.

For Canadians, the polar bear is more than just a nifty wild animal. The polar bear adorns the $2 coin and the $2 stamp; it features prominently in everything from children's books to political campaigns. Canadians see themselves in the bear—rugged, self-sufficient, existing at the frozen limits of mammalian survivability. People in Canada are a few generations closer to the bush than Americans—many have an uncle with a freezer full of moose meat, or a grandparent who homesteaded some scraggly patch of dirt up north. Losing the polar bear would be more than another generic environmental tragedy for Canadians. And Shona, the most important Canadian I know, had never seen one.

Brian pulled the chain aside, and we rolled down the hill in neutral, our tires making heavy crunching noises in the snow. And then, right in front of us, he appeared.

"My God," Shona whispered, as if she were in church. She reached out to grab my arm. "He's so much bigger than I ever imagined."

Twenty feet away from our window, a male polar bear was stretched out on the ground. This was one of the big nasties, a bruiser with a bent nose and an air of weariness. His head, when he lifted it, swung on the end of his neck like a pendulum, and I could almost hear the creaking of his bones above the wind. He reminded me of an old boxer with wounds that never fully heal. The passage of years masked enormous power and a barely suppressed violence. When he yawned, we all sat up a little straighter and tried not to focus on the size of his teeth.

Mac was transfixed. Shona seemed barely able to breathe. I'd seen dozens of polar bears already, but I'd begun to forget how beautiful they are, how that first glimpse blindsides you like a punch to the gut.

We followed the bear as he ambled over to check on the dogs, who were situated a hundred yards down slope. Ignoring the howls of the dogs, the bear surveyed his domain and then lay down. There would be no picturesque lovefest today; the bear was keeping his distance.

"That's a polar bear," Percy declared in a matter-of-fact voice. "I'm glad we're inside a van and not out on one of those ATVs."

"Percy!" Mac cut in, briefly emerging from his reverie. "Don't say ATV. Say quad."

"Oh, OK. Quad. I'm still glad we're inside a van. Can we go home now?" I scrounged a hard candy from the linty depths of my pocket and purchased a few minutes of quiet compliance.

"I don't know why everybody gets so excited about polar bears," she continued. "They're not colorful at all or fun to draw and they just lie there all the time."

"What would you rather see them doing?" I asked.

"I don't even know. I just like ducks and dolphins better, that's all." With that as her final word on one of the world's most celebrated animals, Percy sucked at her peppermint and turned back to her books.

Mac, on the other hand, had been transported. He stood with his face pressed against the glass and a finger buried in his nose well past the first knuckle. He flinched every time the bear moved, as if the two of them were connected by a string.

"He's really, really big," Mac whispered.

"I told you that," I said.

"He's bigger than you said. Way bigger." The window fogged and defrosted with each tiny breath. "How many seals did he have to eat to get that big?"

"I don't know," I said. "A lot, I think."

"'A lot' isn't actually a number, Dad," Mac scolded. "A polar can kill a walrus, too. Or a whale." He'd made careful mental notes at the Parks Canada museum, and he was taking it upon himself to educate me. "If you're going to write a book about them you need to find out how many seals they eat," he said before going silent as we watched the bear yawn and stretch. Another bear approached from the opposite side of the vehicle, and a third slept amid the dogs a hundred yards in front of us. We were surrounded.

Eventually, Caleb wandered over and rapped on the passenger window. He was a good-looking young man from New Zealand who had initially come to Churchill as part of a wide wandering, and he ended up returning multiple times to help Brian with his kenneling operation. Inside his coat, he cradled a tiny pup, not more than a few weeks old. Its eyes were open and bright, and the soft down of its fur stood on end from the static electricity of Caleb's clothes. He passed the dog through the window, and Shona held it gingerly in her lap. Mac was torn between watching the bear and petting the pup, but Percy came alive, stroking and tickling the dog eagerly.

"Some drunk idiot ran over his mom yesterday," Caleb said. "We tried to get another dog to adopt him but she wouldn't do it. We even rubbed her all over with Vick's so she wouldn't be able to smell that it wasn't hers, but it didn't work." Shona passed the puppy into the back seat, where Percy cooed and fussed over it with delight. Mac lost interest and turned back toward the window. Outside, the dogs howled for food and tamped out wide arcs in the snow, like crop circles, at the outer limits of their chains.

"I'd better have that one back now." Caleb reached through the window to take the puppy. Brian was coming, and I got the feeling that Caleb maybe shouldn't have given us the dog. Even Brian's friends act a little on edge around him. We handed the dog through the window, and Caleb got into Brian's truck.

The two of them were in and out of their vehicle without any concern about the three big bears hovering in the margins. If they had a mind to, any of those bears could have been on them in an instant, and Brian, his hands full of frozen chicken parts, would have been in serious trouble.

"Do you ever worry about getting attacked?" I asked Brian.

"I do not," said Brian, his voice clipped and indignant. He must have answered these same questions hundreds of times, posed by incredulous tourists who had taken to heart the warning that stepping out of the vehicle was akin to offering yourself up on a platter. "I know these individual bears. I have known them for many years, and they know me. We have an understanding and they are not dumb. I have a safe working distance that I observe, and if they come closer I will shoot a cracker shell at them. But they don't want to get killed and they know not to overstep their boundaries. They know that they are safe here."

Brian drove off, and we toured the kennel area for a while longer, looking at the bears assembled there. The tide rose quickly over the flats, obscuring the rocky plain with the still waters of Hudson Bay. Mac never took his eyes off the bears. Even his typical running commentary on the world fell to the occasional hushed murmur. Like any boy his age, he spends most of the day pinballing off walls and making explosion noises; I'd never seen anything hold him this enthralled. Top-notch Dad-work, I told myself. I may build a lousy tree house, but I did get my boy twenty feet away from a big-ass male polar bear. Check it off the list; point for Dad. "Everybody ready to go?" I asked.

"Not really," Mac said. There was a sadness in his voice that brought me up short. "If we leave now will I ever see a polar again?"

"Sure you will," I said reflexively. "I mean, maybe you will. Maybe not, I guess. I really don't know."

"I want to see them again. I want to see them all the time."

I hoped he'd be able to. I hoped I would, too. "Try really hard to re-member them," I said. "Get that picture in your brain and work on keep-ing it there."

"I'll try," he said. "But it's not the same as really getting to see one again." This had been possibly the best day of his life, and now Mac looked like he was going to cry.

CHAPTER 26

Circus Bears

*Modern bears, with the exception of polar bears,
have become somewhat chunky
and unspecialized for killing.*

—STEPHEN HERRERO,
UNIVERSITY OF CALGARY, BEAR ATTACK EXPERT

WHEREAS MANY SCIENTISTS and the environmentalists denigrate Brian whenever they can, the locals aren't quite so sure. After all, if you've lived in Churchill for a while, you probably went to grade school with Brian or you've sat next to him in church or you've poured his coffee at the diner every day for a dozen years. Not to mention the fact that he's got intense eyes and a scary scowl, which is fine if you live 2,000 miles away but pretty unsettling if you have to run into him every day in the canned goods aisle. And whatever people think about Brian, the truth is that his operation—his dogs and "his" bears—are the single-biggest selling point for the entire town.

Those famous snapshots are big business, and they drive tourists and photographers northward. Big males are getting harder and harder to find out on the tundra, and knowing that there is a guaranteed money-shot at Ladoon's place has salvaged many a trip. It certainly did for us. I was embarrassed to tell Rupert or Robert Buchanan that I had taken my kids to Brian's place to see polar bears. But the look in Mac's eyes when he saw that bear, the way he talked about it for months afterward are pretty much the reason that being a dad is worthwhile.

Brian understands this, too, and he's not above holding the tour companies over a barrel. "They've had a shitty day out on the tundra, didn't see no bears at all and the people were pissed. Pretty soon they got two or three buses lined up at my gate. And I give 'em a fucking university lecture in there, too, tell the folks everything there is to know about the polar bears, because the guides on those fucking buses sure as hell don't know anything." In multiple trips to Brian's place, I never saw fewer than three vehicles idling on the snow, passengers hanging out of the windows and gawking at Brian's bears. Tour buses, minivans, taxicabs, and Honda Civics—anybody looking for a cheap and easy way to see polar bears made the identical pilgrimage.

When the helicopters hover and the buggy engines whine—hour after hour for weeks on end—the idea that "regular" tourism is different than Brian's model is hard to defend. The helicopter operators and the buggy drivers all tell you that they're absolutely certain that they're not having any bad effect on the bears. And when a scientist chases down a bear from the sky, shoots her in the ass with a tranquilizer dart, cuts a tooth out, tattoos her lip, and wraps a monitoring belt around her neck, they'll invariably say that it's perfectly safe and that the bears don't mind a bit.

But Brian says exactly the same thing. Apart from the fact that he swears a lot and wears a comically retro headband, what's *really* the difference between Brian and all the other people in Churchill who say they love the bears and are working to defend them? If the modern world were designed with the maximum well-being of polar bears in mind, there probably wouldn't be any Brian, and there wouldn't be chicken parts for the bears to scavenge. But there wouldn't be any helicopters full of gun-toting scientists either, and there wouldn't be any Tundra Buggies or flocks of tourists falling over themselves to see who can get a picture of a bear looking the most ferocious. There probably wouldn't be a town called Churchill, either, smack in the middle of what the bears have always considered to be their migratory route.

But there *is* a Churchill and there *is* a Brian, and both of them are tiny pinpricks of intention in the immense Arctic reaches of the polar bear's range. Brian's just one guy. But for an ever-expanding community of do-gooders who are eager to find culprits for the demise of polar bears—without pointing the finger at themselves, of course—Brian makes an easy target. He's a convenient villain in that off-off-Broadway morality play; the other actors can hate him, but they still get a nice cut of the box office. And as for what people think about him . . . Brian absolutely doesn't give a shit.

Later that night, I tucked Mac into his sleeping bag and went to find Brian. Mac was supremely contented, drifting off with visions of polar bears dancing in his head alongside the pirates, jackhammer operators, and demolitions experts that usually live there. I knew where to find Brian; he would be at the Trader's Table restaurant, like always, sitting alone with his back to the wall and an eye on the front door.

Out in front of the restaurant, which was owned by Brian's girlfriend, a single Eskimo dog puppy sat in the snow, a fur ball on a chain, gnawing on an immense piece of meat. It was the cutest thing for miles—a great advertisement for Brian's breeding operation. No tourist could pass by without scratching the little guy under the chin.

Inside, Brian was eating his parsimonious meal, asking the waitress to bring him the smallest piece of meat in the kitchen. The restaurant was nautical-themed, with ship's wheels, lanterns, and heavy ropes dangling from the ceiling. Brian looked at me without expression from beneath his headband and twitched his chin ever so slightly when I asked if I could buy him a beer. I took it for a yes. He'd always been pleasant, if a little odd, yet there was something about him that felt manifestly threatening.

"If everyone says they're so against what you do," I asked, "how come you're still able to do it?"

Brian exploded, almost upending his beer. He leaned forward and hissed that nobody would ever be able to stop what was going on. "It's got nothing to do with me," he said. "It's all about what the *bears* want, and you can't never change that. They've come at me three times like it's

World War III," he said, referring to the law enforcement authorities. "Riot gear, machine guns, semiautomatic rifles like it's D-fucking-Day. They come in and take my bears, put 'em in jail, fly 'em the fuck outta town. But those bears come right back. They're not stupid. Come right back to where they know they're safe and they won't get hassled. If the fucking cops think they can keep those bears away from that spot, they are wrong. Bears go where they choose."

A lot of people make a lot of tough talk about Brian, but for years now it's been easier to leave him alone. He keeps the tourists happy, he keeps the cameras snapping, and he's just scary and unpredictable enough that if you're a petty bureaucrat with a bone to pick, it's always easier to go get yourself another slice of pie and leave the Brian problem to whoever has the job after you. And, in his way, Brian's one of the only people in Churchill who has the guts to deal with the polar bears on their own terms. No buggies, no helicopters, no radio collars. Just a guy who spends every day in waist-deep snow, feeding his dogs and talking softly to the bears that surround him. The scientists might not like to admit it, but there's probably no one on earth with a better innate understanding of polar bear behavior than Brian Ladoon.

AND YET. AS ONE LONGTIME LOCAL resident put it to me, "You just want to love Brian, you really want to be able to pull for him, but then he goes and does something crazy to mess it all up and you start to wonder what you ever saw in him."

I'd heard a lot of dark allegations that Brian mistreated his dogs, that he ran some sort of puppy mill as a cover for the bear-watching business. PETA and various other animal rights organizations were constantly lighting up the Internet with vaguely sourced complaints about how Brian mistreated his dogs. But, in fairness, the dogs always seemed healthy and well cared for, and I was ready to dismiss all the griping as sour grapes. Until I found a woman named Colette Weintraub; the story she told made my heart sink. What she told me about was just one single incident, yet I couldn't help but think about the local who had told me that whenever you start to love Brian, something always happens to muddy up the picture.

Colette is from Santa Monica, and she's a marketer for digital media companies (whatever that means). But more important, she's an inveterate traveler and self-styled eco-blogger, determined to spread the word about environmental depredations she's seen. In short, she's the kind of person I usually have an easy time ignoring.

At the tail end of the season, as the sea ice was thickening and the bears were becoming more and more frantic, Colette and her tour group were watching bears along the coast. They spotted a mom and her cubs walking along the shoreline. "We figured we should move the bus and meet them a mile or two up the coast," she told me. "I guess that was the edge of Brian Ladoon's property there." As usual, a few big males were bedded down near the dogs, and fifteen minutes later the mom and cubs came traipsing along.

"The dogs went nuts," Colette told me. The bears waded into their midst and chaos erupted. These weren't the calm, well-fed bears that the dogs were used to. This was a rogue element, an upsetting of the careful order that Brian allegedly maintains. A few of the dogs broke their chains, and "one of the dogs started going really crazy and lunged at the cub." The bears knew where they wanted to go—and it was directly through the middle of the dog pack. As they walked, the dogs harried them, chasing the bears. Colette figured that the hungry bears were coming onto Ladoon's property in hopes of finding food, or perhaps they could already smell it. The bears moved in, and the dogs went crazy.

In the midst of the confusion, the mother bear reached out her paw and swatted a dog, as carelessly as a person would swat at a fly. "It wasn't exactly an aggressive move," Colette said, and afterward the bears continued along their path, as if the incident in the dog yard had been the merest of distractions. Colette didn't think too much about it, either. Until she heard the howling.

"I've never heard an animal howl the way this dog was howling," Colette told me later, still very much upset by what she'd witnessed. "It was the shriek of a dying animal. It was really one of the most horrible things I've ever heard." What may have been intended as a casual smack from the bear was a life-ending attack for the dog. In the wake of the mauling, Brian Ladoon was nowhere to be found.

Colette and her group headed straight for the offices of Manitoba Conservation. The officers had already heard about the incident, and about similar ones in the past. Despite Brian's vociferous (and rarely believed) assertions that he'd never had a dog killed by a bear, on this particular occasion at least one dog was dead, and others were seriously wounded. But what were the rangers supposed to do about it? It's not illegal to run into bad luck, and nobody expects life to be easy on the tundra. I wanted to ask Brian about this, but he never returned my call, and I wondered what must go through his mind on days like this. Was losing dogs in bear attacks the cost of doing business, or did he feel remorse? "Those dogs never die out there alone," he told me once. "If one of them dies, he dies in my arms. Nobody cares about those dogs the way I do."

But the dog that Colette described didn't die in Brian's arms. And if losing dogs was the cost of doing business, just what *is* Brian's business anyway? Is he a dog breeder who has a sideline in polar bears, or are the dogs the bait to lure in the main attraction? I'd been telling myself that Brian was one of the only honest people in the whole Churchill tourist scene. But as I heard the description of the dog's death howls, and as I thought of that desperate mother bear being lured toward danger by the promise of a meal for her cubs, it was hard to see him as any kind of hero.

"Look, I saw those pictures like everybody else, and I wanted to believe them," said Colette, referring to the iconic shots of polar bears and dogs in happier times. "I wrote about it on my blog and I thought it was great. But now I know it's just not the way that animals coexist in nature, they're not cuddly, lovey friends." In fact, she was having doubts about the entire Churchill experience, which had seemed tailor-made for someone like her. She had wanted to go on a helicopter ride, but in the end, she thought they were hovering too low, disturbing the bears. Even a day on the Tundra Buggy gave her qualms, and she wrestled with her complicity in reducing the bears to circus animals.

"A big part of me feels like it's unnatural and unnecessary," she said. "There's enough going on with bears and global warming without having to add in all this other stuff. When I think about human impact I want it to have a point. I want it to be *positive* impact. We're doing these things just to satisfy ourselves sometimes, and it ends up putting bears and dogs at risk. It's so unnecessary . . . so irresponsible."

BACK AT THE APARTMENT, I sat on the floor with Mac and we looked at the photos of Brian's playful bears, set to music by someone on the Internet. As I watched, I remembered what Tom Smith, the bear behaviorist, had told me about Brian. It could just as easily have applied to anybody else in the tourism business, as well as those of us on the receiving end. "What you're seeing out there is circus-bear behavior," he'd said. "You can make them dance, juggle, and ride bikes if you want them to. And they'll do it, they'll think to themselves 'OK, I'll ride your bike, I'll eat your food.' But what you have to remember when you're watching them ride that bike is that no matter how it looks, those aren't tame bears. Whenever they want to, they'll come right off that bike and kill you. End of circus."

CHAPTER 27

Bear in
the Air

Y OU DIDN'T HEAR IT FROM ME, but there's going to be a bear
lift tomorrow," one of the helicopter pilots said in a low, conspiratorial voice. It had been a bad season for them; fog and whiteouts
had kept them grounded and unpaid for days on end. I'd gotten used to
running into them at the bars and restaurants as they wandered around
in stir-crazy agony, desperate to get in the sky again. But the upcoming
bear lift was big news, not to mention a closely guarded secret.

The bear lifts (or "bear drops," depending on who you talk to) are
the ultimate tool in the Polar Bear Alert's arsenal. The truly incorrigible
bears, the repeat offenders, and the animals that have been languishing
in jail for thirty days or more are tranquilized, put into a net, slung beneath a helicopter and physically removed from the community. Before
helicopters were easily available in Churchill, bears were removed with
fixed-wing aircraft, but that limited the final destination to preexisting
landing strips. Because most of those strips were to the south, the bears
would shake off the narcotics and march right back into town, often
arriving less than a day after their deportation. Now bears are flown
thirty miles to the north, which is the direction their natural migration would be taking them. Nonetheless, some bears still manage to
find their way back.

Bear lifts are kept quiet because they have a way of turning into car-nivals. Given the possibility for mayhem in the combination of helicopter travel and (mostly) unconscious bears, the wildlife officers like to keep the scene quiet. But inevitably, word leaks out, and by the time the chopper is ready to go, there's usually a cheering section several hundred strong.

Helicopter travel is expensive, even for the government, so in an at-tempt to defray the cost, the wildlife officers often introduce the biggest variable of all: television cameras. Film crews that agree to pay for the cost of the flight are given exclusive access to the bear drop, including behind-the-ropes VIP access, interviews with conservation officers and scientists, and—the biggest prize of all—the chance to ride along in a helicopter and film the release of a groggy bear into the wild.

"It's that British crew," the pilot told me, rubbing his hands together. "Or maybe it's the Germans. It's the one with the really cute little pro-ducer. Natalie, I think." I thanked the pilot and promised I wouldn't tell anybody. Seeing a narcotized bear dangling in a net was the hottest ticket in town, and I had to get myself out there. I knew Robert Buchanan and PBI had to be central to any plan like this, and hadn't he always said that he'd do anything he could to help me out?

I called up Krista, Buchanan's assistant and all-around savior. Buchanan might have been the visionary, but I had to wonder whether he'd be able to get coffee in the morning without Krista's guidance.

"So what time are we heading out there tomorrow?" I asked when she answered the phone.

"Out where?"

"To the bear lift!"

"I didn't know you were coming along for that," she said, her voice darkening.

"I wouldn't miss it," I bluffed. "It's totally fine for me to come along."

"All right then . . ." And before she could change her mind, I made her give me the details.

THE NEXT MORNING, I piled into Krista's truck alongside a couple of low-level functionaries from the World Wildlife Fund. The weather was cold

and crisp, perfect for flying. The film crew—British, as it turned out—
was getting set up. And, as promised, Natalie the producer was indeed
quite cute; she also appeared to be in a foul mood. Dressed in designer
jeans and a thin coat, she was smoking a cigarette and cursing the
weather, which, hovering just around freezing, felt positively balmy compared to the past few weeks of storms. Shaun Bobier, the Manitoba Conservation officer, told her where her crew could stand and where she
could set up her cameras. Every time he turned away, she edged closer
to the front door of the jail, only to have him order her back into place.
Complicating the scene was a Korean film crew scuttling about, as well
as a group of Germans with big video cameras and matching wilderness-
chic Jack Wolfskin parkas, which, like Natalie's outfit, were fashionable
but almost completely useless.

Waiting for the action to begin, Natalie danced in a circle and blew
against her hands. She wasn't someone who did well with downtime.
"Bears, bears, bears. Hassle, that," she said. Turning to one of her crew
members she asked, "What've you got next? Gorillas, is it? Brilliant.
Sharks and then gorillas and then whales, that's the bloody life."

From what I understood, Natalie had cut a deal with the Germans
to share some footage. But the Koreans absolutely had to go. "I've paid
too bloody much for this whole thing to have them come in and steal
my shots," she said. She complained to Shaun, who, with a pained expression, sent the offending film crew behind a distant rope. He also
reminded Natalie that one of her guys was getting a little close to the
door. Natalie wrinkled her nose and pouted; big-money television
types don't like to be told what to do by midlevel game wardens in
khaki pants. In turn, babysitting pushy moviemakers had to be the
worst part of Shaun's job. If only he had tiny tranquilizer darts just for
them . . .

"And you're . . . who?" Natalie asked, noticing me for the first time.

"I'm with PBI," I said, which was my best shot at getting to stay. It
had the added virtue of being almost true. I wiggled my notebook at her.
"I'm just a writer. No camera." She gave me a hard look as I tried to melt
into the crowd of the legitimate Polar Bears International people.

As predicted, a crowd had assembled behind the rope. A few tour buses, a handful of vans, and close to a hundred people craning their necks to get the best view. They stood a hundred yards off, a solid wall of fleece. There had to be $1 million worth of Patagonia gear in that crowd.

When the specks of two approaching helicopters appeared on the horizon, Natalie's stress level ramped up still further. "I need you gone *now*," she barked at the Koreans, who were pretending not to speak English and hoping they might be forgotten. But in the face of her wrath, they packed up and moved dutifully behind the rope line. I stuck as close to Robert Buchanan as possible.

After the helicopters landed, there was a flurry of logistics as people shuffled from one camera angle to another. A large cargo net was laid on the ground, and the pilot rechecked his rigging. Nothing would be worse than to go aloft and lose your bear midflight. On camera. You'd make every newscast on earth.

At last everything was ready. The British were in place, the Koreans were in exile, and I was still on the inside of the rope. The prison door opened and out rolled a quad with a small flatbed trailer hitched to the back. The crowd exhaled in unison.

"Oh, that's horrible," said a woman standing next to me. She covered her mouth with her hand. "I think I'm going to be sick."

An enormous bear was stretched out on the trailer. He lay on his stomach, paws splayed out and head wobbling from side to side as the vehicle bumped over the dirt. He might as well have been dead. An uneven green mark stained the hump of his spine, like an alien blood spot. It was meant to warn Native hunters away from eating this bear's tranquilizer-poisoned meat. I'd seen resting bears before, but this was different. He looked defenseless and naked, more like a pig on a spit than a sleeping bear. He was meek and flabby, without muscle tone, and worse, without any awareness of the world around him. I had thought that he would be quiet like a child. Instead, he was as comatose as a drunk. He was hard to look at.

The mood of the crowd was gladiatorial, simultaneously aghast and enthralled. Everything was done as professionally as possible, but still it felt as though the bear were being paraded before us, a tease for the com-

moners in the cheap seats and so close that those of us in the royalty section could almost smell his wet flesh. I wanted him to raise his head or
struggle a little; anything to show he wasn't dead. Death might have been
better than this absence of spirit. Churchill was a model of polar bear
best-management practices; these were the most highly experienced
rangers and scientists on earth. So why did watching this process make
me feel so dirty?

The wildlife officers maneuvered the bear off the trailer and into the
net. He was as toneless as pudding, and the men heaved and grunted to
wedge him into position. The net was tied in place around him, the pilot
made his final checks, and the helicopter lifted off. There was a moment
when the cord pulled taut, but the bear had yet to leave the earth; a radical departure was under way. I looked away, not wanting to see the bear
smashed into the tightening sutures of his net. When I looked back, the
helicopter was chopping away northward, the bear hanging below like
a fat teardrop.

"That's brilliant," Natalie said, squinting hard at the disappearing
bear. "Absolutely bloody brilliant." Natalie had stayed behind while her
film crew boarded a chase helicopter and took off to capture the bear's
release into the wild. As the sound of the blades died out, she turned to
me and said, "If any of them put photos of me on Facebook with no mas-
cara and looking like the Michelin Man in all these clothes, I swear
they're absolutely dead."

At a restaurant later that night, I found myself seated near Natalie
and her crew. I couldn't help but overhear their conversation. They were
planning to rent a buggy for a special tour, to go out early the next
morning "not just for the sunrise but to get rid of all the tracks and the
sound of the buggies." What they wanted was their own untrammeled
wilderness playground, a world where the bears are alone and unmo-
lested and it's almost possible to pretend that filmmakers don't exist.
With buggies and helicopters and shoulder-mounted cameras, they'd
re-create a fake version of the real world as it was in the days before we
all descended upon it. They'd give the viewing public what the rest of
us had long since destroyed.

CHAPTER 28

All Creatures
Great and Small

THE YEAR 2008 was a confusing time to be a polar bear. The winter had been good—cold and long and full of seal blubber—and the bears arrived in Churchill looking fat and trailing healthy cubs behind them. "I had been thinking I wouldn't come back to Churchill anymore after last year," one member of PBI's Advisory Council told me. "The bears were looking so skinny and desperate that it was making me too sad to come see them. But now they look fantastic and I feel really good about being here again." The fall and early winter would not be so providential. Warm temperatures and shifting winds kept the bay from freezing. The bears lolled about near town, miserable and edgy with hunger.

"It's over," Fred Da Silva told me one day when I was loading up with bear claws at Gypsy's Bakery. "The ice is freezing up and they'll all be gone." Something in the air had changed, and ice choked the waters as far as I could see. Losing two weeks of tourist business would hurt. But Fred needed the sleep.

But the ice taunted the bears, freezing and thawing like a cruel trick. Again and again an endless ice-sheet formed, and the shopkeepers worried over their bottom lines. Then overnight the wind would shift and the ice would vanish, blown out to sea on a falling tide.

One day as the kids played on the indoor jungle gym, I stood at the back window of the Complex and watched a bear struggle through the shallows. He took two steps and broke through the ice, dragged himself out only to break through again. His heart was set on distant ice floes, out where he could stalk his prey on the shifting plates. Instead, he hauled himself from the water and flopped down on the beach, exhausted and frustrated. I stared at him as he stared at the sea. Soon an Alert truck rolled up and hazed the dispirited animal off to the north and out of sight.

On the first Sunday in November, I took myself for a midmorning walk around town. It had snowed lightly overnight, and the streets were empty beneath crystalline blue skies. I had the north of town entirely to myself. I walked behind the Complex, down toward the beach. It was a bad idea to go down there alone, but the day was too exquisite to spend on yet another circular stroll to nowhere, up Button Street, down Selkirk, up Hearne, down Laverendrye, past broken snowmobiles and piles of trash and dilapidated tin sheds. It felt more like early spring than hard fall, probably 40°F and calm. I wore a light jacket, removing my hat as the sun filtered through spindrifts of snow that danced in the wind. Climbing up on the lowest arm of the inukshuk, I stared out over the bay. With the sun on my face, the water looked almost inviting. Not even the merest hint of ice was in evidence—no bergs out in the bay, no crystals clinging to the shoreside rocks. Instead, the waters lapped the shore gently; the solid ice of the day before had been swept out to sea. To my left, the port stood like a silent granite tower. Despite the open waters, shipping had long since ended for the season; the risk of getting frozen in place was too great. To my right was nothing but rock and water, an endless expanse of cold loneliness.

Looking at the bay on a day like this, it's hard to believe that the water will ever freeze. It's too big, too deep, and too far across to ever turn to ice. *Maybe this is the year it won't freeze at all,* I thought. Maybe it would just keep bumping along like this until summer, a degree above freezing, a degree below. *Maybe,* I thought, *I'll be here the year the polar bears don't make it out to sea at all.*

But that's the fallacy shared by adventurers since time began; the hope and the myth that this year will be different. It's been the downfall of many a sailor. The bay might freeze a few days late, or even a few weeks, but one hundred times out of one hundred, it's always going to freeze. And the bears will always go out to hunt, with more or less success from one year to the next. One way or another, those bears are going to leave. Looking down from the inukshuk, I saw a single set of tracks; they came up from the water and turned in a circle, almost as if the bear had stopped to take stock of his surroundings. The footprints reentered the sea ten feet away from where they emerged.

Prudence dictated that it was time to leave the beach—the last thing I wanted was to be a cautionary tale of stupidity. I found myself standing outside the Anglican Church, which stood on a low bluff at the northern extreme of town. I'm not much for organized religion, but there is something about the lonely church house standing against the wilderness that moves me. And this particular one is a beauty. It was bought in England in 1889 as a do-it-yourself kit for 200 pounds sterling. The Hudson's Bay Company shipped it to Churchill, where the Reverend Joseph Lofthouse fitted it together almost entirely by himself. At that time, most of the town was located across the river from its present location. When the population center migrated, so did the church, which was sledged across the frozen river as a single unit in 1933. It was resettled again a few years later, and then reached its current location in 1973, at which point its parishioners bestowed upon it the title of World's Most Well Traveled Church. I had been inside only once before, when I had run into a diminutive young tourist, a music teacher who was desperate to stretch his fingers on any piano he could find. Afterward we stood outside, staring into the teeth of an oncoming gale. When I remarked that this place, in bear country, in a whiteout, might well be the most dangerous place he'd ever been, he looked shocked and then replied: "They wouldn't dare hurt us this close to a church, would they?"

But today the skies were clear. It was hard to believe that polar bears could survive in the face of a morning as lovely as this. But polar bears don't think like that. They don't do statistical analyses or try to make sense of changing weather trends. When times are good they flourish, and when times are lean they starve. They have the luxury of being able to ignore the newcomers like me, who descend upon the region to decry what we see and then vow to fix what we've broken in the first place.

I climbed the ice-slicked steps and took a spot in an empty back pew. It was a simple church, ornate without being ostentatious. Eight exquisite stained-glass windows filtered the incoming light, and a metal engraving on the wall memorialized the deathbed sermon of the pastor on Jens Munk's ill-fated voyage. A bit of embroidery showed a mother polar bear with two cubs looking to her for guidance. Beneath a sky that glittered with aurora, they stood next to a bay that was rocky, blue, and ice free to the horizon line. "All creatures great and small," it read. "The lord God made them all."

The pastor ascended to the pulpit and the service began. A small congregation sang hymns and collected coins for the poor, reading from a prayer book written partly in Cree syllabics. They prayed for peace in Sri Lanka, for comfort for the shut-ins, for the relief of headaches suffered by a woman in the community. As the service progressed, I stared out the stained-glass window, just able to discern the hazy image of the inukshuk through the colored panels at the feet of a stained-glass saint. "Where streams of living water flow," the congregants sang, "my ransomed soul he leadeth. And where verdant pastures groweth, celestial food he feedeth." A stream of melting snow kept up a steady drip, drip, drip outside, schussing down the windows and landing in the slurry on the ground. For the bears, water was the enemy. What they needed was ice.

It felt wrong to be sitting here safe and warm, with the promise of coffee cake in the kitchen following the service, while the bears this community depended upon were outside, probably less than a hundred yards away, scrabbling for survival at every turn. "The Lord is my shepherd, I shall not want. He makes me down to lie in pastures green. He leadeth me the quiet waters by."

A WEEK LATER, pastures green were out of the question. The church was heavy with deadly icicles and people darted from their cars into the lobby. On a day like this, Gypsy's is impossible to resist. I put one foot down on the street and literally skated to the bakery with the wind at my back. The front door was crusted with dirty snow, but inside it smelled like doughnuts and chicken soup and everything good. The pastry case gleamed, the shelves heavy with blueberry turnovers, éclairs that glistened with chocolate, and fresh-baked scones studded with crystal sugar. A reporter called from CBC, Canada's national TV station, asking about the weather in Churchill. Apparently, Winnipeg was enjoying record high temperatures for November, but he'd heard the weather farther north was downright foul. The waitress listened to the phone, a quizzical expression on her face. She looked at the assorted locals who were nursing coffees at the front table. "How do we feel about the weather?" she asked, holding the phone away from her ear.

"It's seasonal," said the man sitting at the head of the table. The rest of the locals nodded, mumbled. Yup, seasonal. Then they sorted out their jackets and headed back outside. "What do they want us to say," one guy grunted. "That we've all just given up and the world has stopped?"

Going back home against the gale was considerably more difficult, and not just because my stomach was heavy with pancakes and Nanaimo bars. Snow stung my eyes, so I tried to keep low and perpendicular to the ground. If a bear wanted a piece of me, all he would have had to do was approach from one of the 355 degrees that comprised my blind spot. The wind sawed at my skin, ripping at my exposed cheeks and needling through the layers of my clothing to settle in my bones with a dull ache. By the time I was halfway up the street, I was beyond caring if there were bears around; all I wanted was to get home and collapse on the floor. A school bus drifted past me, gliding silently through an intersection and over a roadside berm of snow. A tiny woman in a thousand layers of fleece was in the driver's seat, her hands spinning the wheel frantically and to no effect. She coasted up into the parking lot of the Eskimo Museum, skidded around end to nose on the way down, and proceeded off in the opposite direction as if she'd planned the maneuver all along.

Forcing my way into the blowing snow, I thought again about how few of the people I'd met in town actually bought into the idea of global warming. These people, for whom global warming would be as easy to observe as looking out their front windows, remained far more skeptical. One man, the editor of a rabble-rousing local newspaper, said that he sometimes felt like a criminal for daring to question the gospel of mainstream scientific dogma. "They call you a 'denier,'" he said. "Even just using that word, denier. . . . It's like you're a Nazi or something."

Beyond that, the idea that global warming was having a measurable effect on the polar bear population was an even tougher sell. The general sentiment was that some years there were more bears and some years there were fewer. But nobody thought extinction was on the horizon. As Rocky had told me, things had always changed and always would. Bears might well show their innate adaptability. In nature, nothing living is ever set in stone.

Just after I left, Canada's environment minister came to Winnipeg to hold a summit on the future of the polar bear. Scientists, Native rights groups, and nongovernmental organizations jostled to be heard, but the mayor of Churchill—the Polar Bear Capital of the World, after all— didn't receive so much as a courtesy call. Feeling snubbed, he was quoted in the *Winnipeg Free Press* as saying, "I think they're sending the wrong message by not including us. . . . The biologists indicate the numbers are down, but we don't see it, in all fairness."

Among the locals, data fatigue had set in. The scientists with their grant money, their whistle-stop tours, and their emerging celebrity were sometimes viewed as being more trouble than they were worth. The numbers and the graphs all told a story, but it wasn't the same story I heard in the coffee shops and hardware stores. One ranger with Parks Canada summed it up for me: "I've got all the respect in the world for what they're doing, but I'm just starting to resent being told that I'm not seeing what I know abso-fucking-lutely damn well that I'm seeing with my own eyes."

CHAPTER 29

The Heavy
Hitters Speak

I don't do this because I want to be a rock star.
If I wanted to be famous I could find easier ways that
pay better. Polar bears have actually been very good
for me. They've given me a career. And I think that for
every bear I've ever caught, I owe them something.
My debt to them is still unpaid. That's one of the
reasons why I publish prolifically . . . that's one of
the debts I have to the bears. The other is to present the
information to a broader audience. . . . Media is a pain
in the ass to what I do, but it's an essential
component to what I do.

—DR. ANDREW DEROCHER, UNIVERSITY OF
ALBERTA (ONE OF THE HEAVY HITTERS)

MY FAMILY HAD BEEN IN CHURCHILL for months, long
enough to grow accustomed to the swaying of the roof beams
each night. The kids had acquired the winter pallor of everyone else in town, a ghostly whiteness overlaid by bright red cheeks and
a dusting of powdered sugar from all the doughnuts. Zeke had learned
not to struggle when it came time to put on his mitts; Mac had made
firm plans to be a polar bear jailer or a helicopter pilot when he grew up;

and even Percy, who had been so lukewarm about the whole enterprise, said she was going to miss coming into a toasty warm house after walking through a blizzard. Shona was feeling nostalgic about life in the North, the scrappy, unpretentious resourcefulness that comes from living in 20° below, the way you see a light on in someone's kitchen and know you're always welcome to drop in and stay for dinner. "The landscape is totally different than back home in Whitehorse," she said. "But it just feels the same. I thought I wouldn't like it here, but now I love it."

As for me, I'd walked grooves into the road between my front door and Gypsy's, and I'd worn out my welcome with anyone who had even the most tenuous connection to polar bears. But despite my efforts, I had yet to speak with Steven Amstrup, the heaviest of the Heavy Hitters. Had Amstrup and the others not written their oft-quoted paper about the 20 percent decline of bears in Hudson Bay, I never would have been here in the first place. But they were proving elusive, overwhelmed by media requests and disinclined to spend time with an unknown like me. Throughout the fall, Robert Buchanan assured me that I'd get an audience if I could just be patient. "They'll usually give an interview if I ask them to," he said, puffing out his chest.

Buchanan had prevailed upon Steven Amstrup to come to Churchill for a few days at the tail end of bear season. He wouldn't be doing any research, but he was pure PR gold, and PBI had all sorts of plans for him. At the time, the Canadian government was spending less than $150,000 a year on polar bear research, despite the fact that the majority of the world's bears could be found in Canada. PBI had emerged as a major scientific funding engine, and when Buchanan called, the Heavy Hitters jumped. Every morning, I would call the PBI house and put in my request for a minute of Amstrup's time. "Wait by your phone," I was always told. "We'll get you some time. It's a promise." Buchanan had never failed to make good on his word to me, and I hoped to continue as the beneficiary of his largesse.

I needed to talk with the Heavy Hitters because I wanted to be reconvinced of what they had to say. I didn't like admitting it even to myself, but ever since my time with Rocky, I'd become a bit of a skeptic. Maybe the bears could change their tactics and dietary habits, I thought. Maybe they could survive somewhere farther north. Maybe the projections were overly pessimistic and maybe the hype had outrun the reality.

And so I found myself in the paradoxical position of wanting to believe the very worst. In that era of faith-based decision-making and gag orders on scientists, my personal biases weren't very deeply hidden. I wanted the scientists to be calm, convincing, and *right*. I wanted them to dismiss Rocky with a carefully measured wave of the hand. I wanted their data to be rock solid and their conclusions pure. I wanted to know that the situation was critical, that polar bears were on their way out.

"You can have an interview with Steven today," said Krista, PBI's chief scheduler. I'd been waiting for this call for two days, barely leaving the house out of worry that I'd miss my window of opportunity. "He keeps saying that you had better be prepared so you don't waste his time. Can you be here at 2:30?" I looked at my watch; it was 2:15. Grabbing my notes, I stuffed myself into winter clothes and stumbled through a series of backyards and snow-choked alleyways to get to the PBI house as quickly as possible.

If my initial attempts to contact the Heavy Hitters had been intimidating, meeting one of them in person was a hundred times more so. Amstrup was tall and angular, with the square jaw and good looks of a star quarterback. The way he stared at me made me feel like I was being humiliated in front of the entire class. Amstrup was something of my idol after all, the kind of man I'd wanted to be when I grew up. For someone who is less of a geek than I am, it would be like meeting Joe Namath or Jimi Hendrix. The only difference was that Amstrup was a whole lot better looking than either of those guys.

I shed my warm clothes in the mudroom while Amstrup looked me over critically. I'd heard so many good things about him from Robert Buchanan and others that I chalked up the chill to his annoyance at having to spend yet another hour talking to a reporter who would ask the same stupid questions as the last thousand reporters. Before I could say a word, Amstrup held up a long finger. He flipped open a notepad and laid it across his knee. "Tell me your name and the publication you are writing for," he said, entering my name into his permanent record. Somehow he had gotten the idea that I was reporting for *Harper's Bazaar*, the glossy women's magazine. He must have thought I was working on the anti-wrinkle secrets of blubber, or what polar bears can teach you about how to please your man in bed. Once I'd cleared up the misconception, the mood lightened appreciably. Still, I couldn't help but long for Rocky Rockwell and his unabashed good cheer. No way was Amstrup going to offer me a shot of Jack Daniels or declare that from here on out I would be a part of his research "family."

I figured that the best place to start was with what had led me—and everyone else—to the story in the first place. Cannibalism. Amstrup's paper (co-written with a gaggle of other Heavy Hitters) had hit the world like a hammer. The idea that bears were so hungry that they were devouring their young was so horrifying that it was impossible to ignore. It's hard to get people to notice shrinking glaciers and incremental upticks in global temperature averages. But polar bears and cannibalism in the same sentence? Now that's sexy.

As I had come to understand more about polar bears, the intense focus on this single story had begun to bother me. It wasn't a controlled experiment, after all. It wasn't exhaustive data collection and analysis. It was only a frozen moment in time, an anecdote that came to represent the whole. It was interesting, but no more definitive than reports from Native hunters that they'd been seeing more polar bears than ever. I asked Amstrup if he was worried about the way the public was ignoring decades of research and paying attention only to the one paper that had blood all over it.

"The important thing with regard to those sorts of snapshots is: Are they consistent with what we might expect to see in a changing environment where the animals are becoming nutritionally stressed?" Amstrup leaned back on the couch and put his hands on his knees as he spoke.

He looked like the statue of Abraham Lincoln on the Washington Mall. His voice was deep, and I felt that if I interrupted him he would smite me with a bolt of lightning.

"There's no way that you could put your finger on it and say, 'Well, that's the fingerprint of climate change or that's caused by global warming,'" he continued. "It happened that the sorts of observations that are reported in that paper were things we hadn't seen before and so they caught our attention. That doesn't mean that they never happened before. It could have been that they happened out there and we just never observed it. So it's the kind of thing that's consistent with what we might expect to see happening in the environment, but you can't necessarily say that that's the cause. And I think that we did a very good job in the paper of making that point. And in the subsequent interviews I think that we made that point very effectively. But it wasn't always carried that way, and it wasn't always translated that way into the general media."

This was exactly what I'd been hoping to hear! I'd been worried that he'd recognized the graphic value of what he'd seen, and that he'd been exploiting it to make his point. I wouldn't have blamed him for it—his only goal was getting as much aid and attention for the polar bears as possible. But Rocky had planted in me a niggling doubt that the Heavy Hitters had crossed the line from science to advocacy, and that they were susceptible to engaging in the sort of pseudo-scientific cheerleading that would spread their message.

When I asked if he was bothered by how the media used his findings, his response was again pitch-perfect. "Scientific credibility suffers because of that," he said. "The point is that you have to present it in a careful fashion, and if the media takes it and embellishes it and spectacularizes it, then you lose the scientific connection . . . and that's really critical to people like us. We have to maintain that." His measured tones and eminently reasonable ideas were a cool rebuke to all those who ever said that the threat to polar bears was overblown, including me.

One by one we ticked off the issues that had been nagging at me. Amstrup reassured me that the data collection and analysis had not been hurried in order to get the polar bear listed as threatened; and he described stable isotope analyses that had been done, proving that although bears might eat berries, they weren't metabolizing them for nutritional benefit. Without mentioning Rocky's name—the last thing I wanted to do was waste my time with Amstrup on an academic pissing match—I asked Amstrup to defend himself against the statistical concerns Rocky had raised. I came away assured that all the variables had been controlled for, that the population projections were as ironclad as could be hoped for in this inexact field. And honestly, though I had been thoroughly convinced by Rocky during my days at Nestor Two, I was in no position to referee this professor-level spat. Maybe Rocky was right, or maybe Amstrup was. I had no way of knowing, but at the very least, this meeting gave me confidence that Amstrup and the rest of the Heavy Hitters weren't exactly winging it.

But what went the furthest toward restoring my faith in the Heavy Hitters was the fact that Amstrup assiduously refrained from using the word *zero*. The specter of zero polar bears, of a complete extinction like dinosaurs and dodo birds, is the extremist fantasy that gives chills of excitement to every television producer looking for a heartstring-tugging top story. And the environmental groups have their radar tuned to the exact same frequency; "significant population decline" is a snoozer, but *zero* can get bleeding hearts from coast to coast to open their wallets.

The Heavy Hitters had produced dozens of journal articles and government reports, but two in particular had gotten the most attention. The first was that 2007 paper suggesting that the Churchill-area polar bear population had declined by 20 percent over seventeen years. The second was Amstrup's paper for the USGS, hypothesizing that two-thirds of the Beaufort Sea bears could be gone by the year 2050. The field notes about deaths by drowning and rampant cannibalism were delicious codas to these tent-pole studies.

But when we talked, Amstrup himself never said *zero*. In fact, when I asked him point blank whether he thought polar bears would go extinct, he was quick to demur. The consensus was that for a long time to come there would be ice somewhere in the high Arctic. And where there is ice, there will be bears. Not very many bears, but not complete extinction, either. "There are likely to be small pockets of bears," Amstrup said, in "places where walrus are going to increasingly haul out on land as the sea ice retreats. Some polar bears will figure that out. So there may be some small pockets of bears that figure out some kind of an equilibrium where they can survive the ice-free period. But it's not very consistent with what we know about polar bears to suggest that whole populations of bears anything like we currently know them are likely to survive in the terrestrial environment." This was fine. I didn't need the Heavy Hitters to be cheery, but I did need them to not spout the same titillating prophecies of doom as the average celebrity eco-flack who decried man's inhumanity toward nature as a way of assuaging his own guilt over having just starred in "Transformers vs. Aliens 3."

This was good. Order had been restored to my universe. I still thought that Rocky made a lot of sense when he spoke about the integrity of the scientific process, but these guys weren't charlatans—my word, not Rocky's—and they weren't purposefully overselling their research. Were they cocky and a bit prickly? Sure, but they *were* the elite. Were they less than gallant in their scientific collaborations? Maybe. But they wouldn't be the first academics to be like that. Whenever I mentioned Linda Gormezano's methods or hypotheses, the Heavy Hitters would harrumph and go off the record with their choicest comments. But academic rivalry can probably be traced back to the first person who called himself a teacher, and its presence doesn't give much insight into the underlying scientific issues.

"This was actually a pretty good interview," Amstrup said as he unfolded his long frame from the couch. He seemed surprised that I wasn't a complete idiot. "I can tell you've done your homework." It was good that he felt that way; I'd only spent the past year and a half neglecting my family in order to read about polar bears, global warming, and nothing else.

Talking to Amstrup had been a perfect capper to my months of travel and research. Later, I ran into Robert Buchanan's assistant, Krista, at the movie theater, and she said, "Steve was impressed with that interview. You really made me look good in there by being so prepared." Mostly, I was happy that Amstrup had walked back his more radical claims, or at least repudiated the way they were twisted by the media. With me, at least, he hadn't played the Chicken Little role, hadn't come close to saying that every last polar bear would be dead within my lifetime.

Which is why I was so surprised to see Amstrup and fellow Heavy Hitter Ian Stirling on CNN the next night.

NATALIE AND HER BRITISH film team sold a few of their reports to CNN and to the *News Hour* on PBS. The on-camera science reporter was a good natured roly-poly fellow who never emerged from an immense canary-yellow parka. The film was classic Arctic stuff, all blowing snow and near-catastrophe on the tundra. He actually narrated one segment from the back of a moving dogsled. None of that was particularly unusual or up-setting; television is television, after all. But when Amstrup and Stirling came on-screen for their star turns, I was shocked by what they said.

The anchorman assumed his most portentous voice, hyping the cold, describing a bleak tableau of starving polar bears, despite the fact that this had been a relatively fat year. "They're under *stress*," he said, his voice heavy, before turning to Dr. Steven Amstrup, who "has joined me on our Tundra Buggy to explain the evidence behind the decision to list the polar bear as threatened. Evidence like cannibalism."

Cut to Amstrup, handsome and grave, wind in his hair, the Voice of Truth. "Large adult males that were clearly stalking, killing, and eating other bears," he said. "So it wasn't a situation where bears were having a fight over a mate or something like that and one of them was killed in the process and the other bear decided, 'Well, as long as I've got a dead bear here I'll go ahead and eat it.' It was actual stalking and killing and then consuming other animals. That sort of thing we just hadn't seen in all the years I'd been there."

Wait a second. Hadn't Amstrup just finished telling me that he thought the cannibalism thing was getting too much play by a bloodthirsty media? Although I knew he hadn't approved the lead-in claiming that cannibalism and the endangered species listing were directly connected, he wasn't a media naïf, either. He must have known that phrases like "stalking and killing" would only incite the producer's most lurid instincts. At the very least, he wasn't doing a hell of a lot to tamp down the extraneous hype that he'd been decrying to me just hours earlier. The camera cut to a patch of blood-stained snow. Although I could see that the gore was the result of a tooth extraction or some other bit of scientific bear handling, few viewers would fail to connect the blood on the ground with the repetition of the word "cannibalism" in the voice-over.

And it only got worse from there. Amstrup continued: "The projections that we developed last year, based on the data that we have and the climate models projecting what the future of sea ice is going to be . . . those projections suggest that polar bears are going to be absent from the Beaufort Sea of Alaska by the middle of this century." Absent. There it was: the *zero*.

I had his report in front of me, and I flipped to the introduction. "Projections using minimal ice levels forecasted potential extirpation in this ecoregion by year [2050], whereas projections using maximal ice levels forecasted steady declines but not extirpation by year [2100]." Conditional and dispassionate—not exactly the same thing as zero. The paper itself was a model of scientific restraint, pointing out uncertainties, deficiencies in the model, and the potential for alternative outcomes. Amstrup made clear that he was referring to a specific subpopulation of bears—the Southern Beaufort Sea group—rather than the population as a whole, but it's not like the average CNN viewer has a tight grasp of circumpolar geography. Neither Amstrup nor the anchor bothered to point out that the population whose imminent death they were lamenting was *2,000* miles away from the bears that they were currently filming. No mention was made of the fact that polar bears seemed likely to survive in the high Arctic; nothing was said about the subpopulations of polar bears that were holding steady or increasing.

I replayed the video clip online and reread the report a dozen times as the wind shook the walls of our little apartment. The report was exhaustive—nine separate documents comprising hundreds of pages, thousands of citations, and countless tables and figures. And for the television audience, for the 99.9 percent of people who would never bother to do the reading for themselves, it was all being boiled down to one thing. It was all about the *zero*. And, in an edited TV appearance, Amstrup seemed just fine with that.

When Ian Stirling came on camera to close the clip, looking grumpy and annoyed, I threw my hands up in frustration. "This is the most important thing that has ever happened in human history," he said. *The most important thing that has ever happened in human history.* Did he really expect anybody to take him seriously?

Upset as I was about Stirling and Amstrup resorting to cannibalism when the cameras were rolling, I understood why. The public says it has a limitless appetite for polar bears, but all people really want is stuffed toys and half-hour specials on *Animal Planet.* And then they want to see a seal getting its head ripped off or a tourist getting chased down and mauled. Hard science is an impossibly hard sell. From years of dealing with the media, Amstrup had to have known that he'd have only a few minutes to make his sell. And nothing sells like blood.

And to be honest, I'd wanted the cannibalism story to be the beginning and the end of it, too. It was too good a disaster metaphor to ignore. I'd even used it on the very first page of this book.

CHAPTER 30

Apocalypse Now.
Or Maybe Later.

I WANTED THE POLAR BEAR story to be simple and dramatic. But the more I learned, the more complicated it became. I came to Churchill believing that Amstrup's word was gospel, only to be seduced by Rocky's steady chipping away at the assumptions that underlay the conventional wisdom. Steven Amstrup won me back, only to push me away again with his hyperbole. Everything I thought I knew about polar bears and about how an environmental disaster should be sold to a willing public was getting twisted around. Even Brian Ladoon, a tailor-made villain if ever there was one, became impossible to pigeonhole after I got to know him. Because when you got down to it, was he any less interested in money and self-promotion than the environmental groups? A lot of money was changing hands up here. A lot of people were dining out on the bear stories they had to tell. And a lot of people, from high school dropouts to decorated PhDs, were constructing entire lives around selling access to this rarest of animals.

In the end, it all felt like theater. There were guns everywhere, threats from all sides, real and imaginary. Amstrup was the Oracle of Doom; the Greatest Conservation Generation was an ensemble cast of plucky do-gooders with Robert Buchanan as their visionary but offbeat leader; the entire town was a not-so-elaborate stage set; and the helicopter bear lift was a Very Special Episode That You Won't Want to Miss.

Despite their divergent roles, everybody had one thing in common. The skeptics, the cynics, the starry-eyed idealists: they all wanted the bears to prosper and thrive. Every single person I met said they wanted the best for the bears, and without exception, I believed every single one of them.

A FEW DAYS BEFORE it was time for me to fly back to Oakland, I ran into Robert Buchanan on the street. His eyes were bloodshot and he looked exhausted. "When are you leaving?" he asked. I told him. "Is that a firm date?" he pressed.

"I don't know. Not necessarily," I said. "How come?"

"Well, we've got Celebration Manitoba the day after that, and I think it would be really good for you."

"What's Celebration Manitoba?"

"Oh, it's big, it's gonna be really big," he said, grinding his promotional engines into gear, even though he looked as though he might fall asleep in the nearest snowbank. "We've got a lot of big names coming. Josh Duhamel, for one."

"Who?" I asked.

"Josh Duhamel. Big star, big big star. Also the Naked Brothers Band."

"Who?"

"Teen band. You know—Nickelodeon, Disney. The kids love 'em," he gave me a conspiratorial wink. "*Entertainment Tonight* might be coming, too, but that's not for public consumption yet, OK?" I nodded; I couldn't imagine who he thought I might call with the scoop that *Entertainment Tonight* was coming to Churchill to film a teen pop band that apparently sang in the nude. "Actually," Buchanan confessed, "it's *Canadian Entertainment Tonight,* but still." The premier of Manitoba was coming, too, he said. Or the vice premier. Or maybe the minister of tourism, Buchanan wasn't sure yet. The point was that it was going to be big.

"I don't really get it," I said. "Why are they all coming?"

"For the bears, man. For the bears. For PBI. They all want to get involved, they want to do something positive."

"That's great. That's really great. I get it now," I said, not really getting it. Later, I Googled Josh Duhamel. His claim to fame was that he was married to Fergie, the lead singer of the Black Eyed Peas. He had starred in the soap opera *All My Children*. He had piercing brown eyes, a dimple in his chin, and abs of steel. He was stunningly handsome.

I decided not to switch my plane ticket.

WHY DO POLAR BEARS matter so much? If you want to get technical about it . . . they don't. If every polar bear on the planet were to disappear, you might be surprised at how little you'd care. Not to get too deeply into the meaning of life, but it's hard to put a value on the survival of a particular species without relating it to what that animal does for us humans. The most ardent environmentalists say that endangered species have value for their own sake, but that's not the way the average American sees it. The buggy tourists were *getting* something out of the experience, taking away something that they valued. Otherwise, they would have been content just looking at pictures, knowing the bears were out there in the wild doing their thing.

And what exactly is that value? The hole in the ozone layer will give you skin cancer, acid rain will make you sick, and mercury in tuna fish will make your children stupid. But if every polar bear on earth disappeared, the effect on the average citizen would be impossible to detect. Polar bears aren't even really all that important for their own ecosystem. It's not like they're the bottom of the food chain and every other species would collapse without them. Although Arctic foxes rely on what they can scavenge from bear-killed seals, it pretty much ends there. And we care about foxes even less than we care about bears. In a concrete sense, a total extinction of polar bears wouldn't affect us one bit. We might not even notice it had happened.

The vast majority of people on earth will never see a polar bear even once in their lives, no matter what the polar bear population does. According to the Heavy Hitters, the western Hudson Bay population has declined by 20 percent over the past two decades. Maybe so. But if you live in London or New York or even in Winnipeg, the difference between 1,100 bears and 750 bears isn't really a difference at all. For a secretary in Miami or an accountant in San Diego, the difference between 1,000 bears and one bear is purely theoretical. They've always taken it on faith that there are any polar bears on earth to begin with. When the scientists and the environmental groups warn that soon all we'll have left is a small remnant population of bears in the high Arctic, they're missing the point: for most of us, that's already all we've got. If 5,000 bears in one spot becomes 1,000 bears in another, how much has your personal world really changed?

What the advocates always fail to mention is that we experienced the near extinction of polar bears forty years ago. We threw that party already, and nobody came. Although people quibble over numbers, the general consensus is that there are about 25,000 polar bears alive today, as compared to the 5,000 bears that roamed the earth in 1973. If the Heavy Hitters are right, and the global bear population is reduced by two-thirds at midcentury, we'll still have nearly twice as many bears alive as there were in the year I was born.

The evolutionary biologist E. O. Wilson wrote, "We're not just afraid of predators, we're transfixed by them, prone to weave stories and fables and chatter endlessly about them, because fascination creates preparedness, and preparedness survival. In a deeply tribal sense, we love our monsters." But our survival has long since ceased to be the issue, at least in a man-against-beast, hand-to-paw combat sort of way. We carry laptops instead of spears, but we're not so far removed from those days that the fear and fascination with bears has completely evolved out of us. We've mostly figured out how not to get killed by bears, and so the fear ebbs. The fascination remains.

And what we notice when we stare at them is that they're a lot like us. They're smart and tough and they nurture their young. They're cute and cuddly and unpredictably ferocious. They're the top of the food chain, they're without natural predators. This isn't some red-legged frog, warty and swamp dwelling, that faces annihilation. This is a master predator, a carnivore, with hands and feet and hair. This bear is *the boss!* This bear is a lot like us.

So when polar bears go extinct, it's not their absence that worries us, it's our own. As we watch them disappear, we wonder if we're witnessing the first slow step toward our own suicide. And because it's our fault (and because it may be our future), the bears become the most important animals on earth. After ourselves, of course.

FOR WEEKS WE'D BEEN PROMISING the kids that we'd show them the northern lights, but night after night the cloud cover failed to break. There were still weeks to go before the winter solstice, but already I felt as if I were living in a world of perpetual darkness. Instead of going up and over the top, the sun skirted the skyline guiltily, offering a few hours of flat morning light before fleeing back below the horizon. All that darkness . . . and still no lights. Shona and I had seen wisps of neon in the sky, but they'd disappeared before we had a chance to wake the kids. At dusk the clouds would lower, and at midnight they'd lower some more. Nightly windstorms reduced our visibility as the fast-approaching winter kept us locked inside for longer and longer periods. The wind rattled the house like an earthquake that never stopped, and fingers of freezing air leaked through the electrical sockets. The snow piled up in front of our house, crusted over and unshoveled except for the narrow pathway to the door we'd tramped out with our feet.

I slipped boots and a coat over my house clothes and stepped outside for a check of the sky. The clouds were breaking apart, spinning off each other like the icebergs in the Churchill River. A diffuse ball of white-green light flickered in the sky above Ladoon's Castle, resembling the Milky Way, only more so. I tapped on the window and called Shona outside.

"I don't know if it's good enough to wake the kids up," I groused. "They'll be cold and we won't be able to get them back to sleep and they were already up late as it is." A spear of light separated from the mass, flying from the core like a comet.

"It's good enough," Shona said. "It's amazing. I'll get Percy and you get Mac."

Mac was confused when I shook his shoulder. I never wake him up, and when he comes for me in the middle of the night, all I ever do is tell him to go back to sleep. "Wake up," I said. "There are northern lights outside." Without a word he came completely awake, stuffing himself into his boots like a fireman. I stood him briefly on the porch while I checked the shadows on both sides of the house for bears, something I hadn't bothered to do when I was standing outside alone.

Mac leaned against my legs, staring upward. Shona and Percy joined us and did the same. The lights spun madly, dripping out of the sky like candle wax, then consolidating into a ring that spun overhead, a midnight sundog of green, chasing its own tail. Flashes of pink and purple at the edges.

Percy, who had been so underwhelmed by the bears, was instantly transfixed. "It's like a million stars falling down on your head," she whispered.

We stood there for ten minutes, fifteen, twenty, growing numb and stiff in the sharp midnight air. Mac, ever practical, had some things he needed to figure out. "Are those lights right here," he asked. "Or are they way out in space?"

"I don't know," I said. "Maybe somewhere in between?"

"This is a new experience for me," he declared as the lights separated, changed colors, crashed back into each other again. "This and seeing polars are new experiences for me." We watched in silence for a minute before he spoke again. "It's sad that I'll never see these lights again."

"Because we have to go back to Oakland?" I asked.

"Because they're going extinct."

"They aren't going anywhere," I said. "Whenever you come back to the North, you'll be able to see the northern lights again."

He was silent, then grabbed my hand. "Dad?" he said.

"Yes?"

"Do you know what's different about this town?"

"Tell me what's different," I said, crouching down beside him to huddle against the wind.

"What's different is that you wake me up in the middle of the night and we go outside in the snow in our pajamas and there are bears in the backyard. That's what's different about this town."

I OWED ROBERT BUCHANAN one last visit before I left town, and on the final night before I was to head south, I set off for the PBI house. As promised, Buchanan had taken me from zero to Mach Ten in Churchill, introducing me to everyone who mattered.

Unlike the deserted streets, the PBI house was a hive of activity. Celebration Manitoba was just a few days away. Half a dozen people sat around a table topped with bottles of beer and Crown Royal. They faced each other in a circle, clacking away at their laptops in a manic frenzy. Buchanan's operation was humming, and everybody had a role to play. Krista on logistics! Raul on cameras! Rachel doing PR! Somebody handed me a beer, and I plunked down in a chair alongside Buchanan.

"How you doing?" Buchanan asked. He looked happy but almost unwell, constantly scratching his head and rubbing his eyes. He didn't have to be doing this. He could have been somewhere in the sun, playing golf. But this wasn't a vanity project for him. He'd taken on this responsibility years ago and now he couldn't let go, feeling that the polar bears would literally fall off the end of the earth if he eased up for a second.

I asked him how the season had gone, whether he considered it a success.

"Oh it's been great, great," he said, gazing at the activity buzzing around him. "I wish I could have done more with the Koala Foundation, though. I didn't have as much time for them as I thought I would. But I just get so busy with what I've already got going. We're making the generation of the greatest . . . we're generating the greatest conservation of the . . ." He twirled his hands in the air. I knew what he meant to say. The Greatest Conservation Generation in the history of the world.

"What happens to you next after you leave here?" I asked.

"Well, I'm already two days behind on my email and that just won't do. After I leave here I'll fly to Portland and pick up the Tin Kan," he said, referring to the motor home he and his wife lived in.

"Will you stay there for a while?"

He gave me a dazed look. "No, no. We'll get right on the road and head south. There's a woman I've got to see who's breeding white poinsettias. It's a marketing thing."

"What do you mean?"

"You know. *White* poinsettias. Polar bears."

"Oh," I said. "White poinsettias. Polar bears. I get it."

One of the volunteers interrupted with a question. Then another one wanted approval on a press release. Somebody handed Buchanan the phone; he'd just be a second but he absolutely had to take this call. I cupped my hands to the window and peered into the enveloping November darkness. Somewhere the bears were gathering, ready to take to the sea ice at long last. Poinsettias, koalas, naked brothers in a band . . . inside the house the meta-world of the polar bear churned on relentlessly, while outside their real world continued to drift, a little warmer than a generation ago, but a little colder than a year ago. Hunting, followed by waiting, followed by hunting. The life of a polar bear, the same this year as it was the last. Hunting and waiting. Some years more of one, some years more of the other. For a bear, the furthest reach of time is the distance to the next meal. Only humans think in decades.

"I really wish you could stay, buddy," Buchanan said, hanging up the phone and shaking my hand for the last time.

"I wish I could too," I said. But it wasn't true. I wanted to get home. I wanted to go someplace familiar, someplace where people were meant to live. Someplace mine. Someplace a whole lot warmer.

S HAUN BOBIER, the conservation officer, told me that as it got closer and closer to freeze-up, we'd start seeing more bears in town. They'd be exiting "Buggyland" by the dozen, loping through the streets to the newly firm ice on the bay. With the ice going back and forth the way it had, some bears had been forced to swim back to shore after falsely believing their long summer fast was at an end. Already, the number of bear encounters in town was growing, and the polar bear jail was full of antsy inmates. It was time for our Northern adventure to come to an end; real life beckoned. There were jobs to return to, kids to educate, California sunshine to be lounged around in.

"Promise me you'll get a cab on your way home," Shona said as I headed into town.

"Sure, sure," I said, with no intention whatsoever of following her advice. I refused to spend ten bucks to drive what should be a five-minute walk. This is what manhood has come to: Samuel Hearne walked to the North Pole; Jens Munk buried his sailors in the ice; I turned down a taxi when I went for a beer and some French fries. That's the kind of hero that the Arctic produces now.

It was a cold night, and the streets were empty. Snow blew along the ground like tendrils of smoke, wrapping around my legs before flitting into the distance. The tide of tourists had ebbed, and some of the hotels were closing. The lights inside the Seaport Hotel burned brightly. The buggy drivers and helicopter pilots were there, drinking hard, celebrating the end of another short, furious bear season. The pilots would head north to work in the mines and the drivers would head south for the ski resorts. The bears would be leaving as well, moving east, out over frozen waters where the seal pups were nestled in the false security of their dens.

I stopped at Gypsy's to pay the tab I had been running since I arrived. The total was not unexpected, though still shocking; no man should see the written record of how many pastries he has consumed over an entire fall. The waitresses filled the salt shakers and wiped down the tables; in their minds they were already gone. Fred stood behind the counter, wiping a wine glass with a cloth napkin.

"Stay for a beer?" he asked.

"Can't," I said. "Gotta go." Three beers later I was firmly planted in my chair, observing the swirl of activity around me. It had been a good season for Fred, but then again, Fred is the kind of person for whom all seasons are good. He was looking forward to taking a month off, going someplace far away. His uncle was heading back to Montreal until next year. His mother was dreaming of her childhood home in the Azores. They had succeeded once again in their unique niche, feeding and entertaining yet another onslaught of Northern sojourners. And despite the dire predictions regarding polar bears, it was impossible to imagine that Fred and the rest of the Da Silva family would ever go anywhere else.

"Lotsa bears out there this year," Fred said. "As many bears as I've ever seen." I thanked him for his hospitality and for all of the lollipops he'd slipped to my kids when I wasn't looking. I promised to come back another time, maybe in the summer to see the beluga whales. We both knew I never would.

I took one long lap around town, saying a silent good-bye to the landmarks that had so quickly become familiar. I hadn't expected this, but it was going to be hard to leave.

As I crossed the entrance to the alleyway that separated the Catholic Church from the rear entrance to the Complex, I stopped to adjust my hat. During the daytime I would often take the shortcut there, skirting the edge of the rocks to cut a minute off my walk. It was an ill-advised route, I knew, but well traveled by the locals. Even I knew better than to walk that way after nightfall.

But that night something made me pause and look hard into the darkness. It could have been something I heard, but really it was something I *felt*. A tingling on the back of my neck. And this time it was real. Right there ahead of me was a polar bear, less than one hundred yards away, shadowy but visible in the light of a distant streetlamp. He stood beside a garbage cage, a pile of torn plastic and half-eaten leftovers at his feet. The wind was strong, blowing sideways, and for a moment I watched him before he realized I was there.

Thinking back on it now I couldn't tell you whether he was big or small, or even whether he was a male. This was probably the same bear that had been hitting all of the trash bins in town, a youngster killing time until the freeze. Eventually, he raised his nose to the air and swung that big sloped head around to face me. I'd been a hundred times closer to bears in the buggy, but that thin pane of window glass made all the difference. He could have my head in his paws if he wanted, and there would have been nothing I could to do to save myself.

For a long time neither of us moved, each trying to estimate the deadliness of the other. It was the epic face-off between two of the world's most ferocious predators—one of them eating garbage and the other one completely drunk.

Part of me wanted to walk right up to him, to be closer. It was the same magnetic force that makes you want to jump when you're standing at the edge of a sheer cliff. Enough with the Tundra Buggies and the electric fences and the armored houses. This was the interaction as nature intended it to be, terror mixed with awe mixed with admiration. And now with pity, as he turned back toward the garbage at his feet.

I watched for a few minutes more, rooted in place. Soon enough—too soon—the lights of a pickup approached from behind, probably the Alert team guys with their guns. The bear gave the garbage one last sniff and then showed me his backside as he turned down the alleyway, heading out toward the water and alone into the cold.

ACKNOWLEDGMENTS

THIS BOOK TRAVELED a long and tortuous path to publication, and I could not have finished without the help of a great many people. First and foremost, all of the people mentioned by name in this book were incredibly generous with their time and expertise. In addition, I was helped by Kelsey Eliasson, Robert George, Raymond Girardin, Mike Goodyear, the entire extended Gunter family, Murray Horne, Sheldon Kowalchuk, Kevin Moloney, and Martina Tyrrell. I would also like to offer particular thanks to Ila Bussidor; anyone interested in the plight of Canada's First Nations people will find her haunting book *Night Spirits* to be essential reading.

Steadfast agents Kristyn Keene and Sloan Harris never gave up on this project, though there were several points when I did and they probably should have. My peripatetic editors—Jonathan Crowe at Da Capo and Bruce Nichols at Houghton Mifflin—gave this process its middle and beginning, respectively, and John Radziewicz at Da Capo brought it across the finish line. At Da Capo, thanks also to Annie Lenth, Fred Francis, Cisca Schreefel, and Sean Maher. Closer to home, Peter Lemieux and Rebekah Bowman contributed both photography and friendship.

I was lucky to have a number of early readers without whose advice and moral support I would have been deeply screwed: Seema Bhangar, Mikey Bigwater, Jim Downing, Anna Fortner, Kate Galbraith, and Lucien Nunn. Copy editor Michele Wynn saved me from much embarrassment.

In addition, the men and women of Local 55 of the International Association of Firefighters have indulged my frequent absences and kept me from burrowing too deeply inside my own head. There were many others who helped, and I apologize if I have missed anyone.

Finally, to say that this book would not have been possible without my wife, Shona, would be a monumental understatement. She acted as editor, researcher, cheering section, traveling companion, crisis counselor, friend, and all-around superhero. And that's *still* an understatement.